Governmental
and
Judicial Ethics
in the Bible
and
Rabbinic Literature

Governmental
and
Judicial Ethics
in the Bible
and
Rabbinic Literature

by

James E. Priest

KTAV Publishing House Inc.
New York

Pepperdine University Press
Malibu, California
1980

Library of Congress Cataloging in Publication Data

Priest, James Eugene, 1923–
    Governmental and judicial ethics in the Bible and rabbinic
literature.

    Bibliography: p.
    Includes index.
    1. Ethics, Jewish. 2. Jewish law. 3. Bible. O.T.—Ethics
4. Talmud—Ethics. 5. Political ethics. 6. Judicial ethics.
7. Justice (Jewish theology)   I.   Title
BJ1286.L3P74   296.3'85   79–23423
ISBN 0–87068–697–6

Manufactured in the United States of America

To
EDNA
who deserves a Ph.T. for
(P)utting (H)usband (T)hrough

CONTENTS

ACKNOWLEDGMENTS

A work of this kind reflects, to a great extent, the accumulative influences of many people. I am grateful to Dr. J. D. Thomas, Retired Chairman, Bible Department, Professor of Bible, Abilene Christian University, and to Dr. Frank Pack, past Dean, Graduate School, Distinguished Professor of Bible, and Chairman of the Religion Division, Pepperdine University, for excellent biblical teaching during my early graduate studies.

I will always be thankful for those who taught me at The John Hopkins University. With reference to background knowledge necessary for this book, I am especially indebted to Dr. Samuel Iwry and Dr. Delbert Hillers for leading me in Hebrew Scripture studies, and to Rabbi Samuel Rosenblatt for introducing me to Syriac, Biblical Aramaic, and Mishnaic Hebrew. I am also appreciative of a special kindness extended to me beyond the call of academic duty by Dr. Hillers and Dr. Hans Goedicke, Chairman, Near Eastern Studies Department.

My years at the Ecumenical Institute of Theology were rich with learning experiences. Father C. S. Mann, Dean, Ecumenical Institute of Theology, St. Mary's University, was most helpful as one of my teachers and as a patient consultant concerning my research. However, in spite of the rich contributions I received from each of the above-named mentors, the present work would not have been done had it not been for the wise teaching, counsel, and superb guidance through vast areas of literature, including "the sea of the Talmud," by Dr. Moses Aberbach, Baltimore Hebrew College and Ecumenical Institute of Theology. "Thank you" seems so inadequate for the capable and sensitive leadership he gave me throughout the study. Any deficiencies in the final product cannot, in any way, be assigned to him—only to me.

My appreciation for libraries and library staff has heightened tremendously during my research. Without exception, the people at the following libraries where I did research were kind and helpful: The Johns Hopkins University, St. Mary's Seminary and University, Baltimore Hebrew College, Hebrew Union College, Pepperdine University, and the University of California at Los Angeles.

My deep gratitude is hereby expressed to Mrs. Marie Mears, The Johns Hopkins University, for typing the entire manuscript, Hebrew excepted.

I would be an ingrate indeed if I also did not express my deep gratitude to the members of the University Parkway Church of Christ, Baltimore, Maryland, where I served as Elder and Minister during nine happy years. Their generosity and encouragement made it possible for me to continue my project to completion.

Finally, what can be said to a wife who has not only willingly shared the rigors and demands of this literary effort but has remained constant with her help and encouragement? It was truly a work of love on her part, and my love for her has been deepened by our shared experience in this project over the past few years.

FOREWORD

This publication of Dr. Priest's monumental study of judicial and governmental ethics in Hebrew Scripture and rabbinic literature comes at a peculiarly appropriate time. Recent years have seen a renewed interest in retracing our "roots" in an effort to better understand our present state and future aspirations by better understanding our antecedents. This need exists and has validity in the realm of ethical standards as well as lineal ancestors.

The impact of the ethical implications of Judaism has an influence that far exceeds the formal acceptance of that religion. Based on both pragmatic and moral needs of mankind, these ethical principles continue to influence standards of human and governmental conduct even when there is absent a realization of their origins.

Dr. Priest deals swiftly and effectively with a complex subject as he describes the origin and implementation of these judicial and governmental ethical considerations under Judaism. The reader will be impressed anew with the scope, flexibility and magnificent capacity of the principles involved.

The author aids us in realizing again the debt owed to the Hebrew nation by a great part of the world for much of its heritage and time-honored tradition in legal and ethical matters.

Dr. Priest's book is timely, effective, and helps us in better understanding who we are and in better appreciating the factors that have influenced us and our culture.

R. Wayne Estes
Professor of Law
School of Law
Pepperdine University
Malibu, California

INTRODUCTION

"Justice, justice shalt thou pursue," is the preamble of the injunction in the book of Deuteronomy pertaining to the appointment and qualifications of judges. But why "pursue"? Because, as it has been aptly observed, "justice is not without us as a fact, but like the kingdom of God a great yearning within us." In fact, "our whole social life is in essence but a long, slow striving for the victory of justice over force."[1]

IDENTIFYING THE TOPIC

The task of this examination is to trace that "long, slow striving for the victory of justice over force" as it is discerned in biblical and rabbinical literature. The path of the study leads through that particular portion of this literature which is concerned with governmental and judicial ethics. The goal of the inquiry is to so study and analyze the governmental and judicial literature of the Torah and the Talmud, utilizing supplemental writings that have a bearing on the subject, until a clear, critical, comprehensive presentation has been made of the governmental and judicial ethics found in the Hebrew Scriptures and the literature of postbiblical Judaism. This *modus operandi* will allow for a coherent summation of findings and an offering of some valid conclusions from the study.

1. Samuel Rosenblatt, *Hear, Oh Israel* (New York: Philipp Feldheim, Inc., 1958), p. 23.

LIMITATIONS OF THE STUDY

A study of ethics, *per se,* is not the main thrust of this inquiry. However, when one speaks of "the victory of justice over force," there is already presupposed a framework of ethics which has given meaning to justice. Since the Bible makes no formal distinction between ethical, ritual, and legal commandments, this inquiry will necessarily include differentiating among these commandments in order to distinguish the ethical aim which has given meaning to the justice sought after in any particular legislation. This procedure will naturally lead to a study of the biblical materials which emphasize governmental and judicial ethics, while at the same time avoiding commandments dealing with ritual and the like.

Neither is social ethics, as such, central to this study. However, any examination of governmental ethics implies the existence and operation of a distinctive society which is being regulated by laws characterized to some degree by ethical principles. Therefore, it will be necessary to determine whether, or to what degree, the governmental and judicial ethics of biblical or postbiblical Jewish literature are compatible with, or antagonistic to, social reality, and to what extent biblical and rabbinic legislation was translated into reality. In this way social ethics are not arbitrarily eliminated from the study, but rather confined to the valid relationship they tend to have to the central topic.

Similarly, religious ethics will be kept in proper perspective throughout the study and not be allowed to overshadow the main theme. However, ancient religion in general, and Judaism in particular, rarely distinguished between religious and other ethics. Religion permeated *all* spheres of life. Therefore, it will be necessary to study the close ties between governmental and judicial ethics and religious ethics, because, in the study of the main thesis it will become apparent that Jewish law, government, and jurisprudence are all grounded in theological foundations, and religion has not been removed from the social, economic, judicial, and political aspects of Jewish life. As pointed out by Licht,

> In the Bible ethical demands are considered an essential part of the demands God places on man. This close connection between the ethical and religious realms (although the two are not completely identified) is one of the principal characteristics of the Bible; hence, the central place of ethics throughout the Bible.[2]

While ethics has a central place through the Bible and postbiblical Judaism, and there is a close connection between the ethical and religious realms, this work will be considering religious ethics only when reflected in a governmental or juridical way.

Moral theology is of such consequence to the study that it could easily become a major theme. This is because the morals called for through biblical and talmudical legislation were viewed by the Jews as being standards set by God through the Torah or the Tradition. Thus, the theology of the Jews encompassed, among many other things, their morality. As will be shown, this morality was often articulated for them through legal enactments and judicial rulings. In spite of the strong and close relationship of moral theology to the governmental and judicial ethics of the Jews, it will be possible to keep this aspect of the study in its proper place, and allow its influence to be directly felt only where the close relationship between law and morality is under specific consideration.[3]

Thus, the field of inquiry is set out specifically as governmental and judicial ethics in Hebrew Scripture and rabbinic literature. This subject will be influenced, but not overshadowed, by ethics, social ethics, religious ethics, and moral theology. The distinction between governmental ethics in general and judicial ethics in particular will emerge as the overall topic unfolds in succeeding chapters.

2. Jacob Licht, "Biblical Ethics," *Encyclopaedia Judaica,* vol. 6, col. 932 (Jerusalem: Keter Publishing House, Ltd., 1971).

3. Robert H. Dailey, *Introduction to Moral Theology* (New York: Bruce, 1970), pp. 34–67. Dailey, pointing out the intricate relationship of law and morality, states, "In the Old Testament we find collections of laws. These collections contain moral, juridical, and ceremonial laws. The Decalogue is at the heart of the moral demands of the Law. The *juridical* parts of the Law regulate the daily life of the people: domestic, social, economic, and judicial affairs" (ibid., p. 47).

SIGNIFICANCE OF THE SUBJECT

It so happens that the governmental and judicial ethics in Judaism were so germane to the total structure of Jewish life during the eras under scrutiny that the study of this subject inevitably touches the wellsprings of much of what was truly characteristic of Jewish society throughout those centuries. And when those wellsprings are tapped during the course of this inquiry, there comes an overflow, as from an artesian well, that indicates some reasons why this subject is significant.

Even though this inquiry is restricted to an analysis of the governmental and judicial ethics found in biblical and rabbinical literature, nevertheless it affords an opportunity to become aware of how great a debt the world, the Western world in particular, owes to the ancient Hebrew nation for much of its heritage, especially in the fields of ethics and law.

This subject is also important because, by its nature, it portrays a nation that continued over many turbulent centuries largely because its very survival was predicated upon the keeping of law. The central place of law in Hebrew society was a catalyst which eventually, despite many setbacks, created a society from which the grosser evils of paganism had been banished.

The unparalleled historical saga which is discernible in the background of this study serves as a stage upon which the analysis of government and jurisprudence is done. Although history, as such, is not studied, it becomes increasingly apparent, as the study proceeds, that the saga of the Jews was, to a great extent, a continuing implementation of an ethical-legal system that contributed greatly to the cohesiveness and continuity of their history.

Another important dimension of the topic that cannot escape notice is the dynamic blend of ethics, religion, morality, and law which was so sharply focused in the governmental and judicial ethics of Judaism. In Judaism, law will particularize, morals will moralize, religion will vitalize, and ethics will criticize; and, where applicable, government and jurisprudence will standardize. This unifying coherence from the different facets of life made it logical for the government and judiciary to reflect an ethical system touching the totality of Jewish life.

Thus, the actualizing of a Jewish society which incorporated ethics, religion, morality, and law was accomplished within a framework which emphasized governmental order and judicial procedure. Although the above peripheral facets are contributing factors to the importance of this study, its prime significance lies in its analysis of the ethics which characterized the government and judiciary described in biblical and rabbinic literature.

METHODOLOGY

This volume is a comparative study of the governmental and judicial ethics in Hebrew Scripture and rabbinic literature. However, the comparison is not simplistic. The complex nature of the subject and the interrelation of the biblical and rabbinic literature prohibits a simple comparative study. Rather, the comparison is logical. Sometimes the respective literatures are intermingled for an in-depth probe of a particular point. At other times they are set apart to point out contrasting positions. Again, they are progressively unfolded in a thematic way to illustrate the evolutionary character of a particular law or judicial procedure from biblical into talmudic times.

The structure of the material is also designed to follow a logical order. First of all, the concept of law in the Bible and Talmud and the law of government are examined in both of these primary sources. Then the role of the Sages in their legislative activity is analyzed. After these concepts of law have been considered, there is a study of the governmental legal system as it existed in Judaism. The legal ethics of Judaism are examined in relation to the legal system itself. Penal legislation is then used as a vehicle for examining and evaluating the governmental ethics of Judaism.

In logical progression, the next area studied is the enforcement of governmental ethics in Judaism. The place and nature of authority in the system are examined. The actual establishment of the court system is traced in the sources. The ethical quality of the leadership called for within the court system is determined, and the close relationship of the law and morality is pointed out.

Closely related to the enforcement of governmental ethics in Judaism are the criteria and implementation of a system of rewards and punishments in governmental ethics. The sources show that rulers and subjects alike are regarded as subject to divine reward and punishment. The death penalty as articulated in biblical and rabbinic literature is used as a case study for the principle of punishment as set out in this literature. Other case studies relating to the governmental-judicial ethics of punishment equal to the crime, used because of their prominence in the Bible, are the "measure for measure" injunction and the "blood for blood" demand.

The detailed study concludes with an evaluation of the ethics of government in war and peace as determined from the biblical and rabbinic sources. The rules for war are studied as they applied to the people, army, and king. The subject of peace is found to be comprehensive in scope and of major emphasis in the Bible and postbiblical Judaism. The volume closes with a summary and evaluation of findings and a statement of conclusions.

CHAPTER I

THE CONCEPT OF LAW IN THE BIBLE AND TALMUD

INTRODUCTION

According to rabbinic tradition, there was no time in the history of the Hebrew people when they did not have a special "law." The biblical evidence quoted in support of this idea was that Abraham, with whom the Hebrew people began, was said by God to have obeyed his laws.[1] Abram's first recorded deed in history[2] after the death of his father was his response to God's instructions.[3] Abram,

---

1. T.B. Yoma 28b, Rab said: Our father Abraham kept the whole Torah, as it is said: "Because that Abraham hearkened to My voice [kept my charge, My commandments, My statutes, and My laws]" (Gen. 26:5).

2. E. A. Speiser, ANCHOR BIBLE, Vol. 1, "Genesis" [eds. William Foxwell Albright and David Noel Freedman], (Garden City, N.Y.: Doubleday, 1964), pp. 103–108. A strong case for the historicity of Abraham is presented by Speiser upon the basis of his conviction that Genesis 14 shows literary evidence of having a non-Israelite origin; e.g., "Hebrew," as in the phrase "Abraham the Hebrew" (Gen. 14:13), "is not applied in the Bible to Israelites, except by outsiders (e.g. xxxix 14), or for self-identification to foreigners (xl 15, xliii 32)." Speiser's eventual conclusion is, "If Abraham was cited in a historical or quasi-historical narrative that was written not by Israelites but by outsiders, it necessarily follows that Abraham was not a nebulous literary figure but a real person who was attested in contemporary sources."

3. Gen. 11:31–12:4.

according to the biblical account, continued to obey God all his life. As a result, God called him "My friend,"[4] blessed him abundantly[5] and established a covenant with him and his descendants.[6] From the very beginning there was a direct connection between God's instructions to Abram, e.g., "Go from your country . . ." (Gen. 12:1), and his promise as covenanter, "I will establish my covenant between me and you and your descendants . . ." (Gen. 17:7). Hence it follows that the divine covenant required Abram and his descendants to obey the divine law in all its ramifications.[7]

Election

The connection between God's instructions to Abraham and his descendants and his promise to them is aptly described by the word "election."[8] God chose to give Abraham and his descendants specific instructions which he did not give to anyone else. He also chose to make specific promises to them which he did not make to anyone else. He chose the Hebrews to be his special people. This choice was neither predicated upon nor implemented by their inherent worth, as their early history subsequently showed.[9] Neither was it determined by natural lineage once it had been made.[10] Yet, by God's determination, there was to be a reciprocal relationship between him and his people. As for God's part, he

4. Isa. 41:8.

5. Gen. 31:2.

6. Gen. 17:7. "I will establish my covenant between me and you and your descendants after you throughout their generations for an everlasting covenant, to be God to you and to your descendants after you."

7. Cf. Gen. 18:19.

8. G. Ernest Wright, *The Old Testament Against Its Environment* (Chicago: Regnery, 1950), p. 54. "The doctrine of election found its most concrete expression in the Old Testament language of the covenant. This term was borrowed from the realm of law and given a special theological application."

9. Gen. 12:10–20, 20:1–5, 25:27–34, 27:1–36. Cf. especially Deut. 7:6–8.

10. Gen. 25:19–26. Ishmael and Esau were excluded from the special covenant relationship.

had said to Jacob, ". . . I will not leave you until I have done what I have promised you."[11] He promised faithfulness to his covenant. As for their part, they were to give heed to God Almighty as he had spoken to Abram, "Walk before me, and be blameless."[12] They were to be faithful to God's instructions and guidance. Thus, reciprocity was to come about as God's chosen people faithfully responded to his election.[13]

Law

A highlight in the historical development of this process occurred at Sinai. The God of the Hebrews identified himself as the "I AM WHO I AM" (Exod. 3:14). He had brought them to freedom by the hand of Moses. He had encouraged them with the promises of the covenant. He had tested them by statute and regulation.[14] They had become organized and able to cope with judicial matters.[15] Then, in a manner commensurate with their identity as a nation of God, they were given a national law by God at Sinai.[16]

And Moses wrote down all the words of the Lord. . . . Then he took

---

11. Gen. 28:15b—New American Standard Bible (NASB). All other biblical references quoted in this book, independent of Scripture quotations from other writers, are from the Revised Standard Version (RSV), unless otherwise noted.

12. Gen. 17:1b.

13. On the theology of Israel's election, cf. especially Deut. 9:4 ff., 10:12–15, and comments by G. Ernest Wright, "The Book of Deuteronomy," *Interpreter's Bible,* vol. 2 [ed. George Arthur Buttrick], (N.Y.—Nashville: Abingdon-Cokesbury, 1953), pp. 380–381, 400.

14. Exod. 15:25.

15. Exod. 18:13–26.

16. Exod. 20. Cf. Mendell Lewittes, "The Nature and History of Jewish Law," in *Rabbinic Judaism from Talmudic to Modern Times,* ed. Jacob Neusner (New York: KTAV, 1974), p. 248, "The contention of the nineteenth century Biblical criticism that it was impossible, because of the primitive state of Israel's culture, for the Decalogue to have been promulgated in the days of Moses has long been discredited by both textual and archeological findings which substantiate the historicity of the Bible in general, including the Pentateuch."

the Book of the Covenant and read it in the hearing of the people;
and they said, "All that the Lord has spoken we will do, and we will
be obedient!"[17]

These introductory remarks show that the concept of law in the
Bible is basically and essentially a theological concept. To the
Hebrews, the law is nothing more nor less than the expressed will
of God for his people. "We will be obedient" is the ideal response
to that law by which his people would consummate their election
and receive the benefits of all the promises of the covenant.

Covenant

God chose Israel. "The relation between Israel and YHWH is a
covenant relation. . . . YHWH's relation to Israel could be conceived of only in terms of election and free choice."[18] Israel was to
acknowledge him uniquely with the words, "The Lord is our God,
the Lord is one!"[19] The Torah possessed its validity within this
theological framework. God expressed his claim of kingship over
his people by means of the Torah; they were to acknowledge this
sovereignty by willingly submitting to God's will as expressed in
the Torah. This background opens up the way for a consideration
of the divine law of government for the Israelites.

17. Exod. 24:4, 7.
18. Y. Kaufmann, *The Religion of Israel,* [trans. Moshe Greenberg], (Chicago: University of Chicago Press, 1956), p. 298.
19. Deut. 6:4 (NASB). Robert Jamison, A. R. Fausset, and David Brown,
"Deuteronomy," in *Commentary Critical and Explanatory on the Whole Bible*
(Grand Rapids, Mich.: Zondervan, n.d.), p. 125, point out that Deut. 6:1–8,
11:18–21; Exod. 13:2–10 served to remind the Israelites of God's sovereignty,
providence, love, and the central place the law was to have in their everyday lives.
This awareness was heightened by the later custom of the תפילין *tefillin*—i.e., the
writing of these scriptures on parchment and carrying them in a small box tied
around the forehead or around the arm.

THE BIBLE AND THE LAW OF GOVERNMENT

The law of government has always been essential for the survival of the human race. Without law there can be no government. Without government there remains the self-destruction of anarchy.[20] Therefore, one of the elements of an enduring civilization is the law of government. Throughout history there have been various forms of government among men, e.g., absolute or constitutional monarchy, dictatorship, oligarchy, and democracy. In antiquity, theocracy was very common. Awareness of this is important for this study since ancient Israel was a theocracy.[21]

In most cases, the form of government by which a particular nation is governed is a clue to its basic beliefs about humanity in particular and reality in general. This section is concerned with the law of government as found in the Bible and is a study of a system which had as its basic premises the reality of a divine being, the great worth of each individual, and the possibility of harmony between that divine being and his chosen nation by means of its willing submission to his revealed, written law.[22]

---

20. There is a well-known rabbinic dictum which holds that even an oppressive government is preferable to anarchy. Cf. M. Ab. III, 2, "R. Hanina, the captain [Heb. (סגן)—an important Temple office held by a leading priest who was in effect governor of the Temple and day-to-day administrator of its affairs] of the Priests, said: 'Pray for the welfare of the government (viz., the Roman government), for were it not for the fear thereof, one man would swallow up alive his fellow-man.'" Cf. Jer. 29:7: "And seek the peace of the city whither I have caused you to be carried away captives, and pray unto the Lord for it: for in the peace thereof shall ye have peace."

21. *Webster's New International Dictionary of the English Language,* 2d ed., Theocracy is: "1. Government of a state by the immediate direction or administration of God; hence, government or political rule by priests or clergy as representatives of God. 2. A state so governed, as the Hebrew commonwealth before it became a kingdom." Cf. below, pp. 114–117 and notes for further comments on ancient Israel as a theocracy.

22. Cf. Meyer Waxman, "Civil and Criminal Procedure of Jewish Courts," in *Studies in Jewish Jurisprudence,* [ed. Edward M. Gershfield], (New York: Hermon

The Sinai Event

For Israel, the will of God was the law of the land. They were his
people, and he was their God. He had said to them, "Now therefore, if you will obey my voice and keep my covenant, you shall be
my own possession among all peoples; for all the earth is
mine . . . "[23] The Israelites were convinced that by the historical
unveiling of himself[24] and of his law at Sinai, God had established
an intimate communication with his nation. Therefore, the subsequent articulation of the law, with all its varying ramifications,
received its ultimate meaning and its absolute authority from the
Sinai event. They perceived the law as God's gift to his people to
govern them in a way and manner befitting a people of God. In
other words, the sovereignty of God over his people was made
clear in the law, and their acknowledgment of his sovereignty over
them was to be expressed in their submission to his law.[25]

Press, 1971), p. 184, where the author notes: "The basic principle of Jewish law is
that any violation against the commandments or precepts of God as expressed in
the Scriptures is a punishable act. It is a very wide one and covers an extensive
area of all phases of human life. In it, the notion of crime is not distinguished
from that of sin."

23. Exod. 19:5. Solomon Goldman, *The Ten Commandments* (Chicago: University of Chicago Press, 1956). Cf. Goldman's commentary on Exod. 19, which
includes the following: "This passage constitutes both the climax to the Egypt-
Israel saga and the basis of Judaism and Christianity. It is what has been aptly
described as the *Kernstück*—the 'core' or 'kernel'—of Scripture. For if what is
here related goes back to fact, then the Bible and with it also the religion of the
Occident originated with God. If, on the other hand, it is folklore or fiction, then
the one and the other are man-made" (pp. 6–7).

24. Exod. 24:9–12.

25. Shalom M. Paul, *Studies in the Book of the Covenant in the Light of Cuneiform and Biblical Law* (Leiden: E. J. Brill, 1970), p. 36, "Although the Israelite
society was greatly indebted to its Mesopotamian predecessors for its deep
respect for law, . . . the basic concept of law in Israel was radically opposed to all
other systems of jurisprudence. Law in Israel has a divine authorship; . . . God
alone is the ultimate source and sanction of law. The entire law is ascribed directly
to him."

Function of the Law

The function of the law needs to be examined. Its goal was to mold the Israelites into a law-abiding, morally superior nation, serving God by following a law designed to promote justice and loving-kindness among men. Thus, the order of government projected by the law was, in essence, a divine order. To the Israelites, the law was the dynamic expression of a sovereign God by which he creatively instructed, guided, warned, and rewarded his people. Their adherence to this law was a visible confirmation of a transcendent God acting in history; it confirmed his election of his people.

The function of the law can be understood more clearly when viewed against the background of other prominent legal systems of the ancient Near East. Finkelstein explains that the *misharum* institution in the Old Babylonian period and earlier applied to enactments by the kings aimed at economic reform or adjustment.[26] In discussing a text of the Sippar material acquired by the British Museum in the latter part of the nineteenth century, he finds that this institution served, in many respects, the same function as the biblical "jubilee land release" laws (Lev. 25:28 ff.).[27]

This same attitude of concern for redemption of patrimonial land is seen in some of the Eshnunna laws, e.g., "If a man is hard up and sells his house, the owner of the house shall (be entitled to) redeem (it) whenever the purchaser (re)sells it."[28] This closely parallels the biblical provision for land redemption found in Leviticus 25:25–27.

The above examples point to the function of law in the ancient

26. J. J. Finkelstein, "Some New *Misharum* Material and Its Implications," in *Studies in Honor of Benno Landsberger on His Seventy-Fifth Birthday, April 21, 1965,* Assyriological Studies, no. 16, eds. Hans G. Guterbock and Thorkild Jacobsen (Chicago: University of Chicago Press, 1965), p. 233.

27. Ibid., p. 241.

28. Albrecht Goetze, [trans.], "The Laws of Eshnunna," in *Ancient Near Eastern Texts Relating to the Old Testament,* [ed. James B. Pritchard, 2d ed.], (Princeton: Princeton University Press, 1955), p. 163.

Near East in attempting to provide a measure of equity in real estate matters. Further parallels may be noted between biblical law and other Near Eastern laws with regard to person, e.g., "If a seignior has stolen the young son of a(nother) seignior, he shall be put to death."[29] This has parallels in Exodus 21:16 and Deuteronomy 24:7.

There are also interesting examples of legal consideration given to domestic matters. For example:

> If a man married a wife (and) she bore him children and those children are living, and a slave also bore children for her master (but) the father granted freedom to the slave and her children, the children of the slave shall not divide the estate with the children of their (former) master.[30]

This law compares favorably with the episode recorded in Genesis 21.

The above examples from various Near Eastern law formulations show that those laws, paralleled in principle in biblical law, offered some measure of protection against injustice, recourse to judicial procedure, and deterrent to crime. In other words, the examples show the laws contributing to the functioning of an orderly society, whether considered as idealized models of behavior in some cases or as operative legislation.

Finally, when one refers to the "formative nature" of biblical law, more is involved than the common traits of the various law systems of the ancient Near East and their biblical parallels, as illustrated above. This is nowhere more apparent than in the formulation of the direct address of biblical apodictic law. Accord-

29. Theopile J. Meek, [trans.], "The Code of Hammurabi," in *The Ancient Near East: An Anthology of Texts and Pictures,* [ed. James B. Pritchard], (Princeton: Princeton University Press, 1958), p. 141.

30. S. N. Kramer, [trans.], "Lipit-Ishtar Lawcode," in *Ancient Near Eastern Texts Relating to the Old Testament,* [ed. James B. Pritchard, 2d ed.], (Princeton: Princeton University Press, 1955), p. 160.

ing to Shalom M. Paul, formulation of biblical apodictic law has as its purpose

> to shape and form a society, not to state cases and provide remedies. . . . This direct address formulation, while found in several literary genres, is not present in any of the cuneiform juridical corpora, but is unique to biblical legal compilations.[31]

Through this means, especially, the biblical law helped to shape Israelite society. As Paul states,

> Though these apodictic formulations deal primarily with moral and religious commandments, the question still remains as to why they are part and parcel of biblical jurisprudence and are noticeably absent from all Mesopotamian corpora. Once again a unique aspect of a society is explicable only in terms of its entire complex. The Israelite society was founded on a covenantal agreement based on the will of God, who expressed his demands in covenant law declared publicly to the entire community. By making his will personally and directly known to man, an I-Thou relationship is established which characterizes the unique feature of this newly founded nation. Moral and religious prescriptions are directed to each and every member of this nation in categorical imperatives. The constitution for this new polity (i.e., covenant law) incorporates and emphasizes both customary civil law (i.e., casuistic formulations) and moral-ethical admonitions together with religious-cultic obligations (i.e., apodictic formulations). However, whereas casuistic law deals with precedent and what is, apodictic commandments express what must and ought to be. It addresses man a priori as to what is right or wrong. It is prescriptive not descriptive, prospective not retrospective, absolute not relative, categorically imperative and obligatory not conditional, subjective and personal ("Thou shalt [not]," i.e., I-Thou) not objective and impersonal ("If a man . . . ").—God's will not man's. Its purpose is to shape and form a society, not to state cases and provide remedies. No time

---

31. Paul, *Studies in the Book of the Covenant*, pp. 122–123.

limit is placed on its demands. Sanctions are absent; yet it appeals
to the conscience of the individual for constant obedience and
fidelity. It is preventive and precautionary, obliging the responsibility of every member of the community. Hence, to impersonal legislation is added feeling; to the intellect, the heart; and to the letter of
the law is added the spirit and values of metajuristic principles—
together they constitute the charter of the people of Israel. The
apodictic commandment, the I-Thou relationship found only in
biblical legal corpora, would seem to be Israel's contribution to the
"theology of jurisprudence."[32]

Scope of the Law

With the foregoing in mind, it is clear why one of the uniform
characteristics of the law of government in the Bible is the close
relationship of the legal, moral, and ethical norms.[33] The ethics of
government found in the Bible were essentially God-given principles for holy living, while the morals of the government became
the actual expressions of those principles in everyday conduct, at
least in theory. Thus, the legal, moral, and ethical demands laid on
the people were closely related in that they were all backed by the
authority of God and all came to the people by the same route of
revelation. In Hebrew thinking, compliance with a legal, moral, or
ethical principle was actually a response to the divine will.

All of this meant that the total lives of the people were subject
to the law of government. This is another way of saying that the
nation, as well as each individual in it, was "under God." The
phrase "under God" in this context is well illustrated by Shalom
M. Paul in his description of several traits of biblical law. An
abbreviated list of these traits follows:

32. Ibid., pp. 123–124.
33. Cf. S. R. Driver, "Law (in the Old Testament)," *Dictionary of the Bible,*
vol. 3, [ed. James Hastings], (Edinburgh: Charles Scribner's Sons, 1900), p. 66.
Driver speaks of the "judicial, ceremonial, and moral" *threefold* character of the
Hebrew Torah.

1. Since law is an expression of the divine will, all crimes are considered sins.
2. The whole of one's life is directly related to the will of God.
3. Since God is the sole legislator, Israel is held responsible to him and not to any human ruler or legislative body.
4. God selects the entire corporate body of Israel to be the recipients of his law.
5. Publicity is the hallmark of the law. It is not restricted to any professional class of jurists, lawyers, or judges (Exod. 21:1).
6. Law becomes a body of teaching directed to the entire community.
7. Since man is conceived as being created in the divine image, the sacredness of a human being becomes a primary concern of the law.
8. Whereas biblical legislation demands a "life for a life," brutal and multiple punishments are all but absent from Israelite law.
9. Since all men are created by God and thus stand equal before him, class distinction is rejected in the meting out of justice.
10. The sole exception to the principle of equal justice as exemplified in *lex talionis* is the slave (Exod. 21:2–6, 20, 26–27); yet all the laws pertaining to slaves are concerned with furthering their protection and preserving their human dignity.[34]

Paul reminds the reader that these features pertained primarily to the theory of biblical law rather than to its actual practice, "about which there is a paucity of information."[35] Thus, society as a whole was motivated, at least in theory, to remain loyal to God and to take the initiative in restraining lawlessness.

This merging of law, morality, and ethics in the everyday life of the individual and in the corporate life of the nation served to accomplish one of the main goals of the Torah—the maintaining of that unique tie between God and Israel. When the total person responded fully to God's law, this meant that nothing was with-

34. Paul, *Studies in the Book of the Covenant*, pp. 37–40.
35. Ibid.

held, whether religious, social, legal, moral, or ethical.[36] The Israelites saw the bond between God and them as complete and verified by the fact that God had revealed himself in his law and his elected people had responded to that revelation in willing obedience. Thus, the prime motive for keeping the law was a responsive, loving obedience to the one who gave it—God.

Results of the Law

To keep the commandments of the Lord was to recognize that those commandments were absolute, given authoritatively by a divine sovereign. The positive commands required specific action; the negative commands required specific restraint. Encouragement to obedience was provided by promises of blessings; warnings against disobedience took the form of threats and punishment. For example, blessings of life, well-being, longevity, and inheritance were promised for obedience.[37] On the other hand, capital punishment was prescribed for many cases of law violation,[38] and

36. Harry M. Orlinsky, *Understanding the Bible Through History and Archaeology* (New York: KTAV, 1972). Quoting Micah 6:8 ("He hath shewed thee, O man, what is good; and what doth the Lord require of thee, but to do justly, and to love mercy, and to walk humbly with thy God?"), Orlinsky continues, "This basic principle, that the law had to be obeyed in spirit together with the letter, was summed up even more succinctly in Deuteronomy 16:20, in the three Hebrew words *Tsedek tsedek tirdof,* 'Justice, justice shall you pursue'" (p. 256).

37. Deut. 5:33, 12:28.

38. Exod. 21:12, 15–17. Paul, *Studies in the Book of the Covenant,* remarks that these references are from the earliest biblical legal corpus, the Book of the Covenant, the formal legal section of which is Exod. 21:2–22:16. After careful comparative analysis, Paul points out several possible examples of the biblical adaptation of ancient Near Eastern cuneiform law code antecedents of the laws of Lipit-Ishtar, laws of Eshnunna, the Hammurabi code, and Hittite laws, in which he finds many striking parallels. He makes similar observations with reference to the Nuzi *Hapiru* document and the Ugaritic legal texts. However, with reference to Exod. 21:12 he observes, "This absolute ban on composition is considered to be contrary to the divine order (cf. Gen. 9:6), it cannot be atoned for by a pecuniary or property settlement; the murderer must be put to death. The religious precept of sanctity of a human life is here embodied within a legal formula" (pp. 41–42, 61, 102–104).

other kinds of disobedience brought on various forms of severe penalties.[39] These examples highlight the underlying principle of the law of government in the Bible. It was of God.

It has been mentioned that the Israelites saw the Sinai event as the historical occasion when they received the law from God.[40] In addition to the Decalogue which Moses received for the people on that occasion, he was instructed by God, who said,

> But you, stand here by me, and I will tell you all the commandments and the statutes and the ordinances which you shall teach them, that they may do them in the land which I give them to possess.[41]

For texts of the Lipit-Ishtar Law Code, Laws of Eshnunna, the Code of Hammurabi, the Middle Assyrian Laws, the Hittite Laws, and the Neo-Babylonian Laws, cf. James B. Pritchard, [ed.], *Ancient Near Eastern Texts Relating to the Old Testament,* 2d ed. (Princeton: Princeton University Press, 1955), pp. 159–198.

For brief descriptions and a study of interrelationships among the four great Law Codes of Eshnunna, Hammurabi, the biblical Book of the Covenant (Exod. 21–23), and the Talmud, cf. Reuven Yaron, "The Goring Ox in Near Eastern Laws," in *Jewish Law in Ancient and Modern Israel,* [ed. Haim H. Cohn], (New York: KTAV, 1971), pp. 50 ff.

39. Lev. 26:14–33; cf. below, chap. 5, for treatment of this theme.

40. Exod. 20:1–17; Deut. 5:6–21.

41. Deut. 5:31. Mediating positions with reference to the role of Moses as lawgiver and leader have been expressed in this century, both early and late, within the framework of the "History of Tradition" school of thought. Examples from representative authors follow.

Charles Foster Kent, *Israel's Laws and Legal Precedents* (New York: Charles Scribner's Sons, 1907), pp. 32–33. With reference to the relation of Moses to Deuteronomy, Kent states, "Not to have acknowledged the supreme debt to Moses would have been unwarranted. It is but fair to say that they [laws] represent what the great prophet would have taught had he been confronted by the later needs and stood in the light of later revelation. Through all the laws, early and late alike, the same God was making known his will to men. It mattered little who was his spokesman; the laws themselves bore on their face the credentials of their divine origin."

Roland de Vaux, *Bible et Orient* (Paris: Editions du Cerf, 1967), pp. 56–57. " . . . par une longue tradition orale et écrite, les narrations et les lois du Pentateuque remontent au timps où Israël se constitua en peuple. Or cette époque est dominée par la figure de Moïse: il a inspiré à Israël le sentiment de son unité, il lui

Eventually, these commandments, statutes and ordinances were, in written form, referred to by the Hebrews as "a copy of the Law of Moses" (משנה תורת משה).[42]

GUIDELINES. The Law of Moses provided the guidelines for the Israelites in all the areas of their activities. This was the case whether the activity was religious, civil, moral, ethical, or social.[43] This was also true regardless of the position of the particular person through whom the law was being articulated, providing, of course, that person was authorized to teach and interpret the law. It has already been pointed out that according to the Bible and rabbinic tradition, God directed the Hebrews beginning with the patriarchs. Then he gave them a law through Moses, whose authority was validated.[44] Under the law the priesthood was assigned major responsibilities, and Aaron, as the first high priest, was declared, along with his posterity, as having the position of authority in the priesthood.[45] However, all of their duties were prescribed by the Law of Moses, even in the details of the different offerings.[46] Then, as has been pointed out, Joshua set the Law of Moses before

a donné sa religion et ses premières lois. C'est là un fait essentiel, qui est commun à toutes les traditions et qu'on ne peut mettre en doute sans rendre inexplicable toute la suite de l'histoire. Les traditions antérieures à lui et le souvenir des événements qu'il a conduits sont devenues l'épopée nationale, la religion de Moïse a marqué pour toujours la foi et la pratique de peuple, la loi de Moïse a continué de le régire."

42. Josh. 8:32.

43. J. H. Hertz, "Ancient Semitic Codes and the Mosaic Legislation," *Publication of the Society for Jewish Jurisprudence,* November 1928, p. 220. In discussing the Mosaic Law vs. the Babylonian, Assyrian, and Hittite Codes, Hertz gives an overriding principle in Mosaic Law when he states, "Perhaps in no respect is the abyss between these resurrected codes and the Mosaic Law deeper than in their attitude to human freedom. . . . the protection of humanity, that is the aim of the Mosaic Code."

44. Num. 12:5–8.

45. Num. 16:1–18:7.

46. Lev. 6:9, 14, 25 (Heb. Lev. 6:2, 7, 18); Lev. 7:1, 11, 37–38.

the people, urging them to "fear the Lord, and serve him in sincerity and in faithfulness" (Josh. 24:14a).[47]

According to I Samuel, chapter 3, the word of the Lord was revealed to Samuel,[48] who, in his own person, marks the transition from the age of the Judges to that of the Prophets. It was Samuel who chose Israel's first king. At that time Samuel solemnly charged the people and warned them that disobedience to the command of the Lord would cause both king and nation to be swept away.[49]

Law Often Disregarded

The emergence of kingship in Israel did not mean that the law of government would be altered. Indeed, the law had already provided for the eventual transition to the agency of kingship as a channel through which God's law of government would continue to be effective. The law was very precise in stressing that when a king came to the throne in Israel he was to be subject to the law if he expected to be blessed and continue his dynasty.[50] The king's relationship to the law was expressed by de Vaux as follows:

> . . . the king could add nothing to the authority of a law to which he himself was subject (I K. 8:58; 2 K. 23:3). There was no such thing as State law in Israel. . . . On the other hand, the king was a judge, and held judicial power.[51]

47. Cf. George E. Mendenhall, *Law and Covenant in Israel and the Ancient Near East* (Pittsburgh: Presbyterian Board of Colportage of Western Pennsylvania, 1955), pp. 41–42, for analysis of the Covenant of Joshua 24. Mendenhall maintains that there is indication of a continuation of the Mosaic Covenant in the prologue.

48. I Sam. 3.

49. I Sam. 12. Similar warnings were uttered by Moses. Cf. Lev. 26:14 ff., Deut. 8:11–20, 11:26 ff., 28:15 ff.

50. Deut. 17:18–20.

51. Roland de Vaux, *Ancient Israel: Its Life and Institutions,* [trans. John McHugh], (New York: McGraw-Hill, 1961), p. 151.

In spite of this instruction, however, the ideal relationship of king to law often remained merely theoretical. During the time of kingship among the Israelites the Law of God was often lost sight of by king, prophet,[52] and priest. This is illustrated by the fact that the law had been literally lost for a long period.[53] But even when it was available, "the words of the Lord" were rejected and the scroll on which they were written were literally cut into shreds and burnt.[54] In addition, the prophet Ezekiel spoke against the priests of his day, saying, "[The] priests have done violence to my law and have profaned my holy things . . ."[55] At times, in fact, the very people who were supposed to be the channels through which God's law was made known to the public were denounced by the prophet speaking in the name of God. Thus Jeremiah maintains:

> The Priests did not say, "Where is the Lord?" Those who handle the law did not know me; the rulers transgressed against me; the prophets prophesied by Baal, and went after things that do not profit.[56]

This kind of rebellion against their law of government eventually led the Israelites to disaster. The kingdom of Israel fell to the Assyrians,[57] and the kingdom of Judah was conquered by the Babylonians.[58]

Ezra's Reform Work

Following the Jewish return to their homeland from Babylo-

---

52. Orlinsky, *Understanding the Bible,* p. 258. "The prophets, more than any other group, emphasized the fact that the laws expressed God's will . . . "

53. II Kings 22.

54. Jer. 36. However, it should be noted that Jehoiakim's vandalism was not typical even among the more ruthless kings.

55. Ezek. 22:26.

56. Jer. 2:8.

57. II Kings 17:23.

58. II Kings 25:1–21; Jer. 39:1–10; II Chron. 36:17–21.

nia, God's law of government was strongly emphasized.[59] It was apparently at this time that the new profession of the Scribes flourished among the Jews, which had as its *raison d'etre* copying, studying, and teaching the law.[60] It was said of the greatest of the Scribes, Ezra, that he "had set his heart to study the law of the Lord, and to do it, and to teach his statutes and ordinances in Israel,"[61] and that "He was a scribe skilled in the law of Moses which the Lord the God of Israel had given . . ."[62] The importance of Ezra's place in the history of Judaism and in the structuring of the law is affirmed by Albright in the following words:

> He [Ezra] seems to have played an important role in establishing the canonical Torah as the normative rule of Israel's faith. . . . It seems highly probable that it was Ezra who introduced the complete Pentateuch into normative Jewish use. . . . In another direction we may credit Ezra with original literary compilation. . . . It is . . . highly probable that Jewish tradition is in principle correct in identifying Ezra with the Chronicler.[63]

Under his tutelage the Law of Moses became the governing force for the Jews in their homeland. It is likely that it was only from his time on that the Law of Moses was effectively imposed on the people, thanks to the authority granted to Ezra by King Artaxerxes I.

And you, Ezra, according to the wisdom of your God which is in

59. Isidore Epstein, *Judaism: A Historical Presentation* (Baltimore: Penguin Books, 1959), pp. 82–85.

60. Cf. Jacob J. Rabinowitz, *Studies in Legal History* (Jerusalem: R. H. Cohen Press, 1958), p. 16. "The Hebrew סופר (scribe) is used in the Bible in a double sense. . . . The title is applied to one Zadok who was a treasury clerk (Nehemiah 13:13) and to Ezra, 'the priest-scribe' (Ezra 7:11)."

61. Ezra 7:10.

62. Ezra 7:6.

63. William Foxwell Albright, *The Biblical Period* (Pittsburgh: Presbyterian Board of Colportage of Western Pennsylvania, n.d.), p. 54.

your hand, appoint magistrates and judges who may judge all the
people in the province Beyond the River, all such as know the laws
of your God; and those who do not know them, you shall teach.
Whoever will not obey the law of your God and the law of the king,
let judgment be strictly executed upon him, whether for death or for
banishment or for confiscation of his goods or for imprisonment.[64]

During Nehemiah's tenure as governor, Ezra saw to it that the law
was read publicly and explained so the common people could
understand it.[65] As a result, the people confessed their sins and
rededicated themselves according to the law of the Torah, and the
men pledged separation from their foreign wives.[66] Thus, the Law
of Moses became an effective force of government for the people.

Summary

The foregoing discussion has traced the law of government in the
Bible from Abraham and the patriarchal period to Ezra and
postexilic times. It is evident that a basic theological belief of the
Hebrews was that Torah (תורה), as a revelation of God's will, was
not only expressed by God directly, as to Moses at Sinai, but was
often transmitted to the people by way of prophet, priest, and
judge. It is also apparent that the word *Torah* was used in a variety
of ways. In some instances it was merely a specific regulation
about a particular matter.[67] Sometimes it was identified as the
standard which had been violated.[68] And it has certainly been
stressed that Torah was a "book of the law" which one had to
study and obey in order to be successful; e.g., the instructions to
Joshua:

64. Ezra 7:11–28, quote, vv. 25–26.
65. Louis Jacobs, "Torah, Reading of," *Encyclopaedia Judaica,* vol. 15, cols.
1246–47.
66. Neh. 8:9–18; Ezra 10.
67. Num. 5:29–31.
68. Zeph. 3:4.

Only be strong and very courageous, being careful to do according to all the law which Moses my servant commanded you; turn not from it to the right hand or to the left, that you may have good success wherever you go.This book of the law shall not depart out of your mouth, but you shall meditate on it day and night, that you may be careful to do according to all that is written in it; for then you shall make our way prosperous; and then you shall have good success.[69]

This, then, was God's law of government for the Israelites as perceived by them. Its mode of expression varied from time to time throughout the long course of history, and was not its essential characteristic. Its unique feature was its revelatory character, and its supreme authority was due to the divine source from which it came—YHWH.

POSTBIBLICAL AND TALMUDIC CONCEPTS OF THE LAW OF GOVERNMENT

The concept of the law of government in the Talmud is more complex than the concept of the law of government in the Bible. In order to more effectively come to grips with the complexity of the law of government in the Talmud, it will be helpful to see the Torah from a rabbinic point of view.[70] At the outset it is easy to

70. Cf. Neusner, *Understanding Rabbinic Judaism,* p. 7, "The central conception of rabbinic Judaism is the belief that the ancient Scriptures constituted divine revelation, but only a part of it. At Sinai, God had handed down a dual revelation: the written part known to one and all, but also the oral part preserved by the great scriptural heroes, passed on by prophets to various ancestors in the obscure

69. Josh. 1:7–8. John Bright, "The Book of Joshua," *Interpreter's Bible,* vol. 2, p. 555. Bright, although well aware of the literary problems surrounding the structure of this book, notes the basic impact of this introductory material on the subsequent conquest from the writer's point of view, i.e., the ultimate outcome is predicated on keeping the law. Bright states, "If Israel hopes to have success she must yield total obedience to the commandments of God . . . [and] it is clear from vs. 8—*book of the law*—that it is the Deuteronomic law that is meant."

conclude from an examination of some textual evidence that there continued to be a great emphasis on Scripture as law; and, in concomitant fashion, the necessity of obedience to the law remained prominent in Jewish writings.

Evidence from the Apocrypha

The postexilic period of Jewish history provides documentary evidence of these features in the apocryphal writings. For example, one finds a call to "even greater progress in living according to the law" in the following appeal:

> Whereas many great teachings have been given to us through the law and the prophets and the others that followed them, on account of which we should praise Israel for instruction and wisdom . . . those who love learning should make even greater progress in living according to the law.[71]

This encouragement "in living according to the law" in the postexilic period was more than mere suggestion. Obedience to the commandments of God was bluntly set down as the only way to live. With reference to Torah, it was said, "She is the book of the commandments of God, and the law that endures for ever. All who hold her fast will live, and those who forsake her will die."[72]

In addition, the apocryphal-historical work of I Maccabees throws light on the emphasis which was being given to law with reference to religious ritual and life. When the Temple was being purified and renovated for worship under the direction of Judas Maccabeus, it is said that

---

past, finally and most openly handed down to the rabbis who created the Palestinian and Babylonian Talmuds. The 'whole Torah' thus consisted of both written and oral parts."

71. Sir., Prologue.

72. Bar. 4:1.

He chose blameless priests devoted to the law, and they cleansed the sanctuary and removed the defiled stones to an unclean place. . . . Then they took unhewn stones, as the law directs, and built a new altar like the former one.[73]

This careful attention that things be done according to the law by those who were devoted to the law indicates that the Jews, in spite of the disruption of society during their struggle for independence, still clung to the conviction that life must be lived according to Torah, and that worship rituals and religious institutions should reflect this commitment.[74]

Evidence from Josephus

It is true that the exigencies of Diaspora life motivated Samuel to rule in the third century that the Jews were to regard the civil law of the land as binding on themselves.[75] However, as noted below,

73. I Macc. 4:42–47.

74. G. H. Box and W. O. E. Oesterley, "Sirach," in *The Apocrypha and Pseudepigrapha of the Old Testament,* ed. R. H. Charles (Oxford: Clarendon Press, 1913), vol. 1, p. 316, "This expresses the practical aim which governed all the activities of the teachers of the Law. Cf. Josephus (*Contra Apion* II, 8:) 'But, as for our people, if any do but ask one of them concerning our laws he will tell all more readily than his own name, and this because of our learning them at once, as soon as we could understand anything, and because they were, as it were, grave upon our souls.'" Also, cf. D. S. Russell, *Between the Testaments,* rev. ed. (Philadelphia: Fortress Press, 1965), pp. 29–30, where Russell gives examples of the acts of the Hasmoneans in destroying renegades and restoring the Temple cult; e.g., "When a Syrian official came to Modein to enforce heathen sacrifice, Mattathias not only refused to comply but slew a renegade Jew who did sacrifice and at the same time killed the Syrian official. . . . The Revolt which followed was led in turn by three of Mattathias's sons, Judas (166–160 B.C.) surnamed Maccabaeus ('the Hammerer'?), Jonathan (160–143 B.C.) and Simon (142–134 B.C.). Marked success followed their campaigns. On the 25th of Chislev (December), 165 B.C., on the very day on which it had been desecrated three years before (I Macc. 4:54), the Temple was cleansed and rededicated, under the leadership of Judas, and the worship restored (I Macc. 4:36 ff.; cf. II Macc. 10:1–7)."

75. Max L. Margolis and Alexander Marx, *A History of the Jewish People*

this was to be the case only if the civil law was consistent with the principles of Judaism. The basic commitment to Torah as God's law of government for the Jewish people continued to be their supreme standard. The reason for this commitment and the extent to which it would go was stated by a Jewish historian who lived to see the destruction of the Second Temple. He said,

> We have given practical proof of our reverence for our own Scriptures. For, although such long ages have now passed, no one has ventured either to add, or to remove, or to alter a syllable; and it is an instinct with every Jew, from the day of his birth, to regard them as the decrees of God, to abide by them, and if need be, cheerfully to die for them.[76]

Thus, it is clear from documentary sources subsequent to the building of the Second Temple, and extending down in history until the time of the destruction of that Temple, that the Jews never lost sight of Torah as God's law of government for them.

Torah Included Scripture and Tradition

It is now time to stress the fact that in postbiblical Judaism the concept of Torah was broad enough to include all the Hebrew Scriptures identified as Torah (Pentateuch), Prophets, and Hagiographa (תנך), as well as the Oral Tradition. Torah was viewed as the entire Mosaic Law, and from this basic meaning the view of Torah

---

(New York: Jewish Publication Society, 1927), p. 239. "In the field of jurisprudence, Samuel specialized in civil cases, and his early appointment to the bench enlarged his experience and deepened his understanding of legal principles so that his decisions, as well as his pronouncements later during his career as a teacher, became authoritative in this branch of the law. A far-reaching legal maxim of his makes the law of the state, in all matters not affecting religious practice, binding upon the Jew."

76. Josephus, *Against Apion,* bk. I, 8 [trans. H. St. J. Thackeray], (in Loeb Classical Library, vol. 1, pp. 179, 181).

was extended to include the other biblical writings, primarily because they were in harmony with the pentateuchal scriptures. Their basis of authority was their agreement with them. In addition,

> the "traditions of the elders"—rules of Jewish life and religion which in the course of centuries had come to possess a validity and sanctity equal to that of the Written Law and which, as the "Oral Law," were deemed, equally with the Written Law, to be of divine origin and therefore consonant with and, for the most part, deducible from the Written Law.[77]

According to the Tradition, this Oral Law was received by Moses at Mount Sinai and subsequently transmitted from him to Joshua.[78] He committed it to the elders.[79] The elders passed it on to the prophets.[80] The prophets gave it to the men of the Great Synagogue.[81]

CONTINUITY OF TRADITION. This continuity was important for the Jews because it assured them of the authoritative nature of the Oral Law. Unfortunately, the identity of the men of the Great Synagogue is shrouded in obscurity. Ezra, traditionally connected

77. Herbert Danby, *The Mishnah,* rev. ed. (London: Oxford University Press, 1958), p. 446, n. 2.

78. M. Ab. I, 1. Josh. 1:7. Sidney B. Hoenig, [ed.], *The Book of Joshua: A New English Translation of the Text and Rashi with a Commentary Digest,* [trans. P. Oratz, A. J. Rosenberg, and Sidney Shulman], (New York: Judaica Press, 1969), p. 5. "Rabbi Simeon ben Jochai held that not only the Oral Law was received by Joshua from Moses, but that Joshua also received the Written Law (Deuteronomy) from Moses, and that the phrase 'this book of the law' in Josh. 1:8 referred to Deuteronomy." Also, cf. above, pp. 20–21, 24–25.

79. M. Ab. I, 1.

80. Ibid.

81. Danby, loc. cit., n. 5. This author notes that the Great Synagogue was "a body of 120 elders, including many prophets, who came up from exile with Ezra; they saw that prophecy had come to an end and that restraint was lacking; therefore they made many new rules and restrictions for the better observance of the Law."

with this governmental body, was called the Scribe. The work of the Scribes and their relationship to this governing body and the governmental process in general are very vague until about the time of the Hasmoneans. Herford describes the situation which existed at that time as follows:

> In the rabbinical tradition a council was founded by Ezra which lasted for many years. The scanty references to it indicate the assembly mentioned in Neh. iv, x. No such permanent council can be shown to have existed; but the tradition is not wholly worthless. The term "Great Synagogue" may be taken to denote the early Scribes (Sopherim), who developed the religion of Torah on the lines and in the spirit of Ezra, for several generations after his time.[82]

Furthermore, the continuity of the transmission of the Oral Law from the days of the Great Synagogue until the dawn of the common era is implied in the opening passages of tractate Aboth. In fact, the tradition has it that from about 160 B.C.E. until the common era the transmission of the Oral Law was through the "president" and "vice-president" of the Sanhedrin from generation to generation.[83] On the basis of this "chain of Tradition," the Rabbis stressed the "Mosaic" basis of their authority.

---

82. R. Travers Herford, "Pirkē Aboth," in *The Apocrypha and Pseudepigrapha of the Old Testament,* [ed.], R. H. Charles, vol. 2 (Oxford: Clarendon Press, 1913), p. 691.

83. M. Ab. I, 1–12; M. Ḥag. II, 2. The authenticity of this tradition has been disputed; though there is a possibility that there was a religious Sanhedrin in addition to the political one which was presided over by the High Priest. Cf. Isidore Epstein, *Judaism,* p. 100, where Epstein states, "During Herodian times, the political Sanhedrin, composed primarily of the Sadducean aristocracy and presided over by the High Priest, concerned itself with political matters, and with the relations of the State with foreign countries; while the religious Sanhedrin, known as the Great Beth Din, presided over by pairs of teachers, had full control over the religious life of the people, and all civil and domestic issues, in so far as these did not impinge upon the politics of the State."

RABBINIC CHANNEL OF TRADITION. During these centuries the Midrash process was going on. The exegesis and interpretation of the law was accompanied by a growing body of *kabbalah* (tradition) which was also authoritative in nature. The channel through which this comprehensive process continued to have its expression was rabbinical. The *halākhāh* which was produced by the Rabbis in the earlier periods was relatively uniform. This was because the Great Sanhedrin of Jerusalem rendered decisions by majority rule in cases where there was some doubt as to the design of a particular law. However, as times became more tumultuous for the Jews, and especially from the period of the Hellenization of the East onward, Jewish life faced challenges from outside influences it had never faced before. There also developed within Judaism a vigorous debating process with respect to the law which showed itself vividly in the different sects which emerged, such as the Pharisees and Sadducees. Thus, the Pharisees upheld the binding validity of the Oral Tradition; the Sadducees denied it.

> Better educated generally, and more strict than the average Pharisee, the Sadducees accepted the Written Law as binding under all circumstances. New laws and new institutions had, to them, no true authority. Thus they rejected legislation enacted to deal with the existing situations of a changed world. Every action, statement or belief must have the direct authority of the Scriptures or they would have none of it.[84]

After Palestine fell to the Romans in 63 B.C.E., and the authority of the Great Sanhedrin was greatly reduced, the diverse activity of the rabbinical scholars was manifested in opposing schools like those of Beth Shammai and Beth Hillel.[85]

84. Gaalyahu Cornfeld, [ed.], *Daniel to Paul* (Tel Aviv: Hamikra Baolam, n.d.), pp. 161–162. Also, cf. Elias Bickerman, *From Ezra to the Last of the Maccabees: Foundations of Post-Biblical Judaism* (New York: Schocken Books, 1947), pp. 171–172.

85. George Foot Moore, *Judaism,* vol. 1 (Cambridge: Harvard University Press, 1927), pp. 77–81. Also, cf. T.B. San. 88b.

Turbulent Times

After the destruction of Jerusalem by the Roman general Titus in 70 C.E., the Great Sanhedrin no longer existed. After considering the evidence and admitting the existence of alternative views, Hoenig speaks of the exact date of the dissolution of this important body in the following words:

> All proof . . . leads to the conclusion that the Great Sanhedrin functioned in Jerusalem until the beginning of hostilities in the Revolt against Rome. The exact date when the Great Sanhedrin was dissolved may be set as 66 C.E.—four years before the destruction of the Temple.[86]

Rabbis and rabbinical schools were scattered. The features of the early *halākhāh* under a powerful Great Sanhedrin, anonymity and uniformity, were no longer possible to maintain. The threat to the survival of Jewish law as it had come to be was very real. The destruction of much of the framework within which Jewish law had developed was decisive in determining its future evolving process.

Crucial Role of the Sages

The Sages continued to play a crucial role in these and subsequent times. The rationale for their role was grounded in the written Torah itself.[87] Rabbinical comment on Deuteronomy 17:9 indicates they saw it as a mandate to the Sages for preservation, expansion, and implementation of the law in every age.

> Can we then imagine that a man should go to a judge who is not in his days? This shows that you must be content to go to the judge who is in your days. It also says, "Say not, How was it that the for-

87. Sidney B. Hoenig, *The Great Sanhedrin* (Philadelphia: Dropsie College, 1953), pp. 109–113.
    87. Deut. 17:9.

mer days were better than these." (n. I.e., had better judges than these. Eccl. 7:10).[88]

Thus, the Rabbis worked under a strong feeling of commitment to divine directive. However, they did not assume beyond their human powers. They were opposed to direct aid in their task, such as visions, heavenly voices, or prophetic utterances inspired by God.[89] They saw the written Torah as the foundation for the entire Jewish legal system, having its binding authority by virtue of its divine source at Sinai. Therefore, the extensive work of all the halakhic scholars in their continuing development of Jewish law was theoretically in agreement with the principles enunciated in the written Torah. If, on occasion, laws were created without pentateuchal authority, they were nevertheless valid if the motive for their enactment was "to make a fence for the Torah."[90]

The Talmud

At about the beginning of the sixth century C.E.[91] the enormous quantity of rabbinical material found in the Mishnah and Gemara

88. Epstein, I. [ed.], T.B. R.H. 25b [trans. Maurice Simon]. All quotations from the Talmud are from I. Epstein's edition of the Babylonian Talmud, unless otherwise indicated. If the translator's notes are included, e.g., above, the translator is acknowledged for his contribution to the quotation. Translator's notes are enclosed in parentheses within the quotations and begin with the abbreviation "n." Other interpolations in the quotations are enclosed in brackets.

89. T.B. B.M. 59b.

90. T.B. Yeb. 90b.

91. Salo W. Baron, *A Social and Religious History of the Jews,* vol. 2, *Christian Era: The First Five Centuries* (Philadelphia: Jewish Publication Society, 1937), p. 267, "Even during the fifth century C.E. the Jews still generally retained criminal jurisdiction in their courts. The capital sanctions were gone, however. Generally, the rabbis found that flagellation, heavy fines, and a system of excommunication upheld the authority of the courts. In short, Jewish law and judicial administration were much more decisive in the life of the Jewish masses than imperial or local legislation and judicial proceedings."

was brought together in redacted form into a comprehensive corpus known as the Talmud. One theory holds

> that such material had been edited early, each part arranged around its particular mishnah in a precise and finished manner and phraseology. . . . This continual process of Talmudic redaction, begun in the second Amoraic generation, after Rav and Samuel, was carried on till the time of R. Ashi.[92]

Summary

In this section the evolution of Jewish law has been stressed, and the historical path by which the Babylonian Talmud came to be virtually the infallible source for the law of government in Judaism has been outlined.[93] It has also been shown that the end result of this historical process, the formation of the Talmud, was the direct consequence of the work of the Rabbis from the age of the construction of the Second Temple to the end of the age of the *Savoraim*.[94]

Throughout this long process, the Rabbis understood that the force and authority of the *halākhāh* was its continuity. Thus, as the *halākhāh* grew, they were concerned that every rule or regulation added to the body of legal literature sprang, either directly or indirectly, out of its divine origin, the written Torah, or from other *halakhot* which had in turn originated from the Torah. Therefore, it was outside the perspective of the Rabbis to view their work at any stage as a revision of previous work. Rather, they saw their effort in each successive age as a work of continuity. Thus, when the Talmud was finally assembled in its redacted form, it was, by

92. J. Kaplan, *The Redaction of the Babylonian Talmud* (New York: Bloch, 1933), p. 179.

93. From this point the Babylonian Talmud will be referred to simply as the Talmud.

94. Cf. Solomon Schechter, *Studies in Judaism, Third Series* (Philadelphia: Jewish Publication Society, 1924), pp. 194–225, for a more detailed description of the schools from the *soferim* of Ezra's time to the era of the *Savoraim*.

virtue of the philosophy of the scholars who produced it, a compilation. This helps to account for the presence of the contradictory opinions rendered by Rabbis.[95] It also helps one to understand why the enactment of additional laws after the "closing" of the Talmud was in no way contrary to the basic perspective of the Talmud itself.[96]

LAW OF SCHOLAR AND COMMUNITY

The foregoing has dealt with that sequence of historical events which eventually led to the establishment of the Talmud as the law of government in Judaism. It also traced the philosophic concepts of the Rabbis, such as the conviction concerning the divine origin of Torah and the principle of continuity of *halākhāh* in each succeeding age as it grew out of and expanded upon the written Torah. Attention is now turned to one aspect of this dynamic process to illustrate the rationale behind specific laws relating to governmental or judicial ethics and the methodology by which these laws were enacted.

Function of Legislation

Legislation has the function of inaugurating a legal standard where none existed before. Or, where laws already exist which bear on a particular matter, legislation may be designed to repeal or alter

95. Cf. M. Ed. I, 4–6 for further details.

96. Jacob Neusner, "Archaeology and Babylonian Jewry," in *Near Eastern Archaeology in the Twentieth Century,* [ed. James A. Sanders], (Garden City, N. Y.: Doubleday, 1970), p. 332. Referring to the "anti-archaeological bias" of past scholarship concerning Babylonian Jewry, Neusner speaks of "the theological conviction that in the rabbinical schools, the 'whole Torah' revealed at Sinai was preserved, both the written text as we now have it, as well as the oral traditions supposedly handed on alongside. No rational argument about the nature of the Babylonian Talmud as a *historical* source was ever thought necessary, for a fundamentally sacred text obviously contained whatever was so. The text did not merely yield history—it *was* history."

existing laws. In the continuing halakhic system of Judaism, legislative objectives were accomplished by a *takkanah* (enactment) or a *gezerah* (decree). The *takkanah* was a legal source of Jewish law, and, when enacted by Sages, carried the force of law.[97] It was positive in emphasis, encouraging positive action. The legislative action of the *gezerah,* on the other hand, was preventive in nature, and usually thought of as "making a fence around the Torah."[98] A brief overview of the historical process of *takkanah* follows, showing the continuous dynamic aspect of the law of government in Judaism. This kind of development was done by Sages who were convinced that the highest source of Jewish law, the Torah, delegated this authority to them.[99]

Takkanoth

The principle of *takkanah* was seen by the talmudic scholars as going back to pre-Sinaitic times. For example, the Rabbis saw their practice of prayers as originating with Abraham, Isaac, and Jacob.[100] They also took note that after the law was received at Sinai, *takkanoth* continued to be enacted by prominent leaders of Israel. Joshua's action at Shechem, when he "wrote these words in the book of the law of God,"[101] was an example of *takkanah* which the Rabbis taught as one of the many coming from this great leader, who, upon his entry into the land of Israel, "laid down ten stipulations."[102] The *takkanah* tradition continued into the time of kingship, as illustrated by the ruling of King David concerning the sharing of booty by the soldiers during a time of war.[103] The tradi-

---

97. *Encyclopaedia Judaica,* s.v. "Takkanot," vol. 15, cols. 728–734.

98. Julius H. Greenstone, "Gezerah," *Jewish Encyclopedia* (1916), vol. 5, pp. 648–649.

99. T.B. Shab. 23a.

100. T.B. Ber. 26b.

101. Josh. 24:25–26.

102. T.B. B.Ḳ. 80b–81a.

103. I Sam. 30:24–25.

tion of the Sages shows that the role of *takkanoth* continued to have a vital place in legislation after the period of the exile.

A large number of these *takkanoth* are found in the public, criminal, and civil areas of Jewish law. Those prescribed before the destruction of the Temple and Jerusalem were usually anonymous because they were rulings of the Great Sanhedrin. Occasionally, however, the leading Rabbi of that court is associated with a particular *takkanah*. For example,

> In former times a man was allowed to bring together a Beth Din wherever he was and cancel the *Gel*. Rabban Gamaliel the Elder, however, laid down a rule that this should not be done, so as to prevent abuses.[104]

Rulings by a *Nasi* and the *Beth Din* after the destruction of the Temple and throughout the entire tannaitic period (ca. 1–220 C.E.) set a pattern for the type and direction of the *halākhāh* for hundreds of years.[105]

Amoraim

In matters of law, the later *Amoraim* worked out of this framework, but did add a greater legislative dimension to the work of the tannaitic Sages, as the following examples show. They bolstered the Torah injunction "you shall do what is right and good"[106] with decrees which supplemented the existing laws for greater justice, especially in social and economic matters.[107] By deduction from Ezra 10:8, which speaks of the forfeiture of possessions under certain conditions, the *Amoraim* evolved the principle of "arise and do," which meant that they could enact *takkanoth* with positive action which circumvented Torah law if it appeared

---

104. T.B. M. Giṭ. IV, 2.
105. *Encyclopaedia Judaica,* s.v. "Bet Din and Judges," vol. 4, cols. 724–725.
106. Deut. 6:18.
107. T.B. B.M. 108a.

necessary to insure justice and equity. Thus, Hillel the Elder decreed a *prosbul* to circumvent Deuteronomy 15:1–2,

> which declares that the Sabbatical year cancels all debts. This institution was introduced by Hillel because he observed that the effect of the biblical law was to deter people from loaning to the needy, a practice which violates the higher moral command of the Torah (Deut. 15:9) which enjoins upon us not to refrain from lending to the poor.[108]

TAKKANOTH FOR "GOOD ORDER." Also, in the criminal area this principle of enactments was utilized for the purpose of maintaining good order during troublesome times.[109] There could also be the setting aside of a positive command of Torah by a *takkanah* under certain conditions, if the Rabbis believed that by such enactment they were in fact carrying out the spirit of Torah, as in the prohibition of blowing the *shofar* on a Rosh Hashanah that fell on Saturday. Raba said, "According to the Written Law it is allowed, and it is the Rabbis who prohibited it."[110]

TAKKANOTH FOR CHANGING TIMES. The final example of how the Sages utilized *takkanoth* to broaden the legislative dimension is seen in their dealing with certain situations in which application of existing laws was neither satisfactory nor appropriate. These conditions were usually brought about by changing times and conditions. For example, the Torah made it necessary for a person to have at least two witnesses for a testimony to be valid.[111] However, a *takkanah* was decreed and taught by both Beth Hillel and Beth Shammai that

---

108. Jacob Z. Lauterbach, *Rabbinic Essays* (Cincinnati: Hebrew Union College Press, 1951; reprinted, New York: KTAV, 1973), p. 287. Also, cf. B.T. Giṭ. 36a.

109. T.B. Yeb. 90b.

110. T.B. R.H. 29b.

111. Deut. 19:15.

A woman who came from the region of the sea and said: "My husband died"—she may be married again; "my husband died" [without issue]—she must be married by her husband's brother (Deut. 25:5).[112]

Thus, if circumstances indicated that a *takkanah* was needed for matters to be resolved in a just manner, it was often enacted even though it circumvented a teaching of the Torah.

The "Will of the Majority"

The analysis above has dealt with specific laws and the *takkanah* and *gezerah* methodologies by which the Sages implemented these laws. This approach to the Talmud as the law of government in Judaism implies that the immediate source of talmudic law was always the Sages. However, this was not the case. The Sages themselves recognized that the "will of the majority" was to be taken into account in matters where basic religious principles were not involved, and that earlier *halakhoth* contained *takkanoth* based upon this principle. For example, in matters concerning charity

---

112. T.B. M. Ed. I, 12. Also S. R. Driver, *Deuteronomy,* International Critical Commentary, 3d ed. (1902), pp. 281–283. Driver remarks that the law of levirate marriage was an early tribal institution in ancient Israel (Gen. 38, esp. vv. 8, 14b, 26) as well as in many other countries, e.g., India and Brazil. However, the Hebrew institution as expressed through Jewish law was different in three respects: "(1) it was limited to the case where the deceased left no male issue; (2) even then it was only put into force when the two brothers were living on the same family estate; (3) the surviving brother, though he took his deceased brother's widow as his wife, and enjoyed during his lifetime (so far as appears) his brother's estate, did not found a family for himself: the issue of the marriage succeeded in the name and estate of the deceased brother." In stressing the high ethical motivation for such legislation, i.e., "to prevent the extinction of a family," the point is also made that the importance of this legislation for the Hebrews is evident from the fact that "perform the duty of a husband's brother" is expressed in Hebrew by a single word, a verb derived from the Hebrew term for 'husband's brother' (יבם), viz., ויבמה, i.e., 'treat her as a יבם', or 'husband's brother' (so Gen. 38:8)."

and the feeding of the poor, the elected or appointed leaders of a town determined many of the rules by which this was to be done, as well as the penalties for violation of the rules, i.e.,

> The townspeople . . . are at liberty to use the soup kitchen like the charity fund and vice versa, and to apply them to whatever purposes they choose. The townspeople are also at liberty to fix weights and measures, prices, and wages, and to inflict penalties for the infringement of their rules.[113]

The principle of following the majority was derived from the rabbinic interpretation of Exodus 23:2, viz.,

> Whence is derived the principle which the Rabbis have adopted, viz.: Follow the majority? Whence? [you ask]; is it not expressly written, "Follow the majority"? In regard to those cases where the majority is defined, as in the case of the Nine Shops or the Sanhedrin, we do not ask the question.[114]

Thus it is clear that the general rule was to have the majority opinion prevail via the majority ruling of the courts.[115] Or, in situations where the ruling of the community majority was obviously the most equitable and ethical position to espouse, there would eventually arise a *takkanah* which would incorporate that ruling into the continuing halakhic legal system.

Summary

The analysis in this section makes it possible to see the halakhic

---

113. T.B. B.B. 8b.
114. T.B. Hul. 11a. [trans. Eli Cashdan], Hullin, p. 48, n. 2. "If in a particular neighborhood there are nine shops which sell ritually slaughtered meat and a tenth which sells *trefah* meat, any meat found in that neighborhood is *kosher* or permitted, it being presumed to have come from the majority, i.e., one of the nine shops."
115. T.B. San. 3b.

legislation of the Rabbis in two vital dimensions. First, when the conditions of the times had changed so drastically from earlier generations that the existing laws did not provide solutions to current problems, the Sages ruled by *takkanah* and *gezerah* in enacting laws to meet those problems through the legal process. Second, in matters of the moment which were partially covered by existing *halākhāh*, it was often possible for the scholars to legislate amendments to existing laws in order to make them appropriate to the new circumstances of the hour.

The continuing legal activity of the Sages was carried on with the full realization that the Torah contained the prohibition, "You shall not add to the word which I command you, nor take from it; that you may keep the commandments of the Lord your God which I command you" (Deut. 4:2). They did not, however, see the evolutionary character of law in the continuing halakhic traditions of the Talmud as contradictory to that prohibition. They saw themselves, unanimously, as recipients of a sacred trust to interpret, expand, create, and continue the *halākhāh*.[116]

In this framework, the prohibition of Deuteronomy 4:2 applied to those who would try to legislate outside the bounds of rabbinic authority. However, this view was not unanimously held by all Rabbis. Some maintained that it applied to everybody, as well as the courts, and the prohibition applied to any attempt to maintain that an enacted law was actually on a par with the Torah. If, however, the Sages were willing to admit that any enacted law was valid because it was according to the Torah and had been enacted by them as rabbinic law by virtue of the authority entrusted to them by the Torah, this was not to be construed as a violation of the deuteronomic prohibition. This view did not perceive the scholars as engaged in primary legislation. The primary legislation rested in Torah, while their work was that of "fence building"

116. Deut. 17:8–11. G. T. Manley, "Deuteronomy," in *The New Bible Commentary,* [ed. F. Davidson, A. M. Stibbs, and E. F. Kevan], 2d ed. (Grand Rapids, Mich.: Eerdmans, 1954), p. 213.

within the scope of authority vested in them by Torah as a channel for the continuing, dynamic development of the law.

Conclusion

In this chapter on the concept of law in the Bible and Talmud, an historical approach to the subject has been adopted. This approach made it possible to analyze the concept of law in both the Bible and the Talmud without distorting the analysis with subjectivism with regard to the law or psychological speculation with regard to the people for whom the law was intended. Or, in other words, the record was allowed to "speak for itself."

This approach established that the concept of law was, from the very beginning of the Hebrew people, a theological concept. The people were chosen by God. The Torah was given to them by God.[117] After the close of the Hebrew Scriptures, the Oral Law and the rabbinical traditions were eventually recorded in the Talmud. The concept of the Sages was that this development was an authoritative process by which the principles and spirit of Torah were perpetuated into succeeding generations.

Both the introduction and this chapter have touched on the ethics of government in the Bible and the Talmud. More germane to the purpose of the present study, however, is the fact that the concept of law in this literature has been set down as an essential groundwork for the specific analysis of the ethics of government in the Bible and Talmud which follows in subsequent chapters.

---

117. Orlinsky, *Understanding the Bible,* p. 100. In speaking of the form of Israel's legal codes, Orlinsky says, "It is now generally agreed that the formulation of the legal enactments in the Pentateuch fall into two main groups. Numerous laws are introduced by a direct command or prohibition of the Lord, 'You shall (or, shall not) . . .' The Ten Commandments (Exodus 20:1–17) are a case in point. . . . Laws expressed so dogmatically and directly are called *apodictic.* The second major group of laws, called *casuistic,* is characterized by a conditional clause ('If; Provided that'). The Book of the Covenant (Exodus 20:22–23:33; 24:7) is a good example of this formulation . . . ."

CHAPTER II

THE GOVERNMENTAL
LEGAL SYSTEM IN JUDAISM

INTRODUCTION

The governmental legal system characteristic of Judaism is a case history in the implementing of ethical government. This system had a broad base and a long period of historical development. Chapter 1 dealt extensively with the concept of law in the Bible and Talmud. Chapter II enlarges on this concept of law to show that the ethical issues of the governmental legal system in Judaism stand out as central themes in the source materials.

Significance of Halākhāh

The centrality of ethics in the legal aspects of government in Judaism is seen at the outset in the very word that connotes the legal side of Judaism—*halākhāh* (הלכה) = "practice" or "traditional law." This noun is from the verb *hālakh* (הלך) = "to go" or "to walk," and is very often used in the Bible to indicate the way of the righteous.[1] For example: "And Enoch walked (ויתהלך *va-*

---

1. *Hālakh* is also used in the sense of "walking after the sins of" (e.g. Jeroboam), I Kings 16:26; II Kings 13:6. Cf. also Ps. 1:1.

yithalakh) with God; and he was not, for God took him" (Gen. 5:24). Therefore, the noun *halākhāh,* which eventually became a term that included the entire legal system in Judaism, implied, among other things, moral, ethical, and religious ideas. To be precise, it indicated the way one should go, i.e., the right way; but what constituted the right way could be a dogmatic rule as well as ethical principles.

> Halakah itself is a product of the value-concepts' drive toward concretization, and without doubt the most important product. Lacking Halakah, the value-concepts, with their need for steady concretization in actual life, might not have functioned at all.[2]

These moral, ethical, and religious ideas, or "value-concepts," were "concretized" in the life of the nation to the degree that it lived in submission to the word of God.[3] For, according to talmudic teaching, the *halākhāh* was indeed the "word of the Lord."

> And it is said, "And they shall wander from sea to sea, and from the north even to the east; they shall run to and fro to seek the word of the Lord, and shall not find it" (Amos 8:11 f.). "The word of the Lord" means *halachah* . . .[4]

DEVELOPMENT OF HALĀKHĀH. In the perspective of the Sages, this *halākhāh,* or "word of the Lord," was delivered to Moses at Sinai in both written and oral form.

---

2. Max Kadushin, *The Rabbinic Mind* (New York: Jewish Theological Seminary, 1952), p. 80.

3. Harry M. Orlinsky, *Understanding the Bible Through History and Archaeology* (New York: KTAV, 1972), p. 258, "They [Israel's laws] established not only the code of conduct for all Israelites in dealing with one another—especially the relations between members of the ruling classes and the less powerful—but through this code gave expression to the obligation for just and righteous behavior inherent in the Covenant."

4. T.B. Shab. 138b.

Among the several predominant themes and central images within the text of the Talmud the two which stand out as most important are: "the importance of Talmud-study. The second is belief in the divine origin of the substance of Talmudic teaching, that is, in the 'Oral Torah,' which, along with the Hebrew Scriptures, was alleged to have been revealed at Sinai."[5]

The subsequent development, elaboration, and adaptation, plus the application of this original revelation, provides a rich and varied historical saga. A study of the history of this development uncovers three interesting aspects: (1) the Sinaitic laws were given priority; (2) laws developed by the Rabbis were thought to be authoritative elaborations, clarifications, and developments of both the Written and Oral Law; (3) ethical considerations carried heavy weight for the Rabbis as they continued to develop a governmental legal system within Judaism with which to regulate society with equity.

Sources of Halākhāh.

A retrospective analysis of this vast body of biblical and rabbinical material shows five different types of sources which served to provide the totality of *halākhāh.*

1. The Written Law was revealed by God to Moses at Sinai and was eventually viewed as a list of positive and negative commandments totaling 613. More will be said about this codification in Chapter 3.

2. The Tradition found in the Prophets and Writings as commandments or admonitions was viewed as having authority from Sinai; e.g.,

Witnesses sign a *Geṭ* to prevent abuses. [Is this rule only] to prevent

5. Jacob Neusner, [ed.], *Understanding Rabbinic Judaism from Talmudic to Modern Times* (New York: KTAV, 1974), pp. 24–25.

abuses? (n. And so of Rabbinical sanction only.) It derives from Scripture, does it not, since it is written, "And subscribe the deeds and seal them?" (Jer. 32:44).[6]

3. The Oral Law, involving (a) the interpretation of the Written Law, (b) the early *halakhot* which had little, if any, scriptural basis, as in the following:

> May we say that our Mishnah teaches here the same as our Rabbis taught: "That phylacteries should be square is a law set down by Moses at Sinai," and Raba explained [this to mean] in their seam and in their diagonal?[7]

(c) logical deduction where a given teaching is so obvious as to need no scriptural basis.

4. Sayings of the Scribes, as an explanation of a principle from the Torah[8] or as a decree originating with the Scribes. In such a case, the saying would need reinforcement, as the following example indicates:

> New Moon is ordained by the Written Law, and the ordinances of the Written Law do not require reinforcement . . . whereas the others are laid down by the Scribes, and the word of the Scribes require reinforcement.[9]

5. Custom. This source of *halākhāh* is very comprehensive. It is also pertinent to the ethical theme in the governmental legal system in Judaism. In this area of corporate Jewish life one finds that, in effect, the law was often "of the people, for the people, and by the people." For example:

---

6. T.B. Giṭ. 36a [trans. Maurice Simon].
7. T.B. Meg. 24b.
8. T.B. San. 88b.
9. T.B. R.H. 19a.

Where it is the custom to do work on the eve of Passover until mid-day one may do [work]; where it is the custom not to do [work], one may not do [work]. He who goes from a place where they work to a place where they do not work, we lay upon him the restrictions of the place whence he departed and the restrictions of the place whither he has gone; and a man must not act differently [from local custom] on account of the quarrels [which would ensue].[10]

And, in addition, it is noticeable that the customs which developed until they carried the force of law were often the very practices which were expressions of sensitive ethical awareness. Custom usually developed where specific teaching was lacking and was expressed as follows: "What is the law? . . . Go forth and see how the public are accustomed to act."[11]

A custom originating from the social, religious, or legal activities of a specific responsible group in a given locality could very well become the source of new teachings which would be as authoritative as if the early Sages had taught it. This procedure, so common in the development of the *halākhāh,* is a prime example of the sensitive nature of the governmental legal system in Judaism. It shows that the voice of pious, responsible people was a contributing element in the formation of laws which were articulated by the Rabbis and implemented within the framework of the established courts; e.g.,

One who engages labourers and demands that they commence early or work late—where local usage is not to commence early or work late he may not compel them. Where it is the practice to supply food [to one's labourers], he must supply them therewith; to provide a relish, he must provide it. Everything depends on local custom.[12]

10. T.B. M. Pes. IV, 1.
11. T.B. Ber. 45a.
12. T.B. M. B.M. VII, 1.

Summary

These introductory remarks show that the governmental legal system in Judaism was one which was shaped by a complex variety of sources including the Written Law, the Oral Law, traditions handed down in the form of commandments or requirements found in the Prophets and Writings, the teachings of the Sages, and custom.[13] This great body of literature was appropriately called *halākhāh* because, in its composite form, it prescribed a way of life in which the people were "to go" that encompassed the social, religious, and civil expressions of the Jewish nation.[14] The inherent ethical quality pervading the governmental legal system in Judaism has already surfaced by way of implication.[15] It is now time to consider specifically the legal ethics of this governmental system.

LEGAL ETHICS IN JUDAISM

The legal ethics in talmudic Judaism stand out in bold relief when one examines the source materials mentioned in the introduction. There was a sustained effort on the part of the Sages to preserve

---

13. Cf. *Encyclopaedia Judaica,* vol. 7, cols. 1158–1159, for the fivefold classification of *halākhāh.*

14. Jacob Z. Lauterbach, *Rabbinic Essays* ([Cincinnati: Hebrew Union College Press, 1951], reprinted, New York: KTAV, 1973), p. 293, " . . . the halakic laws and regulations concerning man's relation to his fellow-man will convince . . . that the Halakah, in interpreting and applying the biblical laws, as well as in its own legal enactments, was guided by the highest ethical principles."

15. Meyer Waxman, "Civil and Criminal Procedure of Jewish Courts," in *Studies in Jewish Jurisprudence,* [ed. Edward M. Gershfield], (New York: Hermon Press, 1971), p. 187. This author notes, "The development of Jewish civil law presents a remarkable contrast to that of criminal law. While the latter retained all through its course of existence its Mosaic character, the former was practically a Talmudic edifice reared on Mosaic principles. The Bible contains comparatively very few civil laws, and even those mentioned are not stated explicitly but casually." The subsequent examination of halakhic materials will bear this out.

the intimate relationship between legal mandates and ethical behavior. Although it was recognized that ethical behavior could not always be required by law, a great thrust of much of the legislation was actually for the purpose of getting people to act ethically in any given situation.

> The significance, from an ethical point of view, of a symmetrical development and exact statement of the law in all its ramifications is obvious. Private and social life is so profoundly affected by the provisions of the law of property and contracts, of marriage and inheritance, the penal law and the law of procedure, with all their premises and consequences, that their authoritative definition is necessarily antecedent to the foundation of ethical conduct.[16]

Ethical Legislation

The determination of the Rabbis to retain in legal form appropriate expressions of ethical behavior is seen in the way they incorporated within terms of law many activities which had a distinctively ethical emphasis. This was one way of building strong assurances that the legal system in Judaism would continue to maintain high ethical standards.

Unethical/Illegal vs. Ethical/Legal Behavior.

One of the techniques utilized by the Sages to accomplish this strong ethical emphasis was to place in the same context, by way of comparison, unethical and illegal behavior on the one hand, and ethical and legal behavior on the other. This close juxtaposition of the unethical and illegal, or ethical and legal, although not precisely identical, often accomplished the same purpose as if they were identical. This is seen in the rabbinical rules regulating remarriage where a minor was involved.

16. M. Lazarus, *The Ethics of Judaism,* pt. I (Philadelphia: Jewish Publication Society, 1900), pp. 22–23.

> R. Eliezer b. Jacob ruled: In the case of any hindrance [in remarry-
> ing] (n. Lit. "retention [in the house of her husband].") that was due
> to the husband, [the minor] is deemed to have been (n. Lit., "as if
> she was") his wife; but in the case of any hindrance [in remarrying]
> that was not due to the husband she is not deemed to have been his
> wife.[17]

The reason for such a rabbinical ruling lies in a combination of
ethical and legal considerations. An attempt was made to assure
equity for the parties involved according to the varying circumstances of the case, and not merely upon the basis of strict legali-
ties. Thus, under one set of conditions the minor would be considered "as if she was" a wife; under other circumstances she
would not be so considered. With such flexibility, a blending of
legal and ethical principles could be brought to bear to insure a
better application of humane justice.

Legal-Religious Matters.

This same procedure was also utilized by the Rabbis in legal
matters of a religious nature. Prominent in the religious activity of
the Israelites until the destruction of the Second Temple in 70 C.E.
was the sacrificial system of worship. Under this system the people
were required to present burnt offerings, meal offerings, peace
offerings, and sin offerings on a regular basis (Lev. 1–5). If these
offerings were faithfully performed, the sins of the people were
atoned for and they received blessings. With this background of
teaching from the Torah in mind, it is significant to note its ethical
extension by R. Isaac, who said,

> Why is the meal-offering distinguished in that the express "soul" is
> used therewith? Because the Holy One, blessed be He, said, "Who is
> it that usually brings a meal-offering? It is the poor man. I account
> it as though he had offered his own life to me."[18]

17. M. Yeb. XIII, 3 [trans. Israel W. Slotki].
18. Men. 104b. A New Testament parallel is found in Mk. 12:41–44, Lk.
21:1–4.

The equating of one who is a poor man with one who is obedient is not exactly a legal equation; it is, rather, an ethical relationship. The one who is lowly is "as though" he were obedient.

"Minor" Crime vis-à-vis Major Crime.

Also, as one would expect, the principle discussed above applied in criminal law, including capital cases. Often, the enormity of the crime under consideration was heightened by comparing it, in principle, with a more serious offense. This had the effect, not only of deterring the potential offender because of legal retribution, but also of calling him to consider the ethical implications of such a deed and thus causing him to desist on both legal and ethical grounds. A Mishnah concerning the capital offense of murder and warnings to witnesses gives a good example of this kind of legal-ethical concern:

> For this reason was man created alone, to teach thee that whosoever destroys a single life (from Israel), scripture imputes [guilt] to him as though he had destroyed a complete world; and whosoever preserves a single life (from Israel), ascribes [merit] to him as though he had preserved a complete world.[19]

The emergence of these kinds of rulings, whether in the domestic, religious, criminal, or other spheres of activity, clearly points up a deliberate endeavor on the part of the Rabbis to relate ethics and law in such a way as to strongly encourage ethical behavior.

Emphasis on "Judgment of Heaven."

Another type of ruling was developed by the Sages to urge an ethical motivation for action in cases where the legal sanction of the courts would not apply. This procedure emphasized the ethical responsibility for complying with the spirit of the law even though

---

19. M. San. IV, 5. Cf. also Herbert Danby, *The Mishnah,* rev. ed. (London: Oxford University Press, 1958), p. 388, n. 4. "Some texts omit 'from Israel.'"

there were no legal sanctions which could be imposed.[20] The pressure for proper ethical response came when the Rabbis pointed out in their rulings that the person in question was subject to divine retribution even though he could not be legally punished. In this way an individual who had not technically broken the law, but who was obviously under demand for a proper ethical response, would be led to consider the gravity of his refusal to respond properly to the Rabbis' ruling. One's dealing with incompetents and minors is discussed under this principle as follows:

> If a man sent out something burning through a deaf mute, an idiot, or a minor [and damage resulted] he would be exempt from the judgments of man, but liable in accordance with the judgments of heaven.[21]

Rabbis' Commendation or Displeasure.

On the other hand, the Rabbis' encouragement of an enlightened response was often predicated upon their conviction that respect for them and their position would carry weight in leading people to choose the course which they, the Rabbis, preferred. Therefore, they often not only gave a ruling in a particular matter, but also expressed an ethical course of action, which, if followed, would receive their personal commendation. The following Mishnah with reference to the payment of debt is a clear example of this type of legal-ethical persuasion.

20. Saul Berman, "Law and Morality," *Encyclopaedia Judaica,* vol. 10, col. 1480. With respect to the problem of enforcement of "the spirit of the law," the Rabbis were working from an ancient pentateuchal legal base where, we are reminded, "On the critical issue of enforcement, no textual distinction exists on which to base enforced and nonenforced forms or between humanly enforced and divinely enforced ones. The apodictic form, for example, is used both for the prohibition on murder (Ex. 20:13) and the command to love one's neighbor (Lev. 19:18)."

21. M. B.Ḳ. VI, 4.

> If one repays his debts in the seventh year the Sages are well pleased with him. If one borrows from a proselyte whose sons had become converted with him, the debt need not be repaid to his sons; (n. Children of a proselyte are regarded as newly born; accordingly, they are not the legal heirs of their pagan father, and, consequently, cannot claim debts due to him. Nevertheless, if his debt is returned to them, the Rabbis are pleased with the debtor.) but if he returns it the Sages are well pleased with him.[22]

Conversely, the Sages expressed displeasure when unethical behavior was exhibited, especially when it caused hardship on others. Thus, they expressed themselves often in the following fashion:

> If a person gives his estate, in writing, to strangers, and leaves out his children, his arrangements are legally valid, but the spirit of the Sages finds no delight in him.[23]

Beyond the Letter of the Law.

One of the most emphatic methods employed by the Rabbis in their attempts to sustain high ethical standards by associating them closely with legal categories was to urge, not only legal requirements, but action that carried beyond the letter of the law as an expression of the ethical spirit of the law. This procedure reminded the people that the law had its subtle demand, which could not be ignored with impunity. Ethical considerations were part and parcel of law to such an extent that often the highest legal intent could be realized only if one reacted ethically to the principle with which a particular ruling dealt. The emphasis of the philosophy behind this legal-ethical relationship is seen in R. Johanan's statement:

22. M. Sheb. X, 9, [trans. S. M. Lehrman].
23. M. B.B. VIII, 5.

Jerusalem was destroyed only because they gave judgments therein in accordance with the law of the Torah. Were they then to have judged in accordance with untrained arbitrators?—But say thus: because they based their judgments [strictly] upon the law of the Torah, and did not go beyond the requirements of the law.[24]

This kind of emphasis in the talmudic discussions gives a clue to the viability of the legal ethics in Judaism. It gave one a legal framework within which one could achieve the ethical results most desirable in any given case. Thus, by acting beyond the strict requirements of the law one could actually behave within the "margin of the judgment" by surrendering his legal rights to benefit another human being. The high motivation for this principle has been stated as follows:

> ... Rabbinical ethics ... looked with approval on a man who did not insist on his strict legal rights ... and the reason why his action in so doing was approved was that in this way brotherly love was promoted between those who were at variance with each other.[25]

This ethical stimulus to do the "right thing" in a legal matter, even if it meant going beyond the "letter of the law," was a bulwark which helped preserve and perpetuate the entire governmental legal system in Judaism. Indeed, the history of legal development in Judaism shows that what often had been urged on the grounds of ethical considerations was later incorporated into the corpus of legal literature as law; e.g.,

> There was a certain man who sold a plot of land to R. Papa because he was in need of money to buy some oxen, and, as eventually he did not need it, R. Papa actually returned the land to him!—[This is no proof] since R. Papa may have acted beyond the strict requirements of the law. (n. לפנים משורת הדין, lit., 'within the line of the law,"

24. B.M. 30b.
25. R. Travers Herford, *Talmud and Apocrypha* (1933; reprinted, New York: KTAV, 1971, p. 140).

i.e., he surrendered his legal right for the sake of benefiting a fellow man.) . . . And the law is that if a man sold [a plot of land] and [on concluding the sale] was no longer in need of money the sale may be withdrawn.[26]

Social Conditions and Law.

This tendency to legislate ethical requirements was especially apparent in legal matters that were concerned with varying social conditions. The technique used by the Rabbis to accomplish this goal was twofold in nature: the incorporation of ethical principles into new law, as explained in the last paragraph, and by offering ethical explanations for laws which already existed. For example, a rare agreement was reached between the schools of Hillel and Shammai that a half-slave must be liberated by his owner.

> One who is half a slave and half free works for his master and for himself alternate days. This was the ruling of Beth Hillel. Beth Shammai said: You have made matters right for the master but not for the slave. It is impossible for him to marry a female slave because he is already half free. (n. And so an Israelite.) It is impossible for him to marry a free woman because he is half a slave. (n. And so not an Israelite.) Shall he then remain unmarried? But was not the world only made to be populated, as it says, "He created it not as a waste, he formed it to be inhabited"? (Isa. 45:18) To prevent abuses, (n. Lit., "for the better ordering of the world.") Therefore, his master is compelled to liberate him and he gives him a bond for half his purchase price. Beth Hillel thereupon retracted [their opinion] and ruled like Beth Shammai.[27]

It is significant that the resolution of the injustice to the half-slave and the agreement between the two rabbinical schools were based on ethical considerations which became the rule.[28]

---

26. Ket. 97a [trans. Israel W. Slotki].
27. M. Giṭ. IV, 5. [trans. Maurice Simon].
28. Isaac Mendelsohn, *Slavery in the Ancient Near East* (New York: Oxford

Concern About Attitudes.

Sometimes a ruling of the Rabbis showed the intenseness with which they pursued ethical principles as regulating forces within society. Not only did they call for overt behavior governed by ethical demands, as mentioned above, they also pressed for the expression of proper attitudes by parties involved in legal problems or situations. Thus, the Mishnah which held that an object found by a man's wife belonged to him is explained by the Gemara as being based on the reason "that he may entertain no ill feeling towards her."[29] The description of legal positions based on social ethical awareness in an attempt to minimize ill will between parties is of frequent occurrence in the Talmud. It is further evidence of the strong role of legal ethics in Judaism.

Judicial Procedure

Finally, in the realm of judicial procedure, the Sages also showed their concern for the ethical as well as the legal. Some of their rulings illustrating this concern were based on the Mosaic injunction, "And you shall do what is right and good in the sight of the Lord . . ." (Deut. 6:18a). The story is told of a man who deposited jewels with his neighbor. When he asked for them later he was told they could not be found. This was ruled to be negligence and the neighbor's house was confiscated. When the jewels were found they were returned to their owner, but in the interim they had appreciated. The law held that the amount of their appreciation was also returnable to the original owner by the one with whom he had deposited them on the grounds that "you shall do what is right

University Press,1949), pp. 63 ff. This excellent treatment of the subject, esp. the O.T. slave legislations of Exod. 21, Deut. 15, and Lev. 25, makes it clear, by contrast, just how ethical the decision of the Rabbis was in the above-mentioned case.

29. M. B.M. I, 5, 12b.

and good . . ."[30] Thus, ethical action was actually enforced on legal grounds. Another example, this time involving real estate, is that of a man who took possession of ground lying between the fields of two brothers. Rab Judah called him impudent but said he could not be removed. Eventually, however, the ruling came to be that he could be removed on the grounds of "you shall do what is right and good . . ."[31] This recourse to a general biblical principle which is primarily ethical in nature to solve a legal dilemma again illustrates how the Rabbis blended the ethical and the legal together into a system designed to produce equity and justice for all. One final example, to show that the Rabbis were concerned with the ethical as well as the legal aspects of the law, is about

> Some porters (who) [negligently] broke a barrel of wine belonging to Rabbah son of R. Huna. Thereupon he seized their garments; so they went and complained to Rab. "Return them their garments," he ordered. "Is that the law?" he enquired. "Even so," he rejoined, "That thou mayest walk in the way of good men." (n. Prov. 2:20.) Their garments having been returned, they observed, "We are poor men, have worked all day, and are in need; are we to get nothing?" "Go and pay them," he ordered. "Is that the law?" he asked. "Even so," was his reply: "and keep the path of the righteous." (n. Actually they were responsible, but Rab told him that in such a case one should not insist on the letter of the law.)[32]

It must be noted, however, that this was an infraction of the pentateuchal law that the poor must not be favored in a lawsuit on account of his poverty (cf. Exod. 23:3, Lev. 19:15). Conceivably, this was a special case, that of a prominent Rabbi, who was expected to behave with special consideration.

30. B.M. 35a.
31. B.M. 108a.
32. B.M. 83a [trans. H. Freedman].

Ethical Lapse: Rabbinic Controversy

Although this system was designed, in principle, to produce equity
and justice for all, it occasionally fell short of this goal. When individual laws were enacted which contained some basic inequity, the
rabbinic discussions of those laws were usually controversial; e.g.,

> Where an ox belonging to an Israelite has gored an ox belonging to
> a Canaanite, there is no liability, whereas where an ox belonging to
> a Canaanite gores an ox belonging to an Israelite, whether while
> *tam* or *mu'ad,* the compensation is to be made in full.[33]

The rabbinic discussions concerning this Mishnah illustrate "the
horns of a dilemma" which were difficult to remove. Those who
supported it generally held that the Israelite was exempt from
payment of damages even though his ox had gored the ox of a
Canaanite on the grounds that the non-Israelites were not guided
by the universal principles of civilization. Since they did not generally recognize the laws of social justice, they could not claim benefits from a law they did not acknowledge.

> In ancient Israel as in the modern state the legislation regulating the
> protection of life and property of the stranger was on the basis of
> reciprocity. Where such reciprocity was not recognized, the
> stranger could not claim to enjoy the same protection of the law as
> the citizen.[34]

Since the Israelite was bound by the law, he was entitled to the
benefits provided by the law—compensation in this case. The
Rabbis who saw inequity in this Mishnah related the story of how
two representatives from Rome were sent to Israel to learn the
Torah. After having studied it carefully, they praised it generally,

33. M. B.Ḳ. IV, 3.
34. M. Guttmann, "The Term 'Foreigner' Historically Considered," *Hebrew
Union College Annual* 3 (1926): 1–20.

but said concerning the Mishnah about the goring ox, "In no case can this be right."[35] The inequity of the law reflects the religious-political tensions of the time between Jews and Romans and Greeks. That the law was questioned by the Rabbis (even though they cited pagan students) shows that they were sensitive to the lack of fairness.

Conclusion

The above discussion of the legal ethics in Judaism leads one to conclude that the Rabbis thought in terms of legal-ethical relationships in society. These two areas were not distinct and separate categories. They were blended together by the various techniques which have been considered in this section. Because the Talmud does reflect so often this blending of the legal and the ethical in its legislative and judicial writings, it becomes valid to speak of the legislative ethics of Judaism. The next section takes up this topic with emphasis on the ethics of Judaism in penal legislation.

ETHICS OF JUDAISM IN PENAL LEGISLATION

The ethics of Judaism loom very prominently in talmudic penal legislation. There was a concerned regard for the rights of both the accuser and the accused, and great pains were taken to see that there was no miscarriage of justice. The safeguards built into the penal system to maintain equity did, indeed, seem to favor the defendant in most cases.[36] Perhaps this was due to the fact that he

35. Cf. B.Ḳ. 37b–38a for full discussion.
36. Emanuel Rackman, "Talmudic Insights on Human Rights," *Judaism* 1, no. 2 (April 1952): 162: "Trial procedure according to Jewish law did not call for representation by counsel; the judges were usually counsel for the accused as well as his tribunal. It is therefore significant that no one could be convicted in a criminal case unless there was at least one judge who found grounds for acquittal and was the champion of the accused. A unanimous agreement as to guilt meant the prisoner's release—B. Sanh. 17a."

was on the defensive, and therefore his judges had to exercise special caution in determining guilt before the verdict was pronounced.[37]

The Principle of "Thou Shalt Not"

For penal purposes an act was criminal if it was a violation of a negative biblical command. For example, the fact that the Torah stated, "You shall not kill" (Exod. 20:13), made it valid to carry out the injunction, "the murderer shall be put to death" (Num. 35:16b).[38] "It is a recognised principle that no transgression carries with it a [humanly inflicted] penalty unless the relevant prohibition, 'thou shalt not,' is explicitly stated in the Bible."[39] Under this principle, even a plain provision of punishment, such as "the adulterer and the adulteress shall be put to death" (Lev. 20:10b), could not have been carried out had it not been for the negative biblical command, "You shall not commit adultery" (Exod. 20:14, Deut. 5:18). This rabbinical requirement for both a biblical "thou shalt not" and a provision establishing a specific penalty for its violation served as a system of checks and balances in the administration of penal law.

37. "אדם יודע" *Encyclopedia Talmudica,* vol. 1, p. 231. "If a man performs an invalid act, we say that he certainly knows it; *hence he must have a different intention* (emphasis added). . . . if a man sells stolen land which the purchaser knows is not his, we say that he knows that the vendor has no land, and therefore he has given the money either as a bailment, or as a gift, according to Rab and Samuel respectively (B.M. 15b)."

38. Gerald J. Blidstein, "Capital Punishment—The Classic Jewish Discussion," *Judaism* 14, no. 2 (Spring 1965): 159. "'Kill' and 'murder' are words whose integrity is carefully guarded. 'Kill' designates any taking of human life, while 'murder' is reserved for unauthorized homicide, usually of a malicious nature. This fine distinction has become a vital one, serving in both legal and ethical Jewish thought.—The children of Israel were thus commanded at Sinai to desist from unauthorized killing, but they were not commanded regarding homicide of, say, a judicial or military nature."

39. Mak. 13b.

Specific Prohibition Required

Additionally, a prohibition could not be inferred in any way. It had to be specifically stated. For example, sexual intercourse was prohibited as follows, "You shall not uncover the nakedness of your sister, the daughter of your father or the daughter of your mother . . . " (Lev. 18:9a). This, of course, involved relations with one's half-sister. But immediately the text goes on to say, "You shall not uncover the nakedness of your father's wife's daughter, begotten by your father, since she is your sister" (Lev. 18:11). This would be one's full sister. Therefore, it seems clear that prohibition of marriage with one's full sister could not be inferred from the prohibition of marriage with one's half-sister. Otherwise, there would not have been two separate prohibitions.[40]

This close link between negative injunction and penal legislation was not restricted to capital cases. Although they serve as vivid examples, it was noted above that an act was criminal if it violated a negative biblical command. Thus, the whole range of criminal jurisprudence came under this principle.

Exceptions.

The fact that the Rabbis observed and further developed this approach to penal legislation indicates their concern for properly administered justice in this area. As a matter of fact, there developed exceptions to the rule that an act was criminal only if it was a violation of a negative biblical command. However, even the exceptional rulings highlight the Rabbis' determination to act ethically in this regard; e.g., with reference to the roasted flesh of the paschal lamb it was taught:

40. Nathaniel Micklem, "Leviticus," *Interpreter's Bible,* vol. 2, p. 92. This writer holds that vv. 9 and 11 refer to a half-sister relationship, but admits perplexity about v. 11, saying, "Why there should be this second reference is not plain."

"And ye shall let nothing of it remain until the morning; and that which remaineth of it until the morning ye shall burn with fire" (Ex. 12:10). Now Scripture came and provided here a [remedial] act to follow a [disregarded] prohibition; (n. Lit., "a prohibition translated into a positive action.") this [provision] is to convey that no flogging is inflicted for the transgression. These are the words of R. Judah. R. Jacob says: [No!] this interpretation is not relevant, as it is rather an instance of a prohibition contravened without action, and any prohibition contravened without action entails no flogging. (n. I.e., the offence was passive, without any physical act, and therefore not punishable.)[41]

Although these two explanations differed, it is significant that they both sought the same results; that is, elimination of a flogging for the violation of a prohibition if the violation was passive in nature.

The Benefit of Doubt

Another evidence of ethical awareness in penal legislation was the practice of the Sages to give to the accused the benefit of all reasonable doubt when he was under trial for alleged legal violations. This principle had several modes of expression. It was especially apparent in cases where more than one person could possibly have been guilty of liability. The one who proved beyond a reasonable doubt to be guilty was charged, while the other party was exempt. For example, in the case of damages

where there is a pit [in charge of] two partners, if the first one passes by and does not cover it, and the second one also [passes by and does] not cover it (n. And damage occurred later.), the second would be liable.[42]

Thus, the one who undoubtedly, and without any mitigating cir-

---

41. Mak. 4b.
42. M. B.Ḳ. V, 6 [trans. E. W. Kirzner].

cumstances, was negligent to the extent of causing damages, was assigned the guilt. This procedure showed a keen sensitivity for avoiding unjust penalties and also carried with it a reluctance to attach any great significance to circumstantial matters. On the other hand, if it came to light that a crime had been committed by someone through a second party, the one who instigated the crime was also called to account. This was articulated by Shammai the Elder in the following way:

> Now, when it was taught: If he says to his agent, "Go forth and slay a soul," the latter is liable, and his sender is exempt. Shammai the Elder said on the authority of Haggai the Prophet: His sender is liable, for it is said, "Thou has slain him with the sword of the children of Ammon." (n. II Sam. 12:9; the reference is to David, who encompassed the death of Uriah the Hittite through the Ammonites, for which the prophet Nathan held him personally responsible.)[43]

Performance Before Guilt

Ordinarily, the illegal act had to be actually performed before guilt accrued. It was generally held that mere intent to do evil did not, itself, make one culpable. "The Holy One, blessed be He, does not combine an evil thought with an [evil] act. (n. For punishment,— i.e., one is not punished for mere intention.)"[44] Thus, the general principle was operative which held that a crime or offense had to be finalized to be a valid wrong. On the other hand, one was not considered criminally guilty even of a consummated act if it was proved that the act performed was not the one intended by the accused.[45] According to this view, one would not be guilty unless

43. Ḳid. 43a [trans. H. Freedman]. Cf. Shab. 56a, where, *contra* Shammai the Elder, David is exonerated according to the opinion of Hillel and R. Samuel b. Naḥmani.

44. Ḳid. 39b [trans. H. Freedman].

45. Michael Higger, "Intention in Talmudic Law," in *Studies in Jewish Juris-*

he consummated the act according to his intention.[46] This perspective on the part of the Rabbis illustrates their desire to avoid presumptive procedures which might possibly result in assigning punishment upon an innocent party.

Exceptions.

Although, generally speaking, an illegal act had to be actually performed before guilt accrued, there was a considerable number of exceptions to this principle. Some of them, perhaps because they were exceptions, highlight all the more the ethical motivations of penal legislation in Judaism. Brief mention of three exceptions will corroborate this point. In some cases the mere attempt to involve people in certain activities, the doing of which would involve grave consequences, was itself considered a criminal offense; e.g., an attempt to entice others to idolatry, even though unsuccessful, was an offense the penalty for which was stoning (Deut. 13:6–10). In other words, the incitement itself constituted a criminal act. Since

---

prudence, [ed. Edward M. Gershfield], (New York: Hermon Press, 1971), p. 252. "A crime thus consists of two elements—a criminal act, and the mental or the criminal intent. Hence, if A aimed a stone at a part of B's body where a mortal wound could not be inflicted, and the stone struck a more delicate part and caused death, or if one aimed a stone at an animal, and the stone struck a human being and caused death, the individual who threw the stone is not guilty of murder. In other words, there because of the lack of an intent to kill, there can be no crime of murder."

46. Israel Herbert Levinthal, "The Jewish Law of Agency," in *Studies in Jewish Jurisprudence,* [ed. Edward M. Gershfield], (New York: Hermon Press, 1971). The general rule of agency in Jewish law was that an agent could be appointed to do everything that a principal could do himself. . . . However, an important exception to the general rule was that the appointment of agency must not contemplate an illegal object. "Accordingly, an act, which, if done by the principal, would be illegal, cannot be done through the agency of another, and such appointment is consequently void." Therefore, in all cases where the act committed is illegal, the doer of the act is alone responsible, and the one who appointed him to do it is not responsible. However, Shammai the Elder takes strong exception to this ruling (pp. 49, 51–52).

the departure into idolatry was such a serious matter, the Rabbis let stand the injunction of the Torah in this instance without further expansion or alteration. Again, an exception to the general principle of no guilt without an illegal deed is seen in the Rabbis' call for the *lex talionis* upon him who would disturb the domestic tranquility by planning to smite his fellow, viz.,

> He who lifts his hand against his neighbour, even if he did not smite him, is called a wicked man, as it is written, "And he said unto the wicked man, Wherefore wouldst thou smite thy fellow?" (Prov. 22:25) "Wherefore has thou smitten" is not said, but "wherefore wouldst thou smite," shewing that though he had not smitten him yet, he was termed a wicked man. . . . R. Huna said: His hand should be cut off, as it is written, "Let the uplifted arm be broken." (Job 38:15) R. Huna had the hand cut off [of one who was accustomed to strike other people].[47]

This indicates that a peaceful society was a prime consideration in the social-legal ethics of Judaism. This subject will be explored at length in Chapter VI.

Again, the untold havoc that false witnesses could bring into the judicial system of Judaism caused the Rabbis to retain without elaboration the biblical requirement of "measure for measure" upon the witness who testified maliciously against his fellow man. Although what he testified against his brother was false, and proven to be so by the judges' examination, the mere attempt to discredit his fellow man was turned upon him, so that what he had tried to establish against his brother was actually applied against him (Deut. 19:16–19).[48] In another connection, this principle is expanded in Chapter V.

These three exceptions to the general penal legislative rule show that where unusually grave circumstances existed which

47. San. 58b.
48. For further elaboration, cf. Gerhard von Rad, *Deuteronomy: A Commentary* (Philadelphia: Westminster Press, 1966), p. 129.

would result in serious consequences with regard to man's relationship with God, his fellows, and the law, the Rabbis viewed *intent* to do wrong as synonymous with actual wrongdoing, and ruled accordingly.[49] This flexibility of penal legislation to fit the nature of the offense illustrates an ethical strain running through the concept of law in Judaism because it shows, in effect, that the law was to be suited to man's needs, and not the other way around.

An extension of this "accommodation" of law to man is seen in R. Judah's affirmation that any act done inadvertently did not carry liability. The following Mishnah illustrates this point.

> If his pitcher broke on public ground and someone slipped in the water or was injured by the potsherd he is liable [to compensate]. R. Judah says: if it was done intentionally he is liable, but if unintentionally he is exempt.[50]

The above-mentioned instances clearly indicate that the flexibility of penal legislation worked in two directions: if intent to act illegally involved cases of severe repercussions, that intent made one as culpable as if he had committed the act; on the other hand, if an act was actually committed which, for example, caused damages, but was done unintentionally, the person who committed the act was not deemed culpable at all.[51]

Furthermore, the illegal act not only had to be committed intentionally for one to be guilty, but it had to be done with willing consent. This meant that the accused would not be found guilty if

---

49. Waxman, "Civil and Criminal Procedure," pp. 206–207. A thief breaking into a house at night forfeited his right to life, and the owner of the house, or any other person who saw him attempting the act, was permitted to kill him (San. 72a; cf. Exod. 22:1). This was another case where *intent* to do wrong, although obviously unsuccessful, was synonymous with actual wrongdoing in the view of the Sages. See also below, pp. 148–149.

50. M. B.Ḳ. III, 1.

51. Cf., however, a ruling *contra* above in M. B.Ḳ. II, 6, "Man is always *mu'ad* whether [he acts] inadvertently or wilfully, whether awake or asleep."

it was proved that he committed the act contrary to his will. Utilizing Deuteronomy 22:25–26,[52] R. Zera stated, " ... the All-merciful absolves anyone who acts under pressure, as it is written, 'But unto the damsel thou shalt do nothing!' (n. Deut. 22:26, when a betrothed girl was violated in a field)."[53]

It was also recognized that under certain conditions an individual might act contrary to the law and still be exempt because of certain extenuating circumstances. For instance, if one made a false oath, he was exempt from guilt if it was established that he swore falsely in ignorance.

> Our Rabbis taught: ["Whatsoever it be that] a man [shall utter clearly] with an oath" (n. Lev. 5:4 האדם בשבועה) at the time of the oath he must be a man, i.e., have all his faculties, but if he swears falsely by accident (thinking it is the truth), he is exempt.[54]

Ethical Trends

In addition to the varied situations described above, which would free one from guilt even though the letter of the law had been violated, the Rabbis also recognized a much wider range of conditions which would free one from culpability. A few of these are enumerated below in order to emphasize the ethical trend in the penal system of Judaism that continued to value the person as the beneficiary of law instead of its victim.

52. S. R. Driver, *Deuteronomy,* International Critical Commentary, 3d ed. (Edinburgh, 1902), p. 257. With reference to the legislation found in Deut. 22:23–27, Driver points out that this case "is treated as virtually one of adultery, the girl, after betrothal, being regarded as pledged to her future husband, as fully as if she were formally married to him; she is described accordingly (v. 24) as his 'wife,' and the penalty (except in the case, v. 25, where the girl can be reasonably acquitted of blame) is the same as for adultery, viz., death for both parties."

53. A.Z. 54a [trans. A. Cohen].

54. Shebu. 26a [trans. A. E. Silverstone].

If one were forced to act illegally because of torture he was exempt.[55] "A deaf-mute, an idiot and a minor are awkward to deal with, as he who injures them is liable [to pay], whereas if they injure others they are exempt."[56] Failure to give warning beforehand to one who committed a capital offense became judicial grounds for staying the execution.[57] The taking of human life in defense of another person was to act without guilt in the matter, according to rabbinical teaching.[58]

All of these enumerations point to the same thing. The law remained the standard by which conduct was measured. However, the flexibility of application of the law was designed to take into account the many different circumstances which arose, and the varying conditions of the people involved. Thus, by retaining ethical principles within the categories of legal expressions, the goal of justice in Jewish penal legislation remained a practical one, not merely theoretical.

This attempt to blend the ethical, legal, judicial, and practical into a workable system is one reason why there are so many different points of view among the Rabbis expressed in the Talmud. In general it can be said, however, that the majority ruling in penal legislation was usually a sensitive attempt to guard carefully the rights of the accused.[59] In the words of one historian, "In the deliberations of the judges considerations tending to acquittal were given precedence."[60] At the same time, however, the principles of justice with respect to the law were not neglected. It has been well

55. Ket. 33b.
56. M. B.Ḳ. VIII, 4.
57. San. 8b.
58. San. 72b.
59. Rackman, "Talmudic Insights on Human Rights," p. 161, adduces as an example the rule against self-incrimination. "The Talmud establishes this rule against self-incrimination by means of a syllogism (Sanh. 9b). Relatives are incompetent to testify against each other. A man is a relative to himself. Therefore, he is incompetent to testify regarding himself."
60. George Foot Moore, *Judaism,* vol. 2 (Cambridge: Harvard University Press, 1927), p. 186.

said, "Nowhere is the endeavor to develop the highest principles of the Law in ordinances and regulations more conspicuous than in the sphere of judicial procedure."[61]

"Satisfaction" Without Due Process

It is valid to state that "the principles of justice with respect to the law" were not neglected even though the law was tolerant enough in many situations to allow "satisfaction" without due process. However, what may seem like a lapse of legality on superficial examination, often turns out to be an example of ethical and moral considerations being overriding factors in shaping the attitude of law so that justice could speedily prevail. Most of these occasions were well grounded in ancient Torah precedents believed to be required by the exigencies of the times in which they occurred. Many instances of summary punishment separate from legal procedure are recorded in the Torah and the Talmud, e.g., the actions of Simeon and Levi against the house of Hamor after discovering that their sister, Dinah, had been defiled (Gen. 34:25–27).[62] Indeed, on certain occasions, this type of action was viewed as a response to the specific command of God (Exod. 32:27–28). With such precedents before them, the Rabbis felt justified in acting in summary fashion under certain conditions in order to maintain high ethical standards and proper regard for the law.[63]

The rulings of the Sages also gave leeway for various other individuals, under certain conditions, to act outside the normal process of law in order that the intent of the law be maintained.

61. Ibid., p. 182.

62. Cuthbert A. Simpson, "Genesis," *Interpreter's Bible,* vol. 1. This commentator sees this episode, and the larger context in which it is found, as two different stories presented by "J" (J[1] and J[2]) and "P" and conflated by R[P] with the motive of showing why the rights and privileges of the firstborn eventually passed to Judah, the fourth-born son of Jacob. Cf. pp. 733–737 for full development.

63. M. San. VI, 4. Some Sages taught that anyone who was stoned to death was afterward hanged, based on Deut. 21:22. Others held that a man was hanged, but not a woman.

For example, based upon the honor given to Phinehas for his spontaneous action in slaying an Israelite man and a Midianite woman for their gross immorality (Num. 25:6–13), the following Mishnah was taught:

> If one steals the ḳiswah (sacred vessel), or curses by enchantments, or cohabits with a heathen [lit., Syrian] woman, he is punished by zealots. (n. I.e., pious men, zealous for the honour of Judaism, may punish him if they apprehend him in the act; but if they did not, they cannot subsequently charge him therewith at the Beth Din.)[64]

This kind of teaching was in harmony with the conviction of the Sages that they could circumvent a pentateuchal law "in accordance with the need of the hour!"[65]

Taking Matters into One's Own Hands

Another interpretative ruling by the Rabbis allowed individuals, under prescribed conditions, to "take matters into their own hands" and take human life. The basis for this ruling was the biblical statement, "If a thief is caught while breaking in, and is struck so that he dies, there will be no bloodguiltiness on his account."[66] The rabbinical interpretation of this passage not only gave the owner the right to kill the burglar,[67] but, on the grounds that the burglar should be regarded as a potential murderer, granted permission to *anyone* catching him in the act of breaking in to kill him in defense of the owner, as indicated by the following ruling:

> Our Rabbis taught: ["If a thief be found breaking up,] and be smitten,—*by any man*; that he die," by any death wherewith you can slay him. Now, [the exegesis] "And be smitten, *by any man*" is

---

64. M. San. IX, 6 [trans. H. Freedman]. But cf. San. 82a on this Mishnah.
65. Yeb. 90b.
66. Exod. 22:2 (Heb. 22:1).
67. Yoma 85b.

rightly necessary: for I might think that only the owner may be assumed not to remain passive, whilst his money is being stolen, but not a stranger: it is therefore taught that he is regarded as a potential murderer, whom even a stranger may kill [in defence of the owner]. But what need of "that he die—by any death wherewith you can slay him": can this not be deduced from a murderer? For it has been taught: "He that smote him shall surely be put to death; for he is a murderer." (Num. 35:21).[68]

Rulings of this kind help bolster the contention that the supreme motive of talmudic law was basically ethical in nature because they show an overwhelming concern for justice for the victim of a crime.

There is a very strong emphasis on justice in the Jewish tradition. The evidence is so powerful that it seems unnecessary to present it in any detail. What are the great codes of law, from the Pentateuch to the Mishnah to Maimonides and the *Shulḥan Arukh*, if not a great celebration of the demands of justice in human affairs?[69]

This concern for justice was so intense that the Sages could circumvent the letter of the law with their interpretive rulings in order to "build a fence around the Torah" and maintain the spirit of the law with its full integrity.

Conclusion

This kind of basic approach to law in Judaism was a daring experiment in the administration of justice. Although it was characterized by rabbinic controversy, frequent conflicting rulings, and occasional ethical lapses, the legal system of talmudic Judaism was one marked by strenuous ethical and moral ideals grounded in

68. San. 72b.
69. Louis Jacobs, *What Does Judaism Say About . . . ?* Library of Jewish Knowledge (New York: Quadrangle, 1973), p. 195.

integrity and religious convictions. As developed, expanded, and perpetuated by the Rabbis, its success depended on two basic elements: (1) the continued acceptance by the people of Torah, the teachings of the Rabbis, and rabbinical authority; (2) an unhampered legislative and judicial apparatus by which the law could be articulated and applied.

This chapter has been devoted to an examination of the legal system of Judaism. It has stressed the ethical ingredients of that system, especially as they are discerned in its legislative and judicial aspects. The area of penal legislation served as a rich resource for determining and analyzing the basic ethical nature of talmudic law, which always pointed to the high goal of justice.

CHAPTER III

ENFORCEMENT OF JUDICIAL ETHICS IN JUDAISM

INTRODUCTION

The Rabbis were very sensitive to the relationship between God's biblical commandments and man's personal response to them.

> In all parts of the Hebrew Bible, especially in the Pentateuch and the Prophets, the only and eternal God is the God of Israel Who brought His people out of the bondage of Egypt, to Whom it owes allegiance, to Whose voice and will the people as a whole and every individual of it have to hearken, and Whose commandments as the detailed expression of His will every Israelite has to obey. The identity of the obligation to hearken to God's voice and of that to keep His laws is unmistakably assumed on every page of the Pentateuch and the Prophets . . . [1]

The rabbinical tradition held the total number of these com-

---

1. A. Büchler, *Studies in Sin and Atonement in the Rabbinic Literature of the First Century*, Library of Biblical Studies (New York: KTAV, 1967), p. B.

mandments to be 613. The Rabbis also believed that all of them were delivered to Moses by God.

> ["Therefore gave he them Torah (teachings) and many command-ments . . . "] R. Simlai when preaching said: Six hundred and thir-teen precepts were communicated to Moses, three hundred and sixty-five negative precepts, corresponding to the number of solar days [in the year], and two hundred and forty-eight positive pre-cepts, corresponding to the number of the members (n. Joints, or bones, covered with flesh and sinews [excluding the teeth].) of man's body.[2]

Taryag Mitzvoth—613 Commandments

The תרי"ג מצות *Taryag Mitzvoth,* as these 613 commandments were mnemonically called (ת = 400, ר = 200, י = 10, ג = 3), became a virtual code of law as enunciated by the Rabbis. Considerable attention was devoted through the centuries to the proper classifi-cation of these laws in order that they might be clarified and better understood.

As one examines the "613 commandments," one finds two things of special interest with reference to the subject of govern-mental ethics: (1) a large number of the laws are concerned with judicial and ethical matters; (2) many of the commandments are interpreted by the Rabbis in ways which produce meanings not obvious from the biblical text alone. As Rosenblatt points out,

> Some of the exegetical methods of the Mishnaic expositors of the Bible . . . might be called auxiliaries. . . . the Tannaitic exegetes were assisted in their Bible interpretation by traditions regarding the meaning of words and the popular usage, as well as by their knowledge of the neo-Hebrew and Aramaic languages, which were current in their milieu.[3]

2. Mak. 23b [trans. H. M. Lazarus].
3. Samuel Rosenblatt, *The Interpretation of the Bible in the Mishnah* (Balti-more: John Hopkins Press, 1935), p. 26.

Yet, almost invariably, the subtle meanings extracted by the Rabbis indicate a high ethical consciousness. This is especially apparent with reference to judges, courts, judicial legislation, and justice generally.

Laws with Stated Reasons

The Rabbis were desirous of understanding and applying the laws in ways which would assure stable government and justice for all. In this way the intrinsic meaning with which the laws had been clothed would be realized. In their search for the principles contained in this great body of biblical literature, they found evidences of a very high ethical rationale in some of those laws which contained within them reasons for their existence, e.g., "You shall not oppress a stranger; you know the heart of a stranger, for you were strangers in the land of Egypt."[4]

Laws without Stated Reasons

On the other hand, the Sages were aware, of course, that many of the biblical laws did not carry with them the explicit reasons for their presence in Scripture. The rabbinic tradition explained this phenomenon with the following teaching:

> R. Isaac also said: Why were the reasons of [some] Biblical laws not revealed?—Because in two verses reasons were revealed, and they caused the greatest in the world [Solomon] to stumble. Thus it is written: "He shall not multiply wives to himself." (n. "That his heart turn not away," Deut. 17:17) whereon Solomon said, "I will multiply wives yet not let my heart be perverted." Yet we read, "When Solomon was old, his wives turned away his heart." (I Kgs. 11:4) Again it is written: "He shall not multiply to himself horses"; concerning which Solomon said, "I will multiply them, but will not

4. Exod. 23:9. Many other examples may be found in biblical literature, viz., Deut. 4:5–8, 11:16–17, 17:16–17, 23:3–4 (Heb. 23:4–5).

cause [Israel] to return [to Egypt]." Yet we read; "And a chariot came up and went out of Egypt for six [hundred shekels of silver]."[5]

Bases for Legal Equity

The rabbinical schools proceeded on the basis of the conviction that the Torah was of God; that it was given to govern Israel; that merit would result from studying and keeping Torah; and that troubles and even disaster would result if Torah was disregarded. Therefore, the equitable application of the laws (government) was of great concern to the scholars.

> Their strict interpretations of legal portions of the Pentateuch can-not be found fault with. That is the only way to construe a legal document, nor is there anything unnatural about their theory that repetition or redundancy has the effect of emphasis and extension of application.[6]

Ideally, they saw their task as requiring: (1) a general recognition of valid authority, (2) the establishment of a court system func-tioning according to high judicial ethical standards, (3) capable leadership not subject to corruption, and (4) the application of justly administered laws within the various communities. Each of these areas of concern is now considered in the order just men-tioned, as it relates to the ethics of the courts and of the govern-ment.

RECOGNITION OF AUTHORITY

Germane to the ethics of government is the question of duly con-stituted authority. This question is not restricted to ultimate

---

5. San. 21b [trans. Jacob Shachter]. The real reason for the objection to mul-tiplying horses was not trading with Egypt, but the provision of Israelite (or Judahite) mercenaries in exchange for the horses.

6. Rosenblatt, *Interpretation of the Bible*, p. 34.

authority, or source, but is also concerned with the transmission, or perpetuation, of authority. The Sages of Judaism, throughout their long and influential history, were unanimously agreed as to the ultimate source of authority and the channel through which that delegated authority was to flow through the succeeding generations.

God as Ultimate Authority

God is the source of authority in Judaism. "Law and righteousness were the special concern of Yahwè; in his name justice was dispensed and to him were all legal ordinances referred."[7] His will was made specific in the Torah received by Moses at Sinai. The Tradition stated:

> Moses received the Torah at Sinai and transmitted it to Joshua, Joshua to the Elders, and the Elders to the Prophets, and the Prophets to the men of the Great Synagogue.[8]

The Sages agreed that Moses received the Oral Law, as well as the Written Law, at Sinai. The Oral Law was articulated through the ancient traditions from the earliest post-Mosaic generations and also through the formulations of the halakhic scholars of each era. Gray describes this transmission process in the following words:

> According to Hebrew or Jewish theory, Yahwe is the source of all law, Moses the medium through whom it was revealed to Israel. . . . At a later period the Jews formulated the theory that the oral law or tradition . . . as well as the written law or scripture, was in the first instance communicated to Moses.[9]

7. Immanuel Benzinger, "Law and Justice," *Encyclopaedia Biblia* (1902), vol. 3, col. 2714.

8. Ab. I, 1.

9. G. B. Gray, "Law Literature," *Encyclopaedia Biblia* (1902), vol. 3, col. 2714.

This continuing process enabled these scholars to continue to develop principles of law through the ages which were accepted as divinely authorized, and, as time went by, this growing body of literature became more and more encompassing in scope, dealing with almost every detail of life.[10]

Rabbinical Authority

Thus, rabbinical authority was recognized as the constituted channel through which God was to make his will known to his people. The Torah had been given from heaven, but it was no longer *in* heaven.[11] The Rabbis, as the human element, were to develop and cultivate the *halākhāh* within society, while at the same time repudiating any suggestion that mysticism, heavenly voices, or miracles have any place in the formulation of law.

Rabbis and Scripture

The Sages looked to certain biblical passages where, in early times, the people were required to go before judges and priests for decisions about their disputes. According to rabbinic interpretation, that procedure was to remain valid throughout postbiblical Judaism. The following Scripture with a rabbinic comment on it illustrates this point.[12]

10. Meg. 19b.

11. B.M. 59a–59b; cf. Deut. 30:12.

12. R.H. 25b. "The Scripture places three of the most questionable characters on the same level as three of the most estimable characters, to show that Jerubaal in his generation is like Moses in his generation, Bedan in his generation is like Aaron in his generation, Jepthah in his generation is like Samuel in his generation [and] to teach you that the most worthless, once he has been appointed a leader of the community, is to be accounted like the mightiest of the mighty. Scripture says also: 'And thou shalt come unto the priests the Levites and to the judge that shall be in those days.' Can we then imagine that a man should go to a judge who is not in his days? This shows that you must be content to go to the judge who is in your days."

> If any case arises requiring decision between one kind of homicide and another, one kind of legal right and another, or one kind of assault and another, any case within your towns which is too difficult for you, then you shall arise and go up to the place which the Lord your God will choose, and coming to the Levitical priests, and to the judge who is in office in those days, you shall consult them, and they shall declare to you the decision.[13]

The Sages recognized the principle that the solutions to specific problems were disclosed directly by God, and in that way became a part of Torah (Written Law); e.g.,

> Now while the children of Israel or Israelites were in the wilderness, they found a man gathering wood on the sabbath day. And those who found him gathering wood brought him to Moses and Aaron, and to all the congregation; and they put him in custody because it had not been declared what should be done to him. Then the Lord said to Moses, "The man shall surely be put to death; all the congregation shall stone him with stones ouside the camp." So all the congregation brought him outside the camp, and stoned him to death with stones, just as the Lord had commanded Moses.[14]

On the other hand, the Sages held that with the passage of time the law was entrusted to judges and scholars, just as it once had been the responsibility of priest and Levite, as indicated in the Torah.[15]

13. Deut. 17:8–9. S. R. Driver, *Deuteronomy,* International Critical Commentary, 3d ed. (Edinburgh, T & T Clark, 1902), p. 401, comments on this passage as follows: "Two great duties of the priestly tribe are indicated in these words: (1) to decide, in cases brought before them, in accordance with the principles of Jehovah's 'direction,' or 'law,' of which they were the guardians (Jer. 8:8); (2) to maintain the service of the altar. . . . By *judgments* will be meant decisions in civil and criminal causes, or the ordinances founded upon them (See Ex. 21:1; Ez. 44:24; and cf. on 4:1, 17:7)."
14. Num. 15:32–36 (NASB). This principle is also illustrated in Lev. 24:10–16.
15. Deut. 33:8–10.

Rabbis and Halakhic Legal Literature

During talmudic times the Rabbis saw themselves as participants in a long historical line of Scripture and Tradition transmission. They were involved in interpreting and further developing the Torah. This process had its expression within the framework of the Torah in the halakhic legal literature of Midrash, *takkanah,* etc. As Berkovits explains:

> Halakhah is not the Law but the Law applied—and by the manner of its application rendered meaningful—in a given situation. The purpose of the Halakhah is to render the Torah in a given historic situation a) practically feasible; b) economically viable; c) ethically significant; d) spiritually meaningful. . . . Halakhah is the bridge over which Torah enters reality, with the capacity to shape it meaningfully and in keeping with its own intention. . . . while the Torah is eternal, the concrete historic situation is forever changing. Halakhah therefore, as the application of Torah in a given situation, will forever uncover new levels of Torah-depth and Torah-meaning and thus make new facets of Judaism visible.[16]

The implementing of the law as interpreted and developed in this way required the establishment and functioning of an enlightened and equitable court system if a high ethical standard of government was to be maintained. Recourse to biblical and talmudic sources shows the foundation, formation, and operation of the court system in Judaism.

ESTABLISHMENT OF THE COURT SYSTEM

The court system of Judaism had its roots deeply embedded in biblical history. In fact, according to the Book of Exodus, one finds

16. Eliezer Berkovits, "The Centrality of Halakhah," in *Rabbinic Judaism from Talmudic to Modern Times,* [ed. Jacob Neusner], (New York: KTAV, 1974), pp. 69–70.

the interesting phenomenon of judicial activity among the Hebrews before they received the Law at Sinai.[17]

The Role of Moses

Moses is pictured as judge before he became lawgiver. "And it came about the next day that Moses sat to judge the people, and the people stood about Moses from the morning until the evening."[18] His role as judge, however, was not without its difficulties. As indicated, the people were slow in getting their cases heard. Obviously, this was trying for them as well as for Moses.

JETHRO'S ADVICE. From the objective point of view of Jethro, Moses' father-in-law, it was apparent that the single-handed administration of judgment as practiced by Moses was not very efficient. He is reported as saying to Moses:

> What you are doing is not good. You and the people with you will wear yourselves out, for the thing is too heavy for you; you are not able to perform it alone. Listen now to my voice; I will give you counsel, and God be with you! You will represent the people before God, and bring their cases to God; and you shall teach them the statutes and the decisions, and make them know the way in which they must walk and what they must do. Moreover choose able men from all the people, such as fear God, men who are trustworthy and who hate a bribe; and place such men over the people as rulers of

17. Mayer Sulzberger, *The Am Ha-Aretz: The Ancient Hebrew Parliament* (Philadelphia: Julius H. Greenstone, 1909), pp. 7–8. This author sees biblical evidence of an early council, or governing body, in Exod. 3:16–18; 4:10, 16, 29–31; 12:21, etc., to which Moses made his appeal as a "newcomer."

18. Exod. 18:13 (NASB). J. Coert Rylaarsdam, "Exodus," *Interpreter's Bible,* vol. 1, p. 966. The author states that "the function of Moses was comparable to that of the Bedouin tribal sheik today. Each morning such a sheik 'sits' briefly as judge. As Israel gradually became an ever-greater aggregate of clan and tribal units such simple administration by one man became impossible. Moses may here be considered as priest as well as tribal chief or judge."

thousands, of hundreds, of fifties, and of tens. And let them judge
the people at all times; every great matter they shall bring to you,
but any small matter they shall decide themselves; so it will be easier
for you, and they will bear the burden with you. If you do this, and
God so commands you, then you will be able to endure, and all this
people also will go to their place in peace.[19]

MOSES' RESPONSE. The Scripture account implies that Moses took
this sound advice of Jethro and weighed it very carefully in his
mind. After having become convinced of the merits of the propo-
sal, he took the initiative in establishing a graded system of courts
according to the model suggested by his father-in-law. Subsequently, Moses is pictured as implementing this court system in
the following manner:

And at that time I said to you, "I am not able alone to bear you; the
Lord your God has multiplied you, and behold, you are this day as
the stars of heaven for multitude. May the Lord, the God of your
fathers, make you a thousand times as many as you are, and bless
you, as he has promised you! How can I bear alone the weight and
burden of you and your strife? Choose wise, understanding, and
experienced men, according to your tribes, and I will appoint them
as your heads." And you answered me, "The thing that you have
spoken is good for us to do." So I took the heads of your tribes,
wise and experienced men, and set them as heads over you, commanders of thousands, commanders of hundreds, commanders of
fifties, commanders of tens, and officers, throughout your tribes.[20]

19. Exod. 18:17b–23. Rylaarsdam, "Exodus," p. 967. Commenting on the
larger context of this passage, this author states that "to inquire of God" (v. 15)
means "to seek an answer for an issue for which no precedent can suffice. . . . The
outcome of an inquiry . . . had the value of revelation. It was the word of God,
not only in rhetorical fashion but also in effect." In contrast, Rylaarsdam states
that "the statutes of God and his decisions" (v. 16) were apparently "oracular
decisions." Thus, one sees the process and method which Moses utilized that
enabled him to be "judge before he became lawgiver" (ibid.). This coincides with
the stance of the Bible and the Talmud that Moses received the law from God.
20. Deut. 1:9–15.

MOSES' CHARGE. In order to impress upon the judges appointed under this system of judicial procedure the gravity of their responsibility, Moses charged them with strong words, saying,

> Hear the cases between your brethren, and judge righteously between a man and his brother or the alien that is with him. You shall not be partial in judgment; you shall hear the small and the great alike; you shall not be afraid of the face of man, for the judgment is God's; and the case that is too hard for you, you shall bring to me, and I will hear it.[21]

THE PEOPLE'S RESPONSE. The Bible relates how the people rose to the challenge of Moses. The system was established. The people saw this new procedure as a good thing. The appointed judges exercised their responsibility as it had been assigned to them, showing themselves to be wise and experienced men.[22] If, however, a case proved too difficult for the judges of the lower courts, it was eventually presented to Moses himself for final judgment. "And they judged the people at all times; hard cases they brought to Moses, but any small matter they decided themselves."[23]

21. Deut. 1:16–17.
22. Jacob Z. Lauterbach, [ed.], *Mekilta (de-Rabbi Ishmael)*, vol. 2 (Philadelphia: Jewish Publication Society, 1933). Cf. pp. 179–185 for rabbinic commentary on Exod. 18:13–27 dealing with the establishment of the court system. Also cf. A. M. Silbermann, [ed.], *Pentateuch with Rashi's Commentary: Exodus,* [trans. and annotated by M. Rosenbaum, A. M. Silbermann, A. Blashki, and L. Joseph], (London: Shapiro, Vallentine, 1930), p. 95. The rabbinic view of these judges comes to light as follows: "Ex. 18:21—ואתה תחזה MOREOVER THOU SHALL PROVIDE through the Holy Spirit that is upon thee, אנשי חיל MEN OF ABILITY (but חיל may mean 'wealth' and in this sense the words would mean)— rich men who will not need to flatter or to show favour. אנשי אמת MEN OF TRUTH—These are people commanding confidence; who are deserving that one should rely upon their words—appoint these as judges because on account of this their words will be listened to. שנאי בצע HATING LUCRE—men who hate (pay no regard to) their property when it is to be made the matter of a law-suit, in accordance with what we say: Any judge from whom one has to wring the money he owes only by means of a law-suit is no fitting judge."
23. Exod. 18:26.

THE RESULT. Thus, a simple but effective judiciary system was
established very early. The high ethical standards required of the
judges are apparent in the charge given by Moses. Rashi's
remarks, in the following commentary on the text, throw additional light on the qualifications required of the appointed judges.

> Deut. 1:13—Get yourselves ready for the matter . . . Take right-
> eous, desirable men—i.e., men who can understand a matter out of
> (i.e., by comparison with) another matter.—AND MEN KNOWN
> AMONGST YOUR TRIBES—i.e., men who are known to you.
> AND I WILL PLACE THEM AT YOUR HEADS—as chiefs and
> persons honoured by you, i.e., that ye should pay them respect and
> reverence. This teaches that Israel's transgressions (אשם asham) are
> placed upon the heads of their judges, because it is their duty to
> prevent them from sinning, and to direct them into the right path.
> Deut. 1:14—And you answered me and said, "The thing which you
> have said is good."—You at once decided the matter to your bene-
> fit, in that you said, "Many judges will now be appointed over us; if
> one of them does not happen to be an acquaintance of ours, we
> shall bring him a gift and he will show us favour." Deut. 1:15—So I
> took . . . and appointed them heads over you . . . —i.e., that you
> should pay them respect—regard them as first . . . in all matters of
> business. . . . AND OFFICERS FOR YOUR TRIBES . . . these
> are they who bind and flog with the lash at the bidding of the
> judges. Deut. 1:16 THEN I CHARGED OUR JUDGES AT
> THAT TIME . . . be deliberate in judgment: if a certain point of
> law comes before you once, twice, three times, do not say, "This
> point of law has already come before me several times," but discuss
> it well on that occasion also. . . . It is not now as heretofore: hereto-
> fore you were your own masters (lit., under your own control), now
> you are in the service of the Community! Deut. 1:17 YOU SHALL
> NOT SHOW PARTIALITY IN JUDGMENT. . . . This is
> addressed to him whose office it is to appoint judges—That he
> should not say, Mr. So-and-so is a fine or a strong man, I will
> make him a judge; Mr. So-and-so is my relative, I will make him a
> judge in the city,—whilst, really, he is not expert in the laws, and
> consequently he will condemn the innocent and acquit the guilty.
> YOU SHALL HEAR THE SMALL AND THE GREAT
> ALIKE . . . i.e., that a lawsuit regarding a peruta be as dear to you

(shall be as of equal importance) as a lawsuit regarding a hundred maneh—that if it (the former) comes before you first, you shall not set it aside until the last. Or, Ye shall hearken unto the words of the small as to those of the great—i.e., that you should not say: This is a poor man and his fellow (opponent) is rich, and is in any case bidden to support him; I will find in favour of the poor man, and he will consequently obtain some support in a respectable fashion. Or, How can I offend against the honour of this rich man because of one dinar? I will for the moment decide in his favour, and when he goes outside (leaves the court) I will say to him, Give it to him because in fact you owe it to him. YOU SHALL NOT FEAR MAN . . . Ye shall not gather in (shall not restrain) your words before any man. THE JUDGMENT IS GOD'S—Whatever you take from this man unjustly you will compel Me to restore to him; it follows, therefore, that you have wrested judgment against Me.[24]

The regulatory effects of the judicial procedure instigated by Moses were so commendable that he saw the far-reaching potential for good of a similar system on a permanent basis. The biblical account describes how, before he surrendered his leadership to his successor, Joshua, Moses urged the people to continue the system and adapt it to their needs when they were settled in the land to which God was leading them.[25] He said,

You shall appoint judges and officers in all your towns which the Lord your God gives you, according to your tribes; and they shall judge the people with righteous judgment.[26]

24. A. M. Silbermann, [ed.], *Pentateuch with Rashi's Commentary: Deuteronomy,* [trans. and annotated by M. Rosenbaum, A. M. Silbermann, A. Blashki, and L. Joseph], (London: Shapiro, Vallentine, 1934), pp. 5b–7.

25. Driver, *Deuteronomy,* p. 201: "No attempt is made to regulate the details of the institution, such as the method by which the judges are to be selected, their numbers, the organization of the courts, & c.; the Writer contents himself with affirming the broad principle that provision is to be made for the administration of justice, and that this is to be done by the appointment of judges possessing local jurisdiction."

26. Deut. 16:18. Calum M. Carmichael, *The Laws of Deuteronomy* (Ithaca: Cornell University Press, 1974), pp. 96–97. Discussing the close relationship

The Rabbinic Courts

This order given by Moses became one of the focal points around
which Rabbis of later ages shaped their concepts of the court system of the Jews.[27] To appoint judges and officers "in all your
towns . . . according to your tribes . . . [for] righteous judgment"
was a decree which had far-reaching consequences in the subsequent history of Israel.

It is noteworthy that this system, in principle, was operative
among the Israelites into rabbinic times. While in the wilderness,
leaders from each of the tribes, along with the elders and Moses,
met and legislated for the people (Exod. 19:7, Num. 11:16–24,
Deut. 27:1). During the period of Judges, the elders, heads, judges,
and officers of Israel were called together to make a covenant at
Shechem (Josh. 24). Even during the Monarchy one sees in the
legal reforms of King Jehoshaphat the continuation of this system,
i.e.:

> He appointed judges in the land in all the fortified cities of Judah,
> city by city, and said to the judges, "Consider what you do, for you
> judge not for man but for the Lord; he is with you in giving judg-
> ment. Now then, let the fear of the Lord be upon you; take heed
> what you do, for there is no perversion of justice with the Lord our
> God, or partiality, or taking bribes." Moreover in Jerusalem

---

between the D narratives and the D laws, specifically Deut. 1:9 ff. and 16:18 ff.,
Carmichael says, "The beginning of D (1:9–18) contains a historical account of
Moses commanding the people to choose leaders and judges. His address to the
judges there is very similar to D's law on the judges (which is also to be understood as spoken by Moses). It may be assumed that the law alludes to this narrative account, particularly since the law's motive clause promises the inheritance of
the land and this promise recalls the historical situation in 1:8, when Israel was
commanded to possess the land and to appoint leaders and judges (1:9 ff.)"

27. For laws, regulations, and rationale for judges in ancient Israel, cf. Elihu
A. Schatz, *Proof of the Accuracy of the Bible Based on Chronological, Organizational, Prophetic and Legal Analyses* (Middle Village, N.Y.: Jonathan David,
1973), pp. 600 ff.

Jehoshaphat appointed certain Levites and priests and heads of families of Israel, to give judgment for the Lord and to decide disputed cases. They had their seat in Jerusalem.[28]

Epstein sees this division of jurisdiction by Jehoshaphat into "matters of the Lord" and "the king's matters" (II Chron. 19:11) as being the pattern for the governmental senate of the Jews operating during the postexilic period. He states,

At the head of this governing body, which later became known as the Sanhedrin, stood "pairs" of teachers named *Zuggoth,* one of whom was the *Nasi* (Prince) and the other *Ab Beth Din* (Chief of the Court). This dual appointment appears to have been an adaptation to changed conditions of the system introduced by King Jehoshaphat whereby the administration of the strict religious law and that of the civil law were separated from each other . . . [29]

Rabbinical dialogue often centered around the type of judicial government which could be deduced from Moses' statement; e.g.,

The appointment of the Sanhedrin is by seventy-one. Whence do we derive this law?—Since we find that Moses set up Sanhedrins, and Moses had an authority equal to that of seventy-one.
   Our Rabbis taught: "Whence do we know that judges are to be set up for Israel?—From the verse, 'Judges thou shalt make thee' (Deut. 16:18). Whence do we deduce the appointment of officers for Israel?—From the same verse, 'Officers shalt thou make thee.' Whence the appointment of judges for each tribe?—From the words, 'Judges . . . for thy tribes.' (Deut. 16:18). And the appointment of officers for each tribe?—From the words, 'Officers . . . for thy tribes.' Whence the appointment of judges for each town?—From the words, 'Judges . . . in all thy gates.' And the appointment of officers for each town?—From the words, 'Officers . . . in all thy

28. II Chron. 19:5–8.
   29. I. Epstein, *Judaism: A Historical Presentation* (Baltimore: Penguin Books, 1959), pp. 89–90.

gates'" (Deut. 16:18). R. Judah says: "One [judicial body] is set
over all the others, as it is written, . . . 'shalt thou make thee.'"
Rabban Simeon b. Gamaliel said: "[The immediate connection] of
'they shall judge' and 'for thy tribes' indicates that the tribal court
must judge only those of its own tribe."[30]

It is quite logical that specific statements by Moses, such as
Deuteronomy 16:18,[31] became the mainsprings for the development of an intricate and highly sophisticated judicial system in
Judaism. It is well to remember that the evolvement of the court
system in Judaism is historical evidence of a sustained determination to achieve the highest degree of judicial ethics possible. This is
seen, not only in the broad framework and power of the courts,
but also in the minute ways in which the laws were actually
executed. The strenuous ethical demands of the Jewish court system are also seen in the qualifications of judges as discussed
above,[32] their strict jurisdictional regulations, and the strong ethi-

---

30. San. 16b.
31. William F. Albright, *The Biblical Period from Abraham to Ezra,* rev. ed.
(New York: Harper Torchbooks, 1963), p. 18. In speaking of the "considerable
body" of legislation found in the Torah, Albright refers to these laws as having "a
basic similarity about their cultural and religious background which makes it
impossible not to attribute their origin to the beginnings of organized Israelite
monotheism—in other words, to Moses."
32. The rabbinic discussions concerning qualifications for judges eventually
reached the point of idealization, as indicated by S. Mendelsohn, *The Criminal
Jurisprudence of the Ancient Hebrews* (Baltimore: M. Curlander, 1891), pp.
92–95: "Some detailed positive and negative qualifications are given as follows:
worthy, true piety, untarnished character, a Jew, knowledgeable in the written
and unwritten laws, familiar with languages (San. 17a) and contemporary science
(Menahoth 65a), affable but not merely popular (Keth. 105b), good appearance
and not haughty (San. 17a), experienced but not too old (Soṭah 22b; Aboth V,
21), a father (San. 36b), no electioneer, no king (San. 18b), no dishonorable voca-
tion (San. 24b), no deformity (San. 36b), no relatives on the same court (San.
27b)." However, cf. Meyer Waxman, "Civil and Criminal Procedure of Jewish
Courts," in *Studies in Jewish Jurisprudence,* [ed. Edward M. Gershfield], (New
York: Hermon Press, 1971), pp. 193–194, where he states that the qualifications
given above applied only to judges who sat in criminal courts. However, with
respect to civil courts, "Every Jew, even of illegitimate birth (San. 36b), if he but

cal principles governing the conduct of judges. What were the characteristics of this court system when fully developed? A look at rabbinical sources gives the answer to this question.

Just as in the days of Moses, when the courts were grouped as to size with leaders of thousands, hundreds, fifties, and tens, and regulated in jurisdiction in that the more difficult cases were brought to Moses, so the courts in later Judaism were varied in size and regulated in their jurisdiction.

COURTS OF THREE. A court composed of three members was an *ad hoc* court agreed to by the parties to a case.[33]

> Whence do we deduce that three are needed [for the composition of a court]?—From what our Rabbis taught: "It is written: 'The master of the house shall come near unto God (the judge),' here you have one; and again: 'the cause of both parties shall come before God (the judge),' here you have two; and again: 'whom God (the judge) shall condemn,' (Ex. 22:7–8) so you have three."[34]

However, these small courts had a rather wide range of jurisdiction, primarily in civil cases. An examination of some of the areas of their jurisdiction throws light on the high ethical standards they were expected to maintain in administering justice within their particular governmental environment. For example, they had authority to absolve from vows:

> In respect of what law [is this deduced] in the chapter of vows?— Said R. Aḥa b. Jacob: To teach that three laymen are qualified [to grant absolution] . . . Then on the view of Beth Shammai, whence do we know that three laymen are valid?—They deduce it from [the teaching reported by] R. Assi b. Nathan. For it is written, "And

possesses high intellectual and moral qualities (wisdom, modesty, fear of God, love of people, of truth, hate of greed, and respectability), is qualified."

33. M. San. III, 1.

34. San. 3b.

Moses declared unto the children of Israel the set feasts of the
Lord" (Lev. 23:44).[35]

They also handled monetary and other cases.

Monetary cases [must be adjudicated] by three judges; cases of lar-
ceny and mayhem, by three; claims for full or half damages, the
repayment of the double or four- or five-fold restitution [of stolen
goods], by three, as must cases of rape, seduction and libel; so says
R. Meir.[36]

And they ruled in divorce cases.

It has been stated: [On the question] how many persons must be
present when the bearer of the Get gives it to the wife there was a
difference of opinion between R. Joḥanan and R. Ḥaninah, one
holding that a minimum of two were required and the other a
minimum of three. . . . The authority who says that two persons
are sufficient holds that an agent may act as witness and a witness
may act as judge (n. And therefore the bearer of the Get may join
with the two witnesses of the delivery to form a Beth Din.), whereas
the one who insists on three holds that while an agent may act as
witness, a witness may not act as judge.[37]

Examples from other areas could be given. However, these
three show that the courts of three did, indeed, have heavy responsibilities. They were involved with the integrity of the people (in
cases of vows), financial problems (in cases involving monetary
matters), and domestic relations (in questions about divorce). It is
easy to see that the moral tone and ethical quality of life would be
set largely by the actions of the courts, and the small courts
touched the lives of the people at the grass-roots level in much of
their civic relationships.

35. Ned. 78a.
36. M. San. III, 1.
37. Giṭ. 5b [trans. Maurice Simon].

COURTS OF TWENTY-THREE. If a village grew to a population of one hundred and twenty, it was eligible for a court consisting of twenty-three members. However, most villages of such small size, and even bigger ones, did not have courts of twenty-three.

> The Great Sanhedrin consisted of seventy-one members; the Small Sanhedrin of twenty-three. . . . What must be the population of a town to make it eligible for a [Small] Sanhedrin?—one hundred and twenty . . . [38]

In contrast to the courts of three, which dealt chiefly with civil matters, the courts of twenty-three were largely concerned with criminal cases. Just as the examples above illustrate the depth of involvement of the courts of three in civil cases, the following example illustrates the involvement of the courts of twenty-three in criminal cases.

> Capital cases are adjudicated by twenty-three. The person or beast charged with unnatural intercourse, by twenty-three, as it is written, "Thou shalt kill the woman and the beast" (Lev. 20:16), and also, "and ye shall slay the beast" (Lev. 20:15).
>
> The ox to be stoned (Ex. 21:28) is tried by twenty-three, as it is written, "The ox shall be stoned and its owner shall be put to death" (Ex. 21:29)—as the death of the owner, so that of the ox, can be decided only by twenty-three.[39]

Great Sanhedrin: Powers Curtailed

The Great Sanhedrin was the highest court in the land. However, as Hoenig puts it,

> Many of the records pertaining to the functions of the Great Sanhedrin are considered theoretical and academic, voiced by scholars

---

38. M. San. I, 6.
39. M. San. I, 4.

who had lived and taught in different academies in an age subsequent to the era of the Second Temple.[40]

This situation must be kept in mind, as, in the next few pages, a description of the functions of the Great Sanhedrin as found in the Talmud is given.

Great Sanhedrin in Rabbinic Literature

"The Great Sanhedrin consisted of seventy-one members."[41] It met in the chamber of hewn stone at the Temple in Jerusalem. "In the chamber of hewn stone the Great Sanhedrin used to sit and judge [among other things the applicants] for priesthood."[42] In the appellate court arrangement of the judicial system of Judaism, the Great Sanhedrin was the "supreme court."[43] Cases could be

---

40. Sidney B. Hoenig, *The Great Sanhedrin* (Philadelphia: Dropsie College, 1953), p. 85.

41. M. San. I, 6.

42. M. Mid. V, 4.

43. Historically speaking, however, the Hasmonean, Herodian, and Roman regimes left few functions and very little power for the Sanhedrin. After the destruction of Jerusalem (70 C.E.), the Sanhedrin ceased to exist. Therefore, one is again reminded that much of what the Talmud says about the Sanhedrin is academic and hardly reflects real life. Cf. Alexander Guttmann, *Rabbinic Judaism in the Making* (Detroit: Wayne State University Press, 1970), pp. 21–24 for functions of the Sanhedrin. Also, cf. ibid., pp. 17–21 for a brief historical sketch of the Sanhedrin in which, among other things, it is stated, "The history of the Sanhedrin may be divided into several periods. The first major period began with its establishment or endorsement by the Hasmonean rulers about 160 B.C.E. and ended with Herod's rise to power in 37 B.C.E. During Herod's time, after the members of the Sanhedrin that tried him were massacred, a new Sanhedrin was established that continued until, or nearly until, the destruction of the Temple in 70 C.E. . . . . It possessed the greatest power under the Hasmoneans when it enjoyed official recognition. . . . At the beginning of the second major period of the history of the Sanhedrin, Herod assumed dictatorial power. During his rule the new Sanhedrin was no more than a great academy, a *Beth Midrash Gadol,* concentrating on study and regulating religious law, without the benefit of support by the political government."

appealed from one court to another, as the following example concerning a rebellious elder shows, but from a ruling of the Great Sanhedrin there was no appeal.

> An elder rebelling against the ruling of Beth Din [is strangled], for it is written, "If there arise a matter too hard for thee for judgment" (Deut. 17:8), [etc.]. Three courts of law were there (n. In Jerusalem; cf. "Then thou shalt arise, and get thee up into the place which the Lord thy God shall choose" [Deut. 17:8].), one situate at the entrance to the temple mount, another at the door of the [temple] court, and the third in the hall of hewn stones. They [first] went to the beth din which is at the entrance to the temple mount, and he [the rebellious elder] stated, "Thus have I expounded and thus have my colleagues expounded; thus have I taught, and thus have my colleagues taught." If [this first beth din] had heard [a ruling on the matter], they state it. If not, they go to the [second beth din] which is at the entrance of the temple court, and he declares, "Thus have I expounded and thus have my colleagues expounded; thus have I taught and thus have my colleagues taught," if [this second beth din] had heard [a ruling on the matter], they state it; if not, they all proceed to the Great Beth Din of the hall of hewn stones whence instruction issued to all Israel, for it is written, "[which they] of that place which the Lord shall choose [shall shew thee]."[44]

Of course, this court had broad powers.[45] The validity of its existence, like that of the other courts, was grounded in ancient teaching. In the structure and work of the Great Sanhedrin the people could see echoes of that group of men gathered together by Moses under the direction of God for the purpose of bearing the

---

44. M. San. XI, 2 [trans. H. Freedman].

45. Hugo Mantel, "The Nature of the Great Synagogue," *Harvard Theological Review* 60 (1967): 87. "Prior to the Maccabean ascendancy, the city and state courts were under the supervision of the high priest (e.g., The Book of Judith 4:6–8; 11:14), and to him the Pharisaic interpretations of the Torah had no validity." This is, of course, based on the theory (which is not accepted by most scholars) that the origin of the Pharisees goes back to pre-Maccabean times.

burden of the people so that Moses would not have to bear it alone.

> And the Lord said to Moses, "Gather for me seventy men of the elders of Israel, whom you know to be the elders of the people and officers over them; and bring them to the tent of meeting, and let them take their stand there with you. And I will come down and talk with you there; and I will take some of the spirit which is upon you and put it upon them; and they shall bear the burden of the people with you, that you may not bear it yourself alone."[46]

The Great Sanhedrin was the exclusive court of jurisdiction over certain very grave legal cases. If certain persons in high places of responsibility and leadership were indicted, or some particularly reprehensible act was committed which had extremely adverse consequences, the Great Sanhedrin became the sole court of jurisdiction.[47] The Talmud amplifies the exclusive prerogatives of the Great Sanhedrin in these and other areas as follows:

46. Num. 11:16–17. John Marsh, "Numbers," *Interpreter's Bible,* vol. 2, p. 197: "We must note that although this arrangement (vs. 17) is clearly meant to remedy Moses' complaint (vs. 12), it relieves his burden not because Yahweh himself carries some of that burden, but because Moses shares it with the seventy elders. Two complementary truths can be discerned: the service to God cannot be achieved without divine aid; God's work cannot be accomplished without human instruments." These "two complementary truths" are apparent not only here, but throughout the entire judicial and political system as the Jews saw it and practiced it.

47. Mendelsohn, *Criminal Jurisprudence of the Ancient Hebrews,* loc. cit.; cf. pp. 87–91 for further details concerning organization and jurisdiction of the Great Sanhedrin. Also, cf. H. Mantel, "The High Priesthood and the Sanhedrin in the Time of the Second Temple," in *The World History of the Jewish People,* [eds. Michael Avi-Yonah and Zvi Baras], (New Brunswick: Rutgers University Press, 1975). Here involved arguments are presented concerning the problems surrounding the nature of the Sanhedrin during Roman times. The conclusion is reached that during the times of the procurators there was not only a halakhic Sanhedrin in the Temple compound of Pharisaic scholars and headed by their *Nasi;* there was also "a council consisting of the acting and former High Priests—all of them owing their appointments to the procurator—(who) headed the political Sanhedrin of the country" (pp. 274–281).

A tribe, a false prophet and a high priest can only be tried by a court of seventy-one. War of free choice can be waged only by the authority of a court of seventy-one. No addition to the city of Jerusalem or the temple courtyards can be sanctioned save by a court of seventy-one.

Small Sanhedrins for the tribes can be instituted only by a court of seventy-one.

No city can be declared condemned save by a decree of a court of seventy-one.[48]

The Gemara of the tractate Sanhedrin speaks of the authority of trial jurisdiction by the Great Sanhedrin to include the trial of the head of a tribe who had sinned.

"The case in question," says R. Mathna, "is one where the head of the tribe has sinned"; (n. Irrespective of the manner of transgression, provided it carries with it the penalty of death) did not R. Adda b. Ahabah say: "'Every great matter they shall bring unto thee' (Ex. 18:22) means the delinquencies of the great man; (n. I.e., the High Priest [כהן גדול lit., 'great priest'].) so this one [sc. the head of a tribe] too, is a great man." (n. Who, accordingly, is tried by seventy-one.)[49]

Regarding these cases over which the Great Sanhedrin had exclusive jurisdiction there are some meaningful observations which may be made. Individuals subject to trial by this court were a false prophet, a high priest, the head of a tribe who sinned, and a woman under the trial of adultery.

They bring her up to the Great Court of Justice which is in Jerusalem, and [the judges] solemnly charge her in the same way that they charge witnesses in capital cases and say to her, "My daughter, wine does much, frivolity does much, youth does much, bad neigh-

48. M. San. I, 5.
49. San. 16a [trans. Jacob Shachter].

bours do much. (n. I.e., there may be some excuse for your be-
haviour.) Do it (n. Confess if you are guilty, and so make the ordeal
unnecessary which includes the use of the Divine Name.) for the
sake of His Great Name which is written in holiness so that it may
not be obliterated by the water." (Num. 5:23)[50]

Each of these individuals was in a strategic place in society. The
prophet was God's spokesman; the high priest officiated over worship of God; the tribal head was crucial in God's government; the
wife was prominent in the home. If high moral standards were not
maintained by these persons, it was inevitable that society would
degenerate. Thus, the strong defense of a high ethic in all these
areas was sought through exclusive jurisdiction and valid exercise
of authority by the Great Sanhedrin.

Not only were these individuals and their trials under the
power of the Great Sanhedrin, but, as was noted above, "war of
free choice" was subject to the court of seventy-one. Additions to
Jerusalem or to the Temple courtyards were not permitted without
the approval of this court. A city could not be condemned unless
by decree of the Great Sanhedrin. Smaller Sanhedrins for the
tribes could not be set up except by the Sanhedrin.

All of these elaborate arrangements reflected a theoretical
design perhaps to be applied in a reconstituted Jewish state. There
was little, if any, application of these rules under Herodian or
Roman rule.

According to the theory as it applied to the more broad perspectives of society—war, worship, municipality, court systems—
the Great Sanhedrin exercised a pervading governmental authority
which sought, by valid judicial, legislative, and administrative processes, to nurture and maintain a high standard of governmental
ethics within the nation.[51]

50. M. Soṭah I, 4 [trans. A. Cohen].
51. Hoenig, *Great Sanhedrin*. The author speaks of "the problem of the Sanhedrin" as being complex. This is because the scholarly discussions of the Sanhedrin are so numerous and are found in such scattered sources. Cf. Hoenig's

Contributing to the "problem of the Sanhedrin" is

> the apparent conflict between the Hellenistic and rabbinic sources as to its nature and function. While in the Hellenistic sources, in Josephus and the Gospels, it appears as a political and judicial Council headed by a ruler, the tannaitic sources depict it chiefly as a legislative body dealing with religious matters, and in rare cases acting as a Court.[52]

According to Isidore Epstein, the withdrawal of the Pharisees from politics, generally speaking, after the rise of Herod, involved "a separation of the political and religious administration of the country. This gave rise to the two Sanhedrins, the political and religious."[53] The first to advance the theory of the two Sanhedrins was Adolf Büchler in his work *Das Synedrion in Jerusalem* (Vienna, 1902). This view has been favorably, though not unanimously, received.[54]

Judges and Judicial Procedure

The caliber of the judges serving in the court system of Judaism, as indicated earlier by an examination of their qualifications, was required to be exceptionally high.[55] A judge's conduct in office was

---

"Attempts at a Solution of the Sanhedrin Problems," pp. 121–132. Also cf. above, pp. 91–92, 96 where the theoretical nature of much of the discussion about the functions of the Great Sanhedrin is stressed.

52. Hugo Mantel, "Sanhedrin," *Encyclopaedia Judaica,* vol. 14, col. 836.

53. Epstein, *Judaism,* p. 100.

54. Mantel, "Sanhedrin," cols. 837–839.

55. R. Travers Herford, *The Ethics of the Talmud: Sayings of the Fathers* (New York: Schocken Books, 1962), p. 29. Here, in his commentary on Ab. I, 8–9, Herford points out that Aboth speaks of legal rather than ethical maxims, and that their intent is to encourage judges "to foster the most scrupulous sense of justice, the most strict impartiality. They are addressed to such as were called upon to administer the Torah in its application to civil or criminal offences, and they have no immediate bearing upon matters outside the courts."

to be above reproach. In fact, he was expected not only to avoid
misconduct, but to avoid the very appearance of misconduct.

> For it is a man's duty to be free of blame (n. I.e., to give no cause
> for suspicion.) before men as before God, as it is said: "And be
> guiltless towards the Lord and towards Israel," (Num. 32:22) and
> again it says: "So shalt thou find favour and good understanding in
> the sight of God and man," (Prov. 3:4).[56]

Just as in the days of old, when the injunction was, "You shall not
pervert justice; you shall not show partiality; and you shall not
take a bribe, for a bribe blinds the eyes of the wise and subverts the
cause of the righteous,"[57] so the judge in Judaism was expected to
shun the temptation to accept bribes arising out of words, acts, or
gifts.[58]

> Our Rabbis taught: "And thou shalt take no gift"; (Ex. 23:8) there
> was no need to speak of [the prohibition of] a gift of money, but
> [this was meant:] Even a bribe of words (n. Or "acts.") is also for-
> bidden, for Scripture does not write, "And thou shalt take no
> gain." (בצע, which would have meant a monetary bribe.) What is to
> be understood by "a bribe of words"? (n. Or "acts.")—As the bribe
> offered to Samuel. He was once crossing [a river] on a board when a
> man came up and offered him his hand. "What," [Samuel] asked
> him, "is your business here?"—"I have a lawsuit," the other

---

56. M. Sheḳ. III, 2 [trans. M. H. Segal].

57. Deut. 16:19.

58. R. Joseph Caro, "Laws of Judges," in *Code of Hebrew Law: Shulḥan
'Aruk; with Glosses of R. Moses Isserles,* [trans. and commentary by R. Chaim N.
Denberg], (Montreal: Jurisprudence Press, 1955), chap. 9, par. 3, p. 120. "It was
[formerly] customary to provide a fund for the [members of the] Court, [i.e.,]
they [the townspeople] undertake to pay a fixed sum of money for the maintenance of the Court, and they collect it [from the townspeople] at the beginning of
the year and at the end thereof, and it does not bear the designation of a bribe or
the designation of remuneration [for pronouncing judgment], for it is obligatory
for Israel to support its Judges and scholars."

replied. "I," came the reply, "am disqualified from acting for you in the suit."[59]

When a court convened and the judges proceeded to hear a case, they were to observe certain judicial rules of conduct in order to insure a fair trial.[60] For example, they were required to hear all testimony in the presence of both plaintiff and defendant.

"Hear [the causes] between your brethren and judge righteously"

59. Ket. 105b. Other examples from Ket. 105b, showing how careful judges were expected to be to avoid anything that could even remotely be considered bribery, are:

Rab Judah stated in the name of R. Assi: "The Judges of Civil Law in Jerusalem received their salaries out of the Temple Funds [at the rate of] ninety-nine *maneh.* If they are not satisfied they were given an increase. [You say] 'They were not satisfied'? Are we dealing with wicked men? The reading in fact is, [If the amount was] not sufficient an increase was granted to them even if they objected."

R. Papa said: "A man should not act as judge either for one whom he loves or for one whom he hates; for no man can see the guilt of one whom he loves or the merit of one whom he hates."

Raba stated: "What is the reason for [the prohibition against taking] a gift? Because as soon as a man receives a gift from another he becomes so well disposed towards him that he becomes like his own person, and no man sees himself in the wrong."

Mar 'Ukba once ejected some saliva and a man approached and covered it. "What is your business here?" [Mar 'Ukba asked him.] "I have a lawsuit," the man replied. "I," came the reply, "am disqualified from acting as your judge."

60. Büchler, *Studies in Sin and Atonement,* p. 65. After referring to Soṭah 47b, Büchler quotes, "'Since judges increased in number who respected persons in judgment, the observance of the prohibition in Deut. 1, 17b, "Ye shall not be afraid of the face of any man," ceased and the observance of "Ye shall not respect persons in judgment," stopped, and they broke off the yoke of God and put upon them the yoke of man.' The disregard of the authority of God in favour of that of man referred to here points most probably to actual conditions prevailing in Jerusalem in the last decades before the year 70, when, on account of some men of influence and of circumstances otherwise unknown, the administration of justice in the Jewish courts of law in the capital and in the towns of Judaea deteriorated." Thus, the ideal of fairness and justice under the law was not always reflected in reality.

(Deut. 1:16). This, said R. Hanina, is a warning to the court not to
listen to the claims of a litigant in the absence of his opponent; and
to the litigant not to explain his case to the judge before his adver-
sary appears. *Shāmōa'* (n. שְׁמֹעַ) [hear], in the verse, can also be read,
shammēa'. (n. שַׁמֵּעַ. In the Pi'el, which has a causative sense, [make
hear].)[61]

Neither could there be any discrimination shown by the judges
for any of the litigants in a case.

Our Rabbis taught: "And the two men shall stand": it is a precept
that the litigants stand. R. Judah said; I heard that if they desire to
allow them both to sit, they may allow them to sit. What is prohibited? One should not stand, and the other sit; one speak all that he
wishes, and the other bidden to be brief.[62]

Summary

A retrospective glance at the court system in Judaism finds that
system to be one of the key ingredients for the enforcement of
governmental ethics within the nation. This court system also
reached out beyond the borders of Palestine.

A Sanhedrin has jurisdiction within the land . . . and outside it.
What [Scriptural] authority is there for this?—Our Rabbis taught:
[From the text,] "And these things shall be for a statute of judg-
ment unto you throughout your generations *in all your dwellings*"
(Num. 35:29), we learn that a Sanhedrin has jurisdiction both in
and outside Palestine.[63]

Organizationally, the court system in Judaism was well
adapted to the varied living conditions of a rural people. The small
ad hoc adjudicators or referees, the courts of three in the villages,

61. San. 7b [trans. Jacob Shachter].
62. Shebu. 30a.
63. Mak. 7a.

helped the people to live by law and maintain their integrity under law. At the same time, the larger courts of twenty-three wielded sufficient power to command the respect of the people in maintaining law and order, especially in their jurisdiction in criminal cases with authority to apply capital punishment. Finally, the Great Sanhedrin, with its extensive jurisdiction, stood, in theory at least, as a towering citadel of preservation and perpetuation of that which was ultimately just and right in Jewish law.

ETHICAL LEADERSHIP

The admirable organization of the court system in Judaism was made viable by men of conscience and dedication.

Men of Integrity

While the Talmud contains hundreds of examples of Rabbis of comparable competence differing sharply on both small and large matters of law, there is, with but few exceptions, no reason to challenge their dedication, integrity, or conviction. On the contrary, the honorable resiliency of the judges under all kinds of strain and tension through the centuries, together with the efficient organization within which they functioned, indicates a major element in maintaining and enforcing governmental ethics in Judaism. This healthy influence existed in spite of the fact that rabbinical authority was usually confined to judicial and religious matters.[64] They rarely enjoyed governmental authority.

Historical Leadership Precedents

This kind of ethical leadership was not present merely as a matter

---

64. *The Apocrypha,* [ed. Bruce M. Metzger], (New York: Oxford University Press, 1965), Ecclus. 39:1–5 + notes.

of law; it grew out of ancient heritage and biblical example and teaching. Even as early as the wilderness migrations of the Israelites, men of leadership stature were prominent. They were often referred to as "leaders of the congregation" (Exod. 16:22) or "rulers of the congregation" (Exod. 34:31 NASB).[65] On occasion, the importance of their role as "leaders of their ancestral tribes" is apparent as they are listed by name as "heads of the clans of Israel."[66]

The grave responsibility of spying out the land of Canaan rested on the shoulders of men of this stature. When it was time for this information to be gathered, the record states:

> "Send men to spy out the land of Canaan, which I give to the people of Israel; from each tribe of their fathers shall you send a man, every one a leader among them." So Moses sent them from the wilderness of Paran, according to the command of the Lord, all of them men who were heads of the people of Israel.[67]

It seems only natural, then, that when the question of dividing the land of Canaan among the tribes was being considered, the responsibilty for this apportionment fell to men of integrity, leadership, and unquestioned devotion to equity and justice. This helped insure a fair settlement and thus reduced the feelings of ill will within the population that might possibly have resulted had they believed any basic injustice was being thrust upon them through incompetence or dishonesty. So the responsibility for dividing the land was placed upon a group of leaders made up of one from each tribe.

The Lord said to Moses, "These are the names of the men who shall

---

65. U. Cassuto, *A Commentary on the Book of Exodus,* [trans. Israel Abrahams], (Jerusalem: Magnes Press, 1951). Cf. in both Exod. 16:22 and Exod. 34:31 "chieftains of/in the congregation" (pp. 197, 449).

66. Num. 1:5–16.

67. Num. 13:2–3. However, ten out of the twelve men sent turned out to be misleaders rather than leaders.

divide the land to you for inheritance: Eleazar the priest and Joshua the son of Nun. You shall take one leader of every tribe, to divide the land for inheritance."[68]

The Nasi

With reference to the high ethical leadership within the courts of Judaism, it was earlier noted that such leadership was not present merely as a matter of law, but that it grew out of ancient heritage and biblical example and teaching. It is interesting to note that the term applied to these leaders in ancient Israel decribed above was *Nāsī'* (נשיא),[69] and this very same term was also applied to the leaders of the Sanhedrin during much of its history.[70] A Mishnah points out that these early leaders of the Sanhedrin were known by the title of *Nāsī'*,[71] and tractate Aboth gives a list of the names of these leaders.[72]

Summary

The linguistic evidence leads one to conclude that the Jewish

68. Num. 34:17–18.
69. Mantel, "Great Synagogue." The author points out that "The heads of the Pharisaic Sanhedrin, beginning with the Zugot, are reported to bear the title *Nasi*" (p. 90). Also, cf. Hugo Mantel, "The Title *Nasi* in Jewish Tradition," and "The Offices of the *Nasi*," in *Studies in the History of the Sanhedrin,* [Harvard Semitic Series, no. 17], (Cambridge: Harvard University Press, 1965), pp. 1–53, 175–253.
70. E. A. Speiser, "Background and Function of the Biblical *Nasi*," in *Oriental and Biblical Studies,* [eds. J. J. Finkelstein and Moshe Greenberg], (Philadelphia: University of Pennsylvania Press, 1967), pp. 116, 121–122. In this penetrating article on the term *nasi',* Speiser maintains that "in order to qualify as a tribal leader, the *nāsī'* had to be a duly recognized head of a *bēt-'āb* (tribe)." However, he goes on to say, "With clans and tribes the title is best reproduced as 'chieftain.' With larger units, notably political states, 'leader' or 'president' should satisfy the requirements. In no case is 'prince' justified; as a translation of *nāsī',* this term is misleading in its primary sense and meaningless in its customary derivative usage."
71. M. Ḥag. II, 2.
72. Ab. I, 1–12.

nation looked to the ruler of the Great Sanhedrin as a true leader.[73] Ideally, the authority which he possessed and the justice which he represented were to be reflected throughout the entire court system. This exalted view of law not only resulted in an easier enforcement of governmental ethics in Judaism, but also made it possible to relate all facets of the law to the community in a more realistic and acceptable manner.[74] Therefore, an examination of the law and its relationship to the morality of the community is in order.

THE LAW AND MORALITY

The enforcement of governmental ethics in Judaism was made easier because of the close relationship between law and morality. The law in Judaism was not viewed as a mere legal apparatus governing the relationships among men. The law also included the relationships between God and men.

A Close Relationship

This meant that Jewish law and morality sprang from the same source, viz., the Written Law and the Oral Law. There was to be no conflict or ambiguity between law and morality.

The common tie between law and morality in Judaism was

---

73. Hoenig, *Great Sanhedrin*, p. 43: "Proof of the rabbinic leadership can also be found in the assertion that Hillel, Simon, Gamaliel and Simon were *Nesi'im*, heads of the Great Sanhedrin during the century before the destruction of the Temple (Shab. 14b). The mere fact that the phrase 'they appointed him *Nasi* over them' already was used in the ancient story of Hillel's elevation by the Bene Bathyra (Shab. 31a) proves that the position of *Nasi* was an early institution. Hence all passages which record the Zugot of the Second Temple era are authentic sources of the epoch's history."

74. Louis Jacobs, *Jewish Law* (New York: Behrman House, 1968), pp. 140–150.

their common origin—God. This seemed obvious to the Jews; e.g., the Decalogue commandments,[75] "You shall not kill" and "You shall not steal" (Exod. 20:13, 15), were stated with no less divine authority than "you shall love your neighbor as yourself: I am the Lord" (Lev. 19:18b).

Sanction by God and by Court

The close blend of the legal and the moral accounts for an interesting feature of Jewish law with regard to the application of sanctions. Under many laws the sanction by the court was sure and swift in coming; in other cases it was felt that the sanction was not the prerogative of man, but of God. As Rabbi Joshua taught,

> There are four acts for which the offender is exempt from the judgments of Man but liable to the judgments of Heaven. They are these: To break down a fence in front of a neighbour's animal [so that it gets out and does damage]; to bend over a neighbour's standing corn in front of a fire; to hire false witnesses to give evidence; and to know of evidence in favour of another and not to testify on his behalf.[76]

"Beyond the Letter of the Law"

This "holy" view of law held by the people made it much easier to maintain a high legal ethic in the enforcement of governmental regulations. Obedience to law was not merely a civic duty under

---

75. Salo W. Baron, *A Social and Religious History of the Jews,* vol. 1, rev. ed., (New York: Columbia University Press, 1952), p. 227, "Law does not mean . . . ceremonial law exclusively. In fact, it may easily be proved that in Judaism morality, however dependent on specific social attitudes, was the source of law. . . . Judaism, and all its official spokesmen, always taught its children that the first and greatest revelation of God was the pronouncement of the Ten Commandments, the ethical rather than the ritual Decalogue."

76. B.Ḳ. 55b.

this concept; it was a God-given responsibility.[77] Since God was merciful to his people, it was understood that law originating from him should be applied mercifully. This idea led to the practice of going beyond the letter of the law while acting under a moral imperative. The following episode explains how this practice was applied.

> Rab Judah once followed Mar Samuel into a street of wholemeal vendors, and he asked him: What if one found here a purse?—[Mar Samuel] answered: It would belong to the finder. What if an Israelite came and indicated an identification mark?—[Mar Samuel] answered: He would have to return it. Both? [Mar Samuel] answered: [He should go] beyond the requirements of the law. (n. I.e., in saying "he would have to return it" R. Simeon b. Eleazar did not give a legal decision but indicated what he would regard as the proper action to take on the ground of morality. The term used [לפנים משורת הדין] means literally "within the line of justice," i.e., performing a good action even if one is not compelled to do so legally.) Thus the father of Samuel found some asses in a desert, and he returned them to their owner after a year of twelve months; he went beyond the requirements of the law.[78]

This principle of going beyond mere law out of concern for one's neighbor or out of compassion for one's fellow man was more widely practiced when the law beyond which one went in his deed of thoughtfulness had emerged out of scholarly decree rather than from the Written Torah. This was the natural course since the decrees enacted by the scholars were generally more leniently approached than those obviously originating directly from the

77. Charles Foster Kent, *Israel's Laws and Legal Precedents* (New York: Charles Scribner's Sons, 1907), p. 11: "The various processes and stages whereby the different laws attained the final form may be traced in detail; but they are of minor importance compared with the supreme fact that Israel's laws contain God's directions, adapted at each point to the intelligence and needs of the race."

78. B.M. 24b [trans. Samuel Daiches]. For another example of "going beyond the letter of the law," cf. above, p. 53–55, and B.M. 83a.

Written Torah. This principle was taught by Rabbi Joshua b. Karḥa as follows:

> In laws of the Torah (n. Laws explicitly stated in Scripture.) follow the stricter view, in those of Soferim (n. Laws enacted by the Scribes [*sofer*-scribe] from the time of Ezra onward.) follow the more lenient view.[79]

A Rabbinic Debate

However, it must be added that, with the passage of time, there was a tendency for many of the Rabbis to apply to their enactments the force of rules of the Torah.[80] This resulted in a sustained debate which emerges from time to time in the rabbinical writings; e.g.,

> The case of partnership in an alley-way is different, because [the prohibition of taking things out there on the Sabbath] is only Rabbinical. (n. And therefore it does not matter if she did not strictly obtain possession.) R. Ḥisda said: Waradan was reduced to silence. What could he have answered?—[He could have said that] the Rabbis gave to their regulations the force of rules of the Torah. What could the other say to this?—That the Rabbis gave to their regulations the force of rules of Torah in matters which have some basis in the Torah, but not in a matter which has no basis in the Torah.[81]

Although the debate continued, and the position that the

---

79. A.Z. 7a [trans. A. Mishcon].

80. Hugo Fuchs, "Halachah," *Universal Jewish Encyclopedia* (1941), vol. 5, p. 173. Speaking of the growing importance of the rabbinic rulings about the time of the formation of the Mishnah (ca. 200 C.E.), Fuchs says, "Judaism now had an authentic law-book, embodying both the written laws of the Torah and the oral laws of the rabbis, dealing with every phase of life, and the complete embodiment of the idea of God's rule over mankind."

81. Giṭ 64b–65a [trans. Maurice Simon].

enactments or decrees coming directly from the Written Torah were to be more specifically and rigorously applied remained theoretically valid, in practical application the decrees of the scholars came to carry virtually the same legal weight as laws traced directly to the Written Torah.

Summary

Perhaps this emphasis on rabbinical authority seen as emerging out of the same origins as all Jewish law, both Written and Oral, goes a long way to explain why it was often (though not always) possible to enforce a high governmental ethic in Judaism through the centuries. This was the cement for the legal machinery which made the practical application of the legal system possible. The people embraced this system of enforcement because they saw the Rabbis as religious figures as well as judges and lawmakers. For, as already pointed out, Jewish law was considered a matter of faith, seen as having its ultimate origin in divine revelation, and the Rabbis, as duly ordained scholars, were the means by which the law was interpreted, expanded, vitalized, and applied. Thus, whether the law involved religious commands about religious festivals or legal regulations concerning property, obedience was necessary in order to maintain acceptable relations among men and between God and men. Obedience to law was a matter of morals, and this morality of obedience was a matter of religious conviction.

Therefore, within the framework of a governmental system which was a blend of legal and religious responsibilities, the people saw no disparity between such laws as "Remember the sabbath day, to keep it holy" and "You shall not steal" (Exod. 20:8, 15). And, under this legal system in Judaism, the people saw it as fitting that their problems and disputes within both religious and legal areas should be brought to the rabbinical courts for settlement. This philosophy of government made the application of the law and obedience to the law questions of moral and religious ethics. This kind of rule, by its very nature, made it theoretically possible to maintain high judicial and governmental ethical standards.

CHAPTER IV

REWARD AND PUNISHMENT IN JUDICIAL ETHICS

INTRODUCTION

Every ethical system is based on an overriding conviction. The great conviction in the theology of the ancient Israelites was that God is one. "Hear, O Israel: The Lord our God is one Lord."[1] This conviction related their ethical behavior (morality) to obedience to God. They believed that obedience to God brought blessings and disobedience brought punishment.[2] Therefore, with regard to the question under consideration, reward and punishment in judicial ethics, one needs to remember that the regulations of law were based upon theological principles.

The people could not long remain ideally related to God or to each other without encouragement and restraint applied in balanced proportion. It has been well said,

> ... it had to be made clear that ... in spite of certain temporary setbacks that it might entail, honesty was in the long run the best policy, while, on the other hand, whatever immediate advantages crime might appear to bring, it did not, when reviewed from the standpoint of its ultimate effects, really pay.[3]

1. Deut. 6:4.
2. Deut. 7:9–10, 11:13–28, chap. 28, 30:15–20; Lev. 26:3–42.
3. Samuel Rosenblatt, *Hear, Oh Israel* (New York: Philipp Feldheim, 1958), pp. 113–114.

The fact that "it had to be made clear" is a pervading principle which operated throughout the Jewish governmental system. Thus, punishment was a deterrent to lawlessness. Reward was an inducement to lawfulness. In the following analysis of reward and punishment in judicial ethics, these principles will be seen to operate at every level of government.

DIVINE REWARD AND PUNISHMENT
FOR RULERS AND SUBJECTS

It has been pointed out in the preceding chapters that the Israelites saw the system of law under which they lived as derived from God and therefore authoritative.

Rabbinic Jurisdiction via the Courts

Although this authority was of God, the power to implement his laws was exercised by duly appointed leaders, such as Moses, and designated agencies, such as the courts. It was also noted earlier that the Rabbis eventually taught that a "voice from heaven" (or "echo of a heavenly voice") was not to be recognized as having legal authority.[4] This meant that the Torah had been finally given, and its development and application rested under rabbinical authority.[5] They held that this rabbinical authority was derived from Torah, and therefore delegated by God and expressed and enforced within Jewish society through the system of courts described in the previous chapter.

4. Above, p. 78, n. 11.
5. M. Lazarus, *The Ethics of Judaism,* pt. II (Philadelphia: Jewish Publication Society, 1901), pp. 174 175.

God's Direct Justice

This did not mean, however, that they thought God's power or determination to administer direct punishment had been diminished. Indeed, the people were well aware that Scripture placed a heavy emphasis upon God's direct punishment of the wicked in the past.[6] Korah's rebellion was a historical example which reminded them of that truth. That incident, which occurred among the Israelites in the wilderness and involved political and religious issues affecting their government, portrayed the fate of Korah and the corps of leaders who joined him in their rebellion against Moses and Aaron.

> . . . and they rose up before Moses, together with some of the sons of Israel, two hundred and fifty leaders of the congregation, chosen in the assembly, men of renown. And they assembled together against Moses and Aaron, and said to them, "You have gone far enough, for all the congregation are holy, every one of them, and the Lord is in their midst; so why do you exalt yourselves above the assembly of the Lord?"[7]

The wider implications of this rebellion, viz., the claim of the Levites for a share of the priestly privileges, was a recurrent problem in the history of the Jews, as the historian Josephus points out:

> Those of the Levites—this is one of our tribes—who were singers of hymns urged the king to convene the Sanhedrin and get them permission to wear linen robes on equal terms with the priests, maintaining that it was fitting that he should introduce, to mark his reign, some innovation by which he would be remembered. Nor did they fail to obtain their request; for the king, with the consent of those who attended the Sanhedrin, allowed the singers of hymns to

6. Gen. 6:5, 17; 18:20–21, 19:24; Num. 25:3, 9; etc.
7. Num. 16:2–3 (NASB).

discard their former robes and to wear linen ones such as they wished. A part of the tribe that served in the temple were also permitted to learn the hymns by heart, as they had requested. All this was contrary to the ancestral laws, and such transgression was bound to make us liable to punishment.[8]

In the case of Korah's rebellion against Moses and Aaron, who were duly appointed by God to their respective roles as leader and high priest, the punishment was not slow in coming. The rebels were committed by God for destruction,

> . . . . and the earth opened its mouth and swallowed them up, and their households, and all the men who belonged to Korah, with their possessions. So they and all that belonged to them went down alive to Sheol; and the earth closed over them, and they perished from the midst of the assembly. And all Israel who were around them fled at their outcry, for they said, "The earth may swallow us up!" Fire also came forth from the Lord and consumed the two hundred and fifty men who were offering the incense.[9]

It goes without question, in view of the above example, that the nation of Israel had ample opportunity to understand the meaning of this catastrophic phenomenon, namely God's approval of the lawful and disapproval of the unlawful.

---

8. Josephus, *Jewish Antiquities,* bk. XX, ix, 6 [trans. Louis H. Feldman], Loeb Classical Library ed., vol. 9).

9. Num. 16:32–35 (NASB). George Buchanan Gray, *Numbers,* International Critical Commentary (1903), pp. 186–208. This author sees this episode as a blending of several different literary sources in an attempt to present a unified story. Actually, he says, two distinct themes may be detected: (1) "the revolt against the civil authority of Moses under the leadership of Dathan and Abiram and On" (p. 189); and (2) the revolt of representatives of the whole people under Ḳorah against the Levites (represented by Moses and Aaron) in vindication of their equal holiness. With reference to the latter, Gray states, "In these verses all Israel except Levi drop entirely into the background, for they have no concern in this dispute: the struggle is confined to the tribe of Levi. The object of these passages is to condemn the non-Aaronic Levites for seeking the *priesthood"* (pp. 192–193).

Thus, God did "make it clear," by what was believed to be his direct intervention of punishment, that rebellion against proper authority could not be practiced with impunity. However, direct intervention was not the only way this principle was made known. There were, of course, great numbers of laws given in the Torah, the violation of which brought sanctions upon the people as applied by the appointed authorities. This will be discussed later at greater length.

Kareth

In addition to the sanctions of law just mentioned, there occasionally appears in the Hebrew Scriptures a warning of God's act of "cutting off" for the commission of certain crimes; e.g.,

> Say to the people of Israel, "Any man of the people of Israel, or of the strangers that sojourn in Israel, who gives any of his children to Molech shall be put to death; the people of the land shall stone him with stones." I myself will set my face against that man, and will cut him off from among his people, because he has given one of his children to Molech, defiling my sanctuary and profaning my holy name.[10]

However, the meaning of כרת *kareth* (usually translated as "extirpation") is disputed and rather doubtful, suggesting that any attempt to relate this subject to the theme of judicial or political ethics among the Hebrews may be too dubious a task. Goldin's remarks are apropos:

> As the Mosaic Law is not very precise in its definition of that punishment, there has arisen much speculation as to its true nature. Some modern commentators on the Bible maintain that *karet* is nothing less than capital punishment decreed by a legally constituted court of Law (e.g., Gesenius, *Thesaurus,* p. 718). According to

10. Lev. 20:2–3.

the Talmudic authorities, however, the cases punishable by *karet* do not come under the jurisdiction of any human tribunal.[11]

Ancient Israel: A Theocracy

While the Israelites understood that the justice of God required that all violations of his will be punished, they also saw his divine holiness as an incentive for them to follow him; e.g., this instruction through Moses, "Speak to all the congregation of the sons of Israel and say to them, 'You shall be holy, for I the Lord your God am holy'" (Lev. 19:2, NASB).[12] However, God's divine attributes of love, mercy, and holiness were not, *per se,* incentive enough to elicit complete loyalty from his people. Therefore, God's Torah was not only given to instruct, but also to encourage them in righteousness with promises of blessings for obedience, and to warn them about the consequences of disobedience.

Thus, the concept of reward and punishment in the theocracy of ancient Israel was articulated through laws which were believed to be of divine origin. The judicial and political framework within which these laws were operative reflected, theoretically at least, the high ethical standards inherent in their theocratic system of government.

During the theocratic system of government which characterized the Mosaic period of ancient Israel, the people were governed by God through Moses, and the priesthood functioned by divine authority (Exod. 20, Lev. 8, Num. 17–18, etc.). Josephus speaks to this point as follows:

He [Moses] had good reason for thinking that he had God for his

11. Hyman E. Goldin, *Hebrew Criminal Law and Procedure* (New York: Twayne Publishers, 1952), pp. 40–41.

12. R. A. Redford, "Leviticus," in *The Pulpit Commentary,* [eds. H. D. M. Spence and Joseph S. Exell], (Grand Rapids, Mich.: Eerdmans, 1950), vol. 2, p. 310. The writer suggests this injunction is based on two universalities: (1) it is addressed to "all"; and (2) it is predicated on the authority of an "all-holy" God.

guide and counsellor. Having first persuaded himself that God's will governed all his actions and all his thoughts, he regarded it as his primary duty to impress that idea upon the community. . . . There is endless variety in the details of the customs and laws which prevail in the world at large. . . . Our lawgiver, however, was attracted by none of these forms of polity, but gave to his constitution that form of what—if a forced expression be permitted—may be termed a "theocracy" [n. The word was apparently coined by Josephus; the idea goes back to the O.T.], placing all sovereignty and authority in the hands of God.[13]

During the period of the Judges, the tribes functioned in a loose and fluid sort of tribal league somewhat analogous to the amphictyony of the Greek city-states that had a common sacral center at Delphi.

The confederation of the 12 tribes was primarily religious, based upon belief in the one "God of Israel" with whom the tribes had made a covenant and whom they worshiped at a common sacral center as the "people of the Lord" (Judg. 5:11; 20:2). The Tent of Meeting and the ark of the covenant were the most sacred cultic objects of the tribal union.[14]

Oded continues,

In the period of the judges there was no predetermined pattern of leadership among the tribes, except for deliverer-judges sent to them by God in time of need. Such crises forced the tribes into cooperative action against enemies under the leadership of the "deliverers." Shiloh served as a sacral center for all the tribes, housing the ark of the covenant under the priestly family of Eli (I Samuel 1:3, 12; 2:27).[15]

13. Josephus, *Against Apion,* II, 16 ([trans. H. St. J. Thackeray], Loeb Classical Library ed., vol. 1, pp. 357, 359).

14. Bustanay Oded, "Tribes, The Twelve," *Encyclopaedia Judaica,* vol. 15, col. 1383.

15. Ibid., cols. 1381–1382.

Thus the essential features of theocracy were retained through this period.

Throughout the monarchical periods of the Israelites the theocracy technically ceased, although there remained certain theocratic features of government, e.g., the prominent role of Jerusalem as a "holy city," the Temple, and the priesthood.

Epstein speaks of the reestablishment of theocracy in the postcaptivity period in his book, *Judaism: A Historical Presentation.* He points out that the political prerogatives of Zerubbabel, governor of Judea under Persian tutelage when the rebuilding of the Temple began, were "turned over by the Persian authorities to Joshua, who had become High Priest in the rebuilt Temple and who, by virtue of his new position, had vested in him the supreme authority—religious and civil (including political)—held hitherto by the Judean kings."[16]

Epstein states that, under Ezra's efforts,

> slowly but surely the Torah became the final source of every Jewish norm and practice, rule and custom, in all departments of life— religious, moral, political, social, economic, and domestic. . . . the Judean theocratic state—a state ruled by Torah—which, though politically and economically insignificant, was destined not only to give a definite direction to Jewish history, but also to prove a factor of the greatest consequence in the history of mankind.[17]

Zeitlin points out the type of government and authority that prevailed in Palestine at a later time.

> Prior to the Hasmonean period, the high priest had complete civil and religious authority. He was the pontifical head of both religion and the state. As high priest he had the power to appoint judges to try those who transgressed religious law and these judges were

16. I. Epstein, *Judaism: A Historical Presentation* (Baltimore: Penguin Books, 1959), p. 81.
17. Ibid., p. 85.

responsible only to him. In civil matters he had the council, *gerousia,* made up of representatives of the Jewish aristocracy. . . . In matters that involved the vital interests of the state, the high priest would convene a Great Synagogue.[18]

This type of government, of course, had a major feature of a hierocracy—a government by rule of priesthood.

THE DEATH PENALTY

In the previous section it was pointed out in both the introduction and in the discussion concerning divine reward and punishment for rulers and subjects that the fact of capital punishment was a vivid reality in Bible times. In the next chapter, where the principle of "measure for measure" and the statement in Genesis 9:6 are discussed, it will be shown that the practice of capital punishment was a method whereby the principles of both "measure for measure" and "blood for blood" were accomplished.

Introduction

The specific purpose of this section on the death penalty is to see it, as described in the Torah, as a prominent feature of the law with carefully defined rules of application and judicial guidelines.[19] After the biblical perspective of the subject has been clarified, the last part of this section will be concerned with the way the Sages dealt with the judicial question of capital punishment during talmudic times.

In such an inquiry it is obvious that a grasp of the judicial

18. Solomon Zeitlin, *The Rise and Fall of the Judaean State,* vol. 1 (Philadelphia: Jewish Publication Society, 1962), p. 202.

19. W. H. Bennett, "Crimes and Punishments (Hebrew)," *Encyclopaedia of Religion and Ethics,* [ed. James Hastings], vol. 4. Cf. p. 281 for description of the death penalty as legislated and applied under biblical law.

ethics involved in the concept of capital punishment is crucial to an understanding of those who were concerned with it in both the biblical and talmudic eras. Therefore, not only will this analysis deal with the descriptive, legislative, and judicial aspects of the question, but there will also be an examination of the ethics, morals, and motives involved.

It has already been noted that the Hebrew nation understood the Torah as having emanated from God at Sinai.[20] They looked to Moses as the mediator of both the Written and the Oral Law.[21] In this divinely revealed Law of God, the Hebrews found his will and what they should do to stay in his favor and receive his blessings. They also found in the law the assurance of punishment if God was disobeyed. This punishment was varied in method of application and degree of severity. Sometimes it was applied directly by an angry God (Num. 11:33–34); again it was applied indirectly through God's appointed leaders, such as priests (Num. 25:6–13) and prophets (II Kings 5:25–27); more often punishment was meted out through the established judicial channel of courts and judges (Deut. 17:8–13). But in every case, and at all times, the biblical Hebrews saw the law as divine law and were in subjection to it as a religious tenet.

Capital Punishment: The Biblical Perspective

The extreme penalty of death was decreed in the law for many different crimes.

Not only such major crimes as idolatry, adultery, and murder,

---

20. W. F. Albright, *New Horizons in Biblical Research* (London: Oxford University Press, 1966), p. 29. "For the first time in history, we have a series of general laws: the Ten Commandments. Unfortunately for the historian, their exact date is not certain, though their original formulation cannot be later than the tenth century B.C., and may easily go back to the thirteenth."

21. Jacob Neusner, [ed.], *Understanding Rabbinic Judaism from Talmudic to Modern Times* (New York: KTAV, 1974), p. 7.

but even relatively minor transgressions like witchcraft, false prophecy, and rebelliousness against parents (to name but a few) were visited with the extreme penalty.[22]

The fact that a capital offense might be "criminal" (murder), "religious" (false prophecy), "social" (adultery), or "domestic" (rebellious son) did not strike a discord for the Hebrews in that they saw, through the Law of God, that all of these and similar offenses were, in the final reckoning, offenses against the divine will or nature. The distinction between "civil" and "criminal" violations was not significant so far as punishment for disobedience was concerned. This "oneness" of law made for a unity of life so that the Hebrews' response to law was in actuality a moral, ethical, and religious response, as well as legal. Thus, an obedient person's relationship to the courts and institutions of society was an ethical one.

PUTTING AWAY EVIL. In such a climate it was perfectly logical that the ultimate motive for capital punishment was to drive evil away. Very often this is specifically stated as the reason for the death sentence. For example, in the case of the one who disregarded both priest and judge it was said,

> The man who acts presumptuously, by not obeying the priest who stands to minister there before the Lord your God, or the judge, that man shall die; so you shall purge the evil from Israel.[23]

From the ethical point of view, it is worth noting that capital punishment was for the purpose of putting away the evil, and not primarily for the purpose of putting away the evil *one*. This motive for capital punishment did not change the fate of the convicted

22. Moses Aberbach, "Jewish Attitude to Capital Punishment," *Jewish Chronicle* (London), Nov. 28, 1952, p. 15.
23. Deut. 17:12. The punishment was of course of a specific nature, for a specific act, not just for "not obeying."

criminal, but it did mean that this practice in biblical times was based on a higher principle than mere retaliation. This can be illustrated at length with Bible examples. For instance:

> If a man is found stealing one of his brethren, the people of Israel, and if he treats him as a slave or sells him, then that thief shall die; so you shall purge the evil from the midst of you.[24]

THE DETERRENT MOTIVE. Since the supreme motive for capital punishment was ultimately to remove the evil, this meant that one of the most desirable effects forthcoming from an execution was that it be a deterrent against further crime. This is specifically stated in a number of cases; e.g., (1) when the presumptuous one is executed, "And all the people shall hear, and fear, and not act presumptuously again," and (2) when the false witness is executed, "And the rest shall hear, and fear, and shall never again commit any such evil among you."[25]

Hanging

The desire for deterrent benefits as a prime motive for capital punishment becomes obvious when one considers the biblical injunction about hanging, and then compares that legislation with examples of this type of execution among other peoples. The Torah calls for hanging in the following way:

> And if a man has committed a crime punishable by death and he is

---

24. Deut. 24:7. S. R. Driver, *Deuteronomy,* International Critical Commentary (1895), p. 152: "And thou shalt exterminate the evil from thy midst" (ובערת הרע מקרבך) so 17:7, 19:19, 21:21, 22:21, 24; and with 'from Israel' 17:12, 22:22 (cf. 19:13, 21:9),—always at the close of instructions for the punishment of a wrong-doer, and always, except 19:19, with reference to capital punishment. A formula peculiar to Dt., whereby the duty is laid upon the community of clearing itself from complicity in a crime committed in its midst, and of preventing, as far as possible, an evil example from spreading."

25. Deut. 17:13, 19:20.

put to death, and you hang him on a tree, his body shall not remain all night upon the tree, but you shall bury him the same day, for a hanged man is accursed by God; you shall not defile your land which the Lord your God gives you for an inheritance.[26]

From this legislation it is clear that when one had been executed for a sin "punishable by death," he was then hanged on a tree.[27] Since death was not the purpose of the hanging, it appears that the motive was to deter others from committing such crimes. However, the deuteronomic requirement to remove the body by sunset was interpreted by the Rabbis to mean only formal hanging for a moment, and was generally given a remarkable homiletical interpretation.[28]

JUDICIAL HANGING. The judicial practice of hanging *after* execution was in contrast to the hangings or impaling often noted in the Bible among non-Jewish peoples. For example, the Pharaoh of Joseph's time "hanged the chief baker" (Gen. 40:21–22). The Gibeonites also used hanging as a method of execution (II Sam. 21:9). Likewise, in summary fashion the king of Persia ordered the execution of Haman as follows:

26. Deut. 21:22–23.

27. עץ = tree (Gen. 2:9), wood (Gen. 22:7), article of wood (Lev. 11:32), timber (II Kings 12:12), pole (Josh. 10:26), gallows (Esth. 2:23). Cf. Francis Brown, S. R. Driver, and C. A. Briggs, *Hebrew and English Lexicon of the Old Testament* (London: Oxford University Press, 1951), pp. 781–782.

28. San. 46b ([trans. Jacob Shachter], "Scripture says, 'And he be put to death, then thou shalt hang him'—he is first put to death and afterward hanged. And how is this done?—It [the verdict] is delayed until just before sunset. Then they pronounce judgment and put him [immediately] to death, after which they hang him; one ties him up and another unties [him], in order to fulfil the precept of hanging. . . . R. Meir said: A parable was stated; 'To what is this matter comparable? To two twin brothers [who lived] in one city; one was appointed king, and the other took to highway robbery. At the king's command they hanged him. But all who saw him exclaimed, "the king is hanged!" (n. Being twins their appearance was similar. So man has some resemblance to God, having been created in His image. Cf. Gen. V, 1.) Whereupon the king issued a command and he was taken down."'

> Then said Harbona, one of the eunuchs in attendance on the king,
> "Moreover, the gallows which Haman has prepared for Mordecai,
> whose word saved the king, is standing in Haman's house, fifty
> cubits high." And the king said, "Hang him on that." So they
> hanged Haman on the gallows which he had prepared for Mor-
> decai. Then the anger of the king abated.[29]

EXTRAJUDICIAL HANGING. An an extrajudicial action during time
of war, it is recorded that Joshua hanged the king of Ai.

> So Joshua burned Ai, and made it for ever a heap of ruins, as it is to
> this day. And he hanged the king of Ai on a tree until evening; and
> at the going down of the sun Joshua commanded, and they took his
> body down from the tree, and cast it at the entrance of the gate of
> the city, and raised over it a great heap of stones, which stands there
> to this day.[30]

This example stands out in Bible history for two main reasons:
first, it shows a very rare occurrence of death by hanging under the
authority of a Jewish leader; second, it was an extrajudicial
action.[31] Thus, it does not alter the principle which has been established above that hanging as a judicial procedure in the Torah was
not to execute, since the hanged criminal was already dead, but to
deter others from committing similar offenses.

Burning

The other two forms of capital punishment in biblical law were

---

29. Esth. 7:9–10.
30. Josh. 8:28–29.
31. H. Freedman, "Joshua," in *Joshua and Judges,* [ed. A. Cohen], (London:
Soncino Press, 1950), p. 44. Here Freedman reminds his readers that in another
case of wartime execution, involving "five kings of the Amorites," "Joshua smote
them and put them to death, and he hung them on five trees. And they hung upon
the trees until evening; but at the time of the going down of the sun, Joshua commanded, and they took them down from the trees" (Josh. 10:26–27). The point is
made that, in this case, the law of Deut. 21:23 was carried out even with non-
Israelites.

burning and stoning. Burning was required by law for only two crimes, viz.,

> If a man takes a wife and her mother also, it is wickedness; they shall be burned with fire, both he and they, that there may be no wickedness among you. . . . And the daughter of any priest, if she profanes herself by playing the harlot, profanes her father; she shall be burned with fire.[32]

This legislation, which required burning as the means of execution for only two different offenses, was in spite of the fact that it was a practice known to the Hebrews before they received the law (Gen. 38:24).[33] Perhaps the rare demand for this type of execution indicates the relative humaneness of the Torah as contrasted to the extrajudicial practice. Since this legislation was directed specifically against those who were guilty of "harlotry" and "immorality," it may well be a clue to the extreme divine displeasure at such acts. This realization on the part of the people, plus the horrible punishment itself, served to facilitate a higher standard of ethics and morals among the populace. This suggestion is strengthened when one realizes that burning, like judicial hanging, was sometimes utilized *after* execution with the apparent motive of deterrence. For example, when Achan's trespass had been established beyond doubt, the following events transpired concerning Achan and his family:

> And Joshua said, "Why did you bring trouble on us? The Lord brings trouble on you today." And all Israel stoned him with stones; they burned them with fire, and stoned them with stones.[34]

32. Lev. 20:14, 21:9.

33. John Skinner, *Genesis,* International Critical Commentary (1910), pp. 454–455: "Death by burning is the punishment imposed in Hammurabi (law) no. 157, for incest with a mother, and was doubtless the common punishment for adultery on the part of a woman in ancient Israel. In later times the milder penalty of stoning was substituted (Lv. 20:19, Dt. 22:23 ff., Ezek. 16:40, Jn. 8:5), the more cruel death being reserved for the prostitution of a priest's daughter (Lv. 21:9; cf. Hamm. [law] no. 110)."

34. Josh. 7:25.

Stoning

Stoning was the most common type of judicial punishment for capital offenses; e.g., the Torah ordained for the convicted idolater, " . . . then you shall bring forth to your gates that man or woman who has done this evil thing, and you shall stone that man or woman to death with stones" (Deut. 17:5). For one who was guilty of blasphemy against God the sentence was stoning. "He who blasphemes the name of the Lord shall be put to death; all the congregation shall stone him; the sojourner as well as the native, when he blasphemes the Name, shall be put to death" (Lev. 24:16).[35] Also, the Torah legislated that the stubborn and rebellious son, if convicted, was to be stoned to death. "Then all the men of the city shall stone him [the stubborn and rebellious son] to death with stones; so you shall purge the evil from your midst; and all Israel shall hear, and fear" (Deut. 21:21). Many other examples may be found in the Torah.

GENERAL PARTICIPATION. The biblical practice of judicial stoning involved the participation of the witnesses and the people. Some of the above examples show this. Others include the punishment of those who were convicted of participating in the Molech cult of child sacrifice and the similar sentence for those found guilty of other forms of idolatry, i.e., worship of sun, moon, or stars (Lev. 20:1–2; Deut. 17:6–7). This had the effect of placing the witnesses in a very sobering position. It also meant that the execution was communal in effect, although popular approbation was legally not required for them to participate in the execution. Popular participation was optional. This merging of the legislative, judicial, and executive procedures in carrying the requirements of the law to

35. M. Lazarus, *The Ethics of Judaism,* pt. I (Philadelphia: Jewish Publication Society, 1900). Cf. pp. 129–130, where Lazarus stresses that this equality before the law was a broad principle which was a characteristic distinction of the most ancient Jewish legislation, as well as later Judaism. There was " 'one law and one code,' alike for the native and the stranger (Num. 15:15)."

their logical conclusion was a unifying factor within the Hebrew nation. It elevated compliance with the law to a level higher than slavish obedience; and, by involving the community as well as the individual in the application of punishment, greatly reduced the possibility of execution out of vengeance.

NO GUARANTEE AGAINST INJUSTICE. However, in spite of the aforementioned safeguards incorporated into the judicial and penal procedures in criminal cases, there was no absolute guarantee against the miscarriage of justice. Sheer savagery could be practiced under the guise of legal proceedings when the ruling power became corrupt. For example, when king Ahab desired the vineyard of Naboth the Jezreelite, which was near his palace in Samaria, queen Jezebel

> wrote letters in Ahab's name and sealed them with his seal, and she sent the letters to the elders and the nobles who dwelt with Naboth in his city. And she wrote the letters, "Proclaim a fast, and set Naboth on high among the people; and set two base fellows opposite him, and let them bring a charge against him, saying, You have cursed God and the king. Then take him out, and stone him to death."[36]

The elders, nobles, and witnesses obeyed her orders. Naboth was stoned, and the vineyard was seized by Ahab.[37]

Capital Punishment: Rabbinic Perspectives

The biblical period of criminal jurisprudence eventually gave way to the period of rabbinical interpretation, adaptation, restriction, and even elimination of many severe features of the criminal law

---

36. I Kings 21:8–10.

37. A N.T. example of unbridled passion leading to an unjustified execution is the stoning of Stephen, Acts 7:54–60. Thus, popular motivation was not necessarily consistent with ethical behavior.

found in the Torah. It was noted in the previous discussion that the death penalty described in the Bible was by stoning and burning, with hanging as a superimposed action on the criminal after execution. The death penalty applied to a large number of infractions, and many examples are found in the Bible of executions under the law.

> Yet, in spite of the severity of the Law, changing social conditions made the death penalty increasingly inapplicable. Throughout the Biblical period, idolatry and vice were constant problems, and the Sabbath was frequently profaned (cf. Jer. xvii, 19 ff.; Nehem. x, 32, xiii, 15 ff.). The extreme penalty—or, for that matter, any other punishment—for these offences must, therefore, have been in abeyance. Similarly, in pre-Hasmonean times, the power of the Hellenised aristocracy was no doubt an effective check against any serious penalty for religious transgressions.[38]

Therefore, when one considers the question of capital punishment during the talmudic period of Judaism, one sees, perhaps as nowhere else, the struggle of the rabbinical authorities to retain a system of justice while adapting to changing conditions. This struggle was stabilized by the retention of three principles which were applied to the execution of the convicted criminal whether the penalty took the form of strangling, decapitation, burning, or stoning.

FIRST PRINCIPLE: LOVE. The first principle was love. " . . . you shall love your neighbor as yourself . . . " (Lev. 19:18b)[39] was applied even to the one convicted of a capital offense in that the judicial authorities were committed to rendering the capital punishment which was most humane in each individual case.

---

38. Aberbach, "Jewish Attitude to Capital Punishment."

39. James L. Mays, *Leviticus,* Layman's Bible Commentaries (London: SCM Press, 1964). "This single sentence discloses in a crucial way the intention and basis of God's instruction for Israel. It transcends the legal idiom because it is stated positively and summons Israel to a way of love" (p. 60).

When he is about four cubits distant from the place of stoning, he is stripped of his garments. A man is covered in front and a woman both in front and behind: This is R. Judah's view. But the Sages say: A man is to be stoned naked but a woman is not to be stoned naked. Raba said: Is there only an inconsistency between R. Judah's two statements and not between those of the Rabbis?—But, said Raba, R. Judah's two statements are not contradictory, even as we have solved the difficulty. And the Rabbis' views are also not opposed: Scripture says, "That all women may be warned and not to do after your lewdness": (Ezek. 23:48) but here, no greater warning is possible than this [sc. the execution]. (n. Hence there is no need to add humiliation.) And should you say, Let us wreak both (n. Humiliation and stoning.) upon her, behold R. Naḥman said in Rabbah b. Abbahu's name: Scripture says, "Love thy neighbor as thyself": (Lev. 19:18) choose an easy death for him. (n. One entailing as little humiliation as possible.).[40]

SECOND PRINCIPLE: NONMUTILATION. The second principle retained in capital punishment cases was closely connected with the way in which the Rabbis perceived God as taking life—that is, natural death. In natural death there was no external disfigurement or mutilation of the body. Since it was concluded that this was God's way of terminating life, it was accepted as being the proper way to apply God's death penalty laws. The conviction that God's way of taking life was without mutilation of the body had given rise to an ancient teaching that the bodies of Nadab and Abihu[41] had remained intact while their souls were burned.

> What is meant by a wick?—R. Mathna said: A lead bar. ("Lit" in the Mishnah will therefore mean "melted.") Whence do we know this? (n. That death by fire was thus carried out, instead of burning the body.)—It is inferred from the fact that burning is decreed here; (Lev. 21:9 "She shall be burnt with fire.") and was also the fate of the assembly of Korah; (Num. 17:4) just as there the reference is to

40. M. San. VI, 3; 45a [trans. Jacob Shachter].
41. Lev. 10:1–2.

the burning of the soul, the body remaining intact, so here too. R. Eleazar said: It is deduced from the employment of the word "burning" here and in the case of Aaron's sons; (Lev. 10:6 "Let your brethren . . . bewail the burning which the Lord hath kindled.") just as there the burning of the soul is meant, while the body remained intact, so here too. . . . Now he [R. Eleazar] who infers it from the sons of Aaron, whence does he know [that their bodies were not burnt]?—Because it is written, "And they died before the Lord," (Lev. 10:2) teaching that it was like normal death [from within].[42]

NONMUTILATION IN BURNING. In harmony with this principle of leaving the body unchanged by execution, even the teachings concerning execution by burning were meant to assure that no mutilation would result. The rabbinic explanation of how this was to be accomplished is as follows:

> The manner in which burning is executed is as follows: He who had been thus condemned was lowered into dung to his armpits; then a hard cloth was placed within a soft one, wound round his neck, and the two loose ends pulled in opposite directions, forcing him to open his mouth. A wick was then lit, and thrown into his mouth, so that it descended into his body and burnt his bowels. R. Judah said: Should he however have died at their hands [being strangled by the bandage before the wick was thrown into his mouth, or before it could act], he would not have been executed by fire as prescribed. Hence it was done thus: His mouth was forced open with pincers against his wish, the wick lit and thrown into his mouth, so that it descended into his body and burnt his bowels.[43]

As in biblical law, so in rabbinical law, execution by burning was restricted to a priest's daughter convicted of adultery and those guilty of specified forms of incest. According to the Mishnah,

42. San. 52a [trans. H. Freedman].
43. M. San. VII, 2.

The following are burnt: He who commits incest with a woman and her daughter, and a priest's adulterous daughter. There is included in "a woman and her daughter" his own daughter, his daughter's daughter, his son's daughter, his wife's daughter and the daughter of her daughter or son, his mother-in-law, her mother, and his father-in-law's mother.[44]

As was pointed out, care was to be taken that the body not be disfigured in this type of execution. In one recorded case where the proper procedure was not followed in execution by burning, the Mishnah states that the court's ignorance of the law was the reason.

R. Eleazer b. Zadok said: It once happened that a priest's daughter committed adultery, whereupon bundles of faggots were placed round about her and she was burnt. The sages replied, That was because the Beth Din at that time was not well learned in law.[45]

However, R. Joseph stated in a later commentary on this text, "It was a Sadducee Beth Din that did this" (San. 52b). The significance of this statement becomes clear when it is pointed out that the Sadducees, in criminal jurisdiction, "were very rigorous and . . . carried out the penalty of death by fire in a literal manner."[46]

NONMUTILATION IN STRANGULATION. The talmudic reforms of capital punishment resulted in another method of execution which

44. M. San. IX, 1.
45. M. San. VII, 2.
46. I. Epstein, [ed.], *The Babylonian Talmud,* vol. 3, *Seder Nezikin,* [trans. H. Freedman, Sanhedrin], p. 353, n. 2. Also, cf. Josephus, *Antiquities,* XX, ix, 1, where, in speaking of the younger Ananus, he describes the judicial severity of the Sadducees as follows: "The younger Ananus, who . . . had been appointed to the high priesthood, was rash in his temper and unusually daring. He followed the school of the Sadducees, who are indeed more heartless (savage) than any of the other Jews . . . when they sit in judgment."

was supposed to be more humane and less mutilating than any of the others.[47] Strangulation was the sentence imposed upon a criminal who had committed a capital offense the punishment for which was not specified in the law. Thus, if the convicted person had committed a capital offense which was not specifically punishable by burning, decapitation, or stoning, he was to be strangled.[48] The procedure was in some ways similar to execution by burning.

> Strangulation was thus performed:—The condemned man was lowered into dung up to his armpits, then a hard cloth was placed within a soft one, wound round his neck, and the two ends pulled in opposite directions until he was dead.[49]

In addition to applying the mode of strangling to all criminals convicted of a capital offense the punishment for which was not specified, strangulation was also assigned as the definite punishment for a few special capital crimes.

> According to the Mishnah, the following are strangled: He who strikes his father or mother; or kidnaps a Jew [to sell as a slave]; an elder rebelling against the ruling of Beth Din; a false prophet; one who prophesies in the name of an idol; one who commits adultery; witnesses who testified falsely [to the adultery of] a priest's daughter, and her paramour.[50]

47. David Daube, *The New Testament and Rabbinic Judaism* (London: Athlone Press, 1956). Cf. pp. 304–305, where Daube says that "between about 100 B.C. and A.D. 100 a far-reaching reform of the modes of execution was effected by the Pharisees," and describes their manner of stoning, burning, strangulation, and decapitation.

48. San. 52b, "Whenever the Torah decrees an unspecified death penalty, you may not interpret it stringently but leniently: (n. Lit., 'attract it to stringency etc.' Hence strangulation, the easiest of deaths, must be meant.) this is R. Josiah's view. R. Jonathan said: Not because strangulation is the most lenient death, but because by every unspecified death in the Torah strangulation is meant" [trans. H. Freedman].

49. M. San. VII, 3.

50. M. San. XI, 1.

THIRD PRINCIPLE: REMOVAL OF SINS. Before considering the other two methods of execution set forth in the laws of Judaism, it is time to mention a third principle in the governmental system of Judaism with regard to sanctions which showed an ethical ingredient of considerable merit in the ultimate motive for capital punishment.

This principle has already been mentioned earlier in this discussion.[51] Therefore, it needs little elaboration here. The reason it is emphasized is because it illustrates an ethical foundation of capital punishment as it was practiced in biblical and talmudic times. The principle held that capital punishment was primarily to remove the *evil,* rather than the *doer* of evil, from the land. This high motive, if properly followed, meant that no judicial execution in either biblical or rabbinical times could be, theoretically at least, vindictive and lawful at the same time. An example of how the removal of *sins,* rather than the removal of *sinners,* satisfied the Rabbis is found in the life of R. Meir, viz.,

> There were once some highwaymen (n. *Baryone,* a word of doubtful meaning.) in the neighbourhood of R. Meir who caused him a great deal of trouble. R. Meir accordingly prayed that they should die. His wife Beruria (n. *Valeria*) said to him: How do you make out [that such a prayer should be permitted]? Because it is written 'Let *hatta'im* cease'? Is it written *hot'im?* (n. Pres. part. of the verb *hata,* to sin. Hence meaning sinners.) It is written *hatta'im!* (n. Which can be read חֲטָאִים sins. M.T. vocalizes חַטָּאִים [sinners].) Further, look at the end of the verse: "and let the wicked men be no more." Since the sins will cease, there will be no more wicked men! Rather pray for them that they should repent, and there will be no more wicked. He did pray for them, and they repented.[52]

EXCEPTION TO NONMUTILATION: DECAPITATION. Execution with the sword was obviously a method of capital punishment which

51. Cf. above, p. 119.
52. Ber. 10a.

mutilated the body. However, it was specifically stated in the Torah that the inhabitants of a city who had been seduced into abominable idolatry were to be put to "the edge of the sword."

> If you hear in one of your cities, which the Lord your God gives you to dwell there, that certain base fellows have gone out among you and have drawn away the inhabitants of the city, saying, "Let us go and serve other gods," which you have not known, then you shall inquire and make search and ask diligently; and behold, if it be true and certain that such an abominable thing has been done among you, you shall surely put the inhabitants of that city to the sword, destroying it utterly, all who are in it and its cattle, with the edge of the sword.[53]

Indeed, the sword (or war) was described in the Torah as being the very instrument of God. "And I will bring a sword upon you, that shall execute vengeance for the covenant . . . " (Lev. 26:25). With this biblical emphasis before them, the Rabbis specified those who were to be decapitated as follows:

> The following are decapitated: A murderer, and the inhabitants of a seduced city. A murderer who slew his fellow with a stone or an iron, or kept him down under water or in fire, so that he could not ascend thence, is executed.[54]

53. Deut. 13:12–15 (Heb. 13:13–16). Historically, no such action was ever taken. However, there is a dispute about this in T.B. San. 71a, viz. "'There never was a condemned city, and never will be.'—It agrees with R. Eliezer. For it has been taught, R. Eliezer said: No city containing even a single *mezuzah* can be condemned. Why so? Because the Bible saith [in reference thereto], 'And thou shalt gather all the spoil of it in the midst of the street thereof and shalt burn [them]. But if it contains a single *mezuzah,* this is impossible, because it is written ['And ye shall destroy the names of them'—i.e., the idols— . . .] 'Ye shall not do so unto the Lord your God' (Deut. 12:4). R. Jonathan said: I saw it, [a condemned city] and sat upon its ruins."

54. M. San. IX, 1.

And the manner of decapitation was also established in rabbinical law, viz.,

> Execution by the sword was performed thus: The condemned man was decapitated by the sword, as is done by the civil authorities. (n. Under the Empire the Romans practiced various forms of execution, including beheading by axe and sword.) R. Judah said: This is a hideous disfigurement; but his head was laid on a block and severed with an axe. They replied, No death is more disfiguring than this.[55]

THE MOST COMMON TYPE OF EXECUTION. Stoning was the most prevalent form of execution for a capital offense in biblical and talmudic times. However, the Rabbis modified this method of punishment in keeping with their conviction that there should be as little mutilation of the body as possible and that the procedure should be no more humiliating than necessary. They were trying to be humane.[56] To achieve these goals they established a procedure by which the general public would be restricted in its participation in the execution. The role of the witnesses as the ones who did the initial stoning was also regulated so they would, in all likelihood, put the criminal to death in short order with little, if any, mutilation. This entire judicial form of capital punishment was carried out in a place which had been prepared into which the felon was pushed. A description follows:

> The place of stoning was twice a man's height. One of the witnesses pushed him by the hips, [so that] he was overturned on his heart. He was then turned on his back. (n. To see whether the drop

---

55. M. San. VII, 3 [trans. H. Freedman].

56. William F. Albright, *Yahweh and the Gods of Canaan* (Garden City, N.Y.: Doubleday Anchor Books, 1969), p. 181: "One of the most remarkable features of Mosaic legislation—always using the term in its widest sense, of laws approved or introduced by Moses and developed in later Israel—is its humanity to man. It is the most humanitarian of all known bodies of laws before recent times."

brought his death forthwith.) If that caused his death, he had ful-filled [his duty]; (n. I.e., the witness, the obligation of execution lying primarily upon him.) but if not, the second witness took the stone (n. "The" stone, because it was prepared before. This was a very heavy stone, which it required two men to lift.) and threw it on his chest. If he died thereby, he (n. Sc., the second witnesses.) had done [his duty]; but if not, he [the criminal] was stoned by all Israel, (n. I.e., all the bystanders.) for it is written: "The hand of the wit-nesses shall be first upon him to put him to death, and afterwards the hand of all the people." (Deut. 17:7).[57]

ALLEVIATING THE HARSHNESS OF
CAPITAL PUNISHMENT

The attempt to alleviate the harshness of capital punishment as set forth in the Torah was the chief aim of the Sages as they regulated its application and modified the procedures to be used. This is evi-dent in the above analysis. The determination of the scholars to restrict the use of the death penalty still further, or virtually elimi-nate it entirely, is indicated in the history and literature of talmudic Judaism.[58]

A Difficult Task

This was not to be an easy task. For example, during the period of Greek domination, Palestine was subjected to the cross-currents of many different influences. The Hellenizing tendencies brought with them the inevitable relaxation of the strict religious, moral, and ethical codes which had characterized the Jewish nation after

57. M. San. VI, 4.
58. Haim H. Cohn, *Jewish Law in Ancient and Modern Israel* (New York: KTAV, 1971). Cf. pp. 61–82 for an excellent article on "Penology of the Talmud," in which the conclusion is stated (p. 82): "The humanization of punishment . . . is the fundamental concept of talmudic penology."

the great reforms of Ezra and his contemporaries instigated at the building of the Second Temple (Ezra 6:15–21, 9:1–10:14; Neh. 8:1–10:33, 13:1–47). In order to maintain the integrity of the Jewish nation, at times it was necessary for the authorities to apply the law even more severely than was technically intended in order to safeguard the principles of Torah;[59] e.g.,

> It has been taught: R. Eliezer b. Jacob said: I have heard (n. From my teachers.) that the Beth Din may, [when necessary] impose flagellation and pronounce [capital] sentences even where not [warranted] by the Torah; yet not with the intention of disregarding the Torah but [on the contrary] in order to safeguard it. It once happened that a man rode a horse on the Sabbath in the Greek period and he was brought before the Court and stoned, not because he was liable thereto, (n. The prohibition against riding on the Sabbath is only a "shebuth," i.e., a Rabbinical injunction.) but because it was [practically] required by the times. (n. During the time that Palestine was under Greek rule . . .)[60]

In such cases it was understood by the law-abiding citizens that these severe judicial actions were necessary if government was to be ethical as well as legal. Therefore, when the death sentence was applied "not with the intention of disregarding the Torah but in order to safeguard it," the relatives who had lost their kinsman

59. Mordecai M. Kaplan, "The Legal Foundations of Rabbinic Judaism," in *Understanding Rabbinic Judaism from Talmudic to Modern Times,* [ed. Jacob Neusner], (New York: KTAV, 1974), pp. 55–56: "To evaluate properly the significance of a common legal code for Jewish survival, we have to bear in mind that the Rabbis of old succeeded in formulating a code which fulfilled the following functions: 1) It provided the scattered communities of the Jewish people with a sense of unity and solidarity. 2) It called for the leadership of those who were expert in the knowledge and application of Jewish law, and who were authorized to use sanctions as means of enforcing their decisions. 3) It led to the establishment of courts of law which, being sufficiently flexible in structure, were able to adjust themselves to the various contingencies in the life of the Jewish People."
60. San. 46a [trans. Jacob Shachter].

responded positively to the court in the following way to indicate
their conviction that the judges had rendered a true judgment.

> When the flesh was completely decomposed, the bones were
> gathered and buried in their proper place. (i.e., the family vault.)
> The relatives then (n. Soon after the execution.) came and greeted
> the judges and witnesses, as if to say, We have no [ill feelings]
> against you in our hearts, for ye have a true judgment. And they
> observed no mourning rites but grieved [for him], (n. As, in ordi-
> nary cases, before the burial.) for grief is borne in the heart alone.[61]

After the struggles of the Maccabees had resulted in relief from
Greek domination, and a treaty had been confirmed with Rome in
ca. 140 B.C.E., the country was actually ruled by the Sadducean
party.[62] Their period of dominance was characterized by a strict
judicial rule coupled with a literal interpretation of Scriptural law.
With the rise of the Pharisees, however, there was a progressive
development toward a more lenient and humane judicial perspective. This turn of events was the result of a more enlightened rule
on the part of the Pharisees and also of the eventual control of
Palestine by the Roman conquerors.

Judicial Techniques

In their attempt to reduce to an absolute minimum the application
of the death penalty, the judges utilized the following tactics:
(1) they subjected witnesses in capital cases to extensive cross-
examination (M. Sanh. V, 1–2; Aboth I, 9), and if contradictions

61. M. San. VI, 6 [trans. Jacob Shacher]. This is a convenient time to note
that there was much "idealization" literature written by the Rabbis in connection
with legislative rulings. There is no evidence to indicate that this Mishnah was
ever literally followed in real life. The Mishnah states in effect what should be the
case—if there were an execution. But then the Rabbis virtually abolished executions.
62. Zeitlin, *Rise and Fall of the Judaean State,* vol. 1, pp. 144–149.

developed the testimony was thrown out; (2) there was no admission of circumstantial evidence (B. San. 37b); (3) near-relatives and persons of questionable character could not testify (M. San. III, 3–4); (4) a judge who merely expressed a view that the defendant was innocent could not retract his statement (M. San. IV, 1, V, 5); (5) even after conviction by at least a majority of two, any of the judges could recall the condemned, and the condemned man could have himself recalled, if anything else could be said favorable to his case (M. San. V, 5–VI, 1).[63]

Rabbinic Debate Over Capital Punishment

This climate of concern for the defendant gave rise to debates among the Rabbis regarding the propriety of capital punishment in *any* case.[64] For example, in the following excerpt three Rabbis are aligned against one in their affirmation that capital punishment would never have been carried out while they were members of the Sanhedrin.

> A Sanhedrin has jurisdiction within the land [of Palestine] and outside it. A Sanhedrin that effects an execution once in seven years, is branded a destructive tribunal; R. Eleazar b. Azariah says: Once in seventy years. R. Tarfon and R. Akiba say: Were we members of a Sanhedrin, no person would ever be put to death. [Whereupon] Rabban Simeon b. Gamaliel remarked, [Yea] and they would also multiply shedders of blood in Israel![65]

In a similar fashion two Rabbis form a majority against one in

---

63. Aberbach, loc. cit.

64. Sidney B. Hoenig, *The Great Sanhedrin* (Philadelphia: Dropsie College, 1953). Cf. p. 207, where Hoenig says that "many interpretations of the law were introduced in a hope that they would rule out the death penalty." Also, cf. Gerald J. Blidstein, "Capital Punishment—The Classic Jewish Discussion," *Judaism* 14, no. 1 (Winter 1965): 165–166.

65. M. Mak. I, 10.

their contention that the death penalty against a "stubborn and rebellious son" *never was carried out and never would be!*

> With whom does the following Baraitha agree: There never has been a "stubborn and rebellious son," (In the Biblical sense, to be executed.) and never will be. Why then was the law written? That you may study it and receive reward.—This agrees with R. Judah. Alternatively, you may say it will agree with R. Simeon. For it has been taught: R. Simeon said: Because one eats a *tartemar* of meat and drinks half a *log* of Italian wine, shall his father and mother have him stoned? But it never happened and never will happen. Why then was this law written?—That you may study it and receive reward. R. Jonathan said "I saw him (n. A rebellious son who was executed at his parents' demand.) and sat on his grave."[66]

It was stated above that this turn toward the mitigation, and even elimination, of capital punishment in Pharisaic Judaism was the result of enlightened rule on the part of the Pharisees and the eventual control of Palestine by the Romans.[67]

Effect of Roman Rule

Two elements under Roman rule further reduced the use of the death penalty by the courts of Judaism almost to the vanishing

66. San. 71a (trans. H. Freedman).

67. Further evidence of halakhic interpretation requiring greater safeguards in capital cases comes from the Qumran community. Lawrence H. Schiffman's commentary on B. Levine's translation of the Qumran Law of Testimony (Damascus Document IX, 17–22) calls attention to their requirement of three witnesses for a capital offense conviction instead of two. Cf *Revue de Qumran*, no. 32, vol. 8, fasc. 4 (December 1975): 603–605. Cf. also Josephus, *Antiquities* VIII, xiii, 8, where Josephus, in writing about the so-called trial of Naboth (I Kings 21:8–13), speaks of three witnesses in the face of the biblical account, which mentions two. Was this a "historical error" or did he inadvertently record a practice which was prevalent in his day? Be that as it may, there is ample evidence, above, to show that the Rabbis were moving away from a harsh view of the law, and that, as they applied its principles, the sternness of the law was mitigated.

point. One was the fact that the Roman government had the power to inflict the death penalty. If the death penalty was pronounced by a Jewish court, no execution could take place without prior approval by the Roman governor. Another circumstance which prevailed under Roman rule was the destruction of the Temple in 70 C.E.[68] This had far-reaching consequences for the people of Israel in a multitude of ways, and devastating consequences for the functioning of the priesthood and the Great Sanhedrin.

> . . . the following Baraitha: "And thou shalt come unto the priests, the Levites, and unto the judge that shall be in those days": (Deut. 17:9) This teaches that when the priesthood is functioning [in the Temple], the judge functions [in respect of capital punishment]; but when the priesthood is not functioning, the judge may not function.[69]

Effect of Temple's Destruction

In 30 C.E. there had already been a shift in the location of the Great Sanhedrin away from the Hall of Hewn Stones, where it had convened for generations.

> And it has also been taught: Forty years before the destruction of the Temple, the Sanhedrin were exiled (n. From the Hall of Hewn Stones.) and took up residence in Ḥanuth. (n. חנות *Ḥanut.* A place on the Temple Mount outside the hewn chamber where they had temporary residence.)[70]

Then, with the destruction of the Temple, the Great Sanhedrin ceased. The cessation of Sanhedrin activities at Jerusalem led to

68. F. M. Abel, *Histoire de la Palestine Depuis la Conquête d'Alexandre Jusqu'à l'Invasion Arabe,* vol. 2 (Paris: J. Gabalda et Cie, 1952), chap. 2, pp. 22–43, esp. pp. 31–35.
69. San. 52b.
70. San. 41a [trans. Jacob Shachter].

the rabbinic conclusion that the four forms of capital punishment
discussed in this section also ceased.

> Since the day of the destruction of the Temple, although the San-
> hedrin ceased, (n. And capital punishment could no longer be
> decreed by the Jewish Courts.) the four forms of capital punish-
> ment have not ceased? "They have not ceased," [you say]? Surely
> they have ceased![71]

Discussions with respect to the death penalty continued among
the Rabbis in later talmudic times. However, the emphasis was
more and more upon an academic consideration of situations and
laws from the past.

> Speaking of talmudic penology, it is . . . highly relevant to bear in
> mind that criminal jurisdiction ceased with the destruction of the
> Temple in 70 C.E., and the bulk of criminal legislation—and all of
> the penology—in the Talmud dates from then. Thus whatever is
> said in the Talmud about capital punishment, is said without rela-
> tion or reference to actualities, since they were never put into prac-
> tice.[72]

In this kind of climate, the study of the laws relating to capital
punishment was classed with the study of the laws relating to sacrifices, i.e., worthy of study because learning has its own merit, but
not to be applied.

> R. Joseph queried: [Do we need] to fix a *halachah* for [the days of]
> the Messiah? (n. Since the Sanhedrin no longer had jurisdiction in
> capital offences, there is no practical utility in this ruling, which can
> become effective only in the days of the Messiah.)—Abaye
> answered: If so, we should not study the laws of sacrifices, as they

---

71. Ket. 30a [trans. Samuel Daiches].
72. Cohn, loc. cit. However, it is possible that such "actualities" could have
been put into practice during periods of insurrection, e.g., the Bar Kochba War.

are also only for the Messianic era. But we say: Study and receive reward. (n. Learning has its own merit, quite apart from any practical utility that may be derived therefrom.)[73]

SUMMARY

To sum up, this section on the death penalty was a study of the Torah with regard to capital punishment as a prominent feature of the law. Special attention was given to the judicial guidelines and rules of application of the death penalty as found in Scripture. Then, an analysis was made of the talmudic sources to examine the way in which the Sages dealt with the judicial question of capital punishment.

As the descriptive, legislative, and judicial aspects of the whole question were considered, it became obvious that ethics, morals, and motives were closely linked with judicial philosophy, regulation, and application of the laws relating to capital punishment. One of the most outstanding features of the study is the evidence showing how the Sages of talmudic times persistently mitigated the harshness of the death penalty by various procedures. These techniques stand out in very sharp relief when compared to the judicial approaches utilized in handling civil cases.

1. Civil cases may be decided by three; capital cases require at least twenty-three judges.

2. In civil cases they may first discuss the evidence either for or against the defendant; in capital cases they must first discuss that in his favor.

3. In civil cases a majority of one suffices for acquittal or condemnation; in capital cases a majority of one suffices for acquittal but a majority of at least two is required for condemnation.

4. In civil cases a revision of the verdict may take place either in favour of the defendant or against him, if further evidence is produced; in capital cases a revision can only take place in order to free

73. San. 51b [trans. H. Freedman].

him from the death penalty to which he has been sentenced.

5. In civil cases anyone, even a student of law who is listening to the proceedings, may plead either for or against the accused; in capital cases anyone may speak for but not against him.

6. In civil cases a judge may retract his view already expressed whether that was for or against the defendant; in capital cases he may retract only if that was against the accused.

7. In civil cases the judges discuss the evidence by day and may give their verdict after dark whether it be for or against; in capital cases both discussion and verdict must be during daytime.

8. In civil cases the decision may be given whether it be for or against the defendant on the same day as the evidence is discussed; in capital cases this is so only if the veridct is one of not guilty, but if it is found impossible to decide in favour of the accused, the matter must be postponed until the morrow in order to give an opportunity for discovering something in his favor.

9. In civil cases the eldest of the judges is the first to give his views; in capital cases the youngest does this first, for fear lest, out of respect for the President of the Court, he may express an agreement with him that he does not actually feel.

10. In civil cases any Israelite though of illegitimate birth may act as judge; in capital cases only Priests and Levites, and Israelites whose descent is such that they may ally themselves by marriage with a priestly family.[74]

Attention is turned in the next chapter to two methods of punishment mentioned in the Torah and Talmud which are especially susceptible to the criticism of being lacking in ethical quality—"measure for measure" and "blood for blood." The chapter will analyze and evaluate the ethics of these two methods of judicial punishment from the biblical and talmudic points of view.

---

74. A. M. Silbermann, [ed.], *Pentateuch with Rashi's Commentary: Deuteronomy,* [trans. and annotated by M. Rosenbaum, A. M. Silbermann, A. Blashki, and L. Joseph], (London: Shapiro, Vallentine, 1934). This summary of San. IV, 1, is found on pp. 186–187.

CHAPTER V

JUDICIAL ETHICS OF PUNISHMENT EQUAL TO THE CRIME

INTRODUCTION

No legal system long endures unless there is incorporated within it the power to apply sanctions against those who violate the law. There is also the necessity of having a viable system of courts which will dispense justice according to the law. The law and the apparatus to maintain and apply it remain elements within a system of "mere" legalism unless there is some redeeming or saving principle behind them.

Saving Principle in Judaism's Legal System

The saving principle in the legal system of Judaism was held strongly by the Jews to be the ultimate divine origin of both the law and the court system under which that law functioned. Therefore, compliance with the law was not merely a legal matter. To the Jews it was, in the final analysis, a religious way of life regulated by God's will as expressed in the law.

The sages perceived the Torah not as a mélange of sources and laws of different origins, but as a single, unitary document, a corpus of laws reflective of an underlying ordered will. The Torah revealed the way things should be, just as the rabbis' formulation and presentation of their laws tell how things should be, whether or not that is how they actually are done. The order derives from the plan and will of the Creator of the world, the foundation of all reality. The Torah was interpreted by the Talmudic rabbis to be the architect's design for reality: God looked into the Torah and created the world, just as an architect follows his prior design in raising a building.[1]

As has already been pointed out in the previous chapter, incentives to obedience were offered in the form of promised blessings from God.[2] Warnings against disobedience were expressed in the form of threats of calamities and destruction.[3] If these warnings did not suffice, and one turned from following the law, the sanctions expressed in the law for that disobedience were to be applied in full measure. In many cases this meant "measure for measure," in other words, a punishment equal to the crime.

> This principle may seem and is often said to be extraordinarily primitive. But it is actually not in the least primitive. Whereas the beginnings of *lex talionis* are found before Israel, the principle was now extended by analogy until it dominated all punishment of injuries or homicides. In ordinary Ancient Oriental jurisprudence, men who belonged to the higher social categories or who were wealthy simply paid fines, otherwise escaping punishment. . . . So the *lex talionis* [is] . . . the principle of equal justice for all![4]

1. Jacob Neusner, *Invitation to the Talmud* (New York: Harper & Row, 1973), p. 226.
2. Lev. 26:3–13.
3. Lev. 26:14–39.
4. W. F. Albright, *History, Archaeology, and Christian Humanism* (New York: McGraw-Hill, 1964), p. 74. Cf. also, pp. 98–99.

Divine Justice Commensurate with Crime

This biblical principle was sustained by the ethical demand for justice commensurate with crime.[5] Although this required stern action which seemed harsh at times,[6] there was no question that Scripture demanded it. In fact, this is often expressed biblically as being God's way of personally dealing with criminality on both a national and personal level. This was acknowledged to be God's way of retribution for evil even by those who ruled over other nations. In the post-Joshua conflict, Judah and Simeon led their forces against the Canaanites in the south. The description of their taking and punishing Adoni-bezek shows that this man believed God was dealing justly with him "measure for measure."

> Adoni-bezek fled; but they pursued him, and caught him, and cut off his thumbs and his great toes. And Adoni-bezek said, "Seventy kings with their thumbs and their great toes cut off used to pick up scraps under my table; as I have done, so God has requited me." And they brought him to Jerusalem, and he died there.[7]

Also, the prophets expressed the "measure for measure" principle; e.g., "For the day of the Lord is near upon all the nations. As you have done, it shall be done to you, your deeds shall return on your own head" (Obad. 15). And again, "I the Lord search the mind and try the heart, to give to every man according to his ways, according to the fruit of his doings" (Jer. 17:10).

5. Ibid., p. 99; "In the Hebrew Bible we never find use of the common Babylonian and Hittite assumption that a man can escape a severe penalty if he is rich or well-born, a penalty which would fall without mitigation on the poor man or the slave. Equal justice for all is at the heart of Mosaic jurisprudence."
6. W. F. Albright, *The Biblical Period from Abraham to Ezra* (New York: Harper Torchbooks, 1963), pp. 18–19. It is pointed out that Hebrew law, such as that found in the Book of the Covenant (Exod. 21–23), was "much more humane than the draconic Middle Assyrian laws . . ."
7. Judg. 1:6–7.

"MEASURE FOR MEASURE"

The Jews saw the "measure for measure" principle as rooted and grounded in the very nature of God and applying to all people.[8] Since it was clear that God himself acted on the principle of "As you have done, it shall be done to you," it was not startling to the Jewish nation to find this type of punishment incorporated in the law which they were convinced was of divine origin; e.g.,

> When a man causes a disfigurement in his neighbor, as he has done it shall be done to him, fracture for fracture, eye for eye, tooth for tooth; as he has disfigured a man, he shall be disfigured.[9]

As in other legal matters, it was also understood that they were not to stand by for God's direct action of punishment; but, on the contrary, they felt the responsibility under law to carry out the penalty as prescribed by law.

> If any harm follows, then you shall give life for life, eye for eye, tooth for tooth, hand for hand, foot for foot, burn for burn, wound for wound, stripe for stripe.[10]

8. Haim H. Cohn, *Jewish Law in Ancient and Modern Israel* (New York: KTAV, 1971), p. 74: ". . . by punishing the offender according to the measure of his offence, God's fury is exhausted and His anger 'accomplished' (Ezekiel 7, 8). The vengeance of the Lord can be satisfied by doing unto the offender exactly as he himself has done (Jeremiah 50, 51). Thus, measure for measure can be said to be God's own way of doing justice . . ."

9. Lev. 24:19–20. J. K. Miklisanski, "The Law of Retaliation and the Pentateuch," *Journal of Biblical Literature* 66 (1947): 296, 300. The author faces squarely the impact of pentateuchal texts usually cited as examples of the *lex talionis* legal genre, e.g., Exod. 21:22–25; Lev. 24:19–20; Deut. 19:21. However, he insists that "the *lex talionis* was obsolete in Biblical times," and argues that "the only unquestionable law of retaliation in the Mosaic code refers to *intentional* murder for which there is no other retribution but *life-for-life* in the literal sense."

10. Exod. 21:23–25. W. F. Albright, *Yahweh and the Gods of Canaan* (Garden City, N.Y.: Doubleday Anchor Books, 1969). With reference to the *lex talionis*

Punishment Equivalent to Crime

It is obvious from the above remarks and sources that punishment was very often a case of identical "measure for measure."[11] However, even in biblical times it was clear that an identical punishment for crime was not the only sanction which would meet the qualifications for "measure for measure." Indeed, the law often specified that the punishment was not to be identical to the crime, but equivalent to it. For example:

> When men fight with one another, and the wife of the one draws near to rescue her husband from the hand of him who is beating him, and puts out her hand and seizes him by the private parts, then you shall cut off her hand; your eye shall have no pity.[12]

This type of sanction related the punishment directly to the offense. The "measure for measure" action was not identical, but equivalent in that the member of the body which caused the offense

---

formula of Exod. 21:23–25, Albright states, "In the Hebrew formula, we have what may be the earliest enunciation of a generalized legal principle known anywhere in the world. Though it has not yet attained the level of a generalized abstract proposition, it reaches its purpose by listing several related concrete propositions to illustrate the scope of the generalized principle. Since the Old Testament shows little trace of protological thinking after the thirteenth-twelfth centuries B.C. but is throughout a monument of empirical logic, we need not have any hesitation about tracing the legal generalization back to the beginnings of the Mosaic revolution—either to Moses himself or to a 'school' of interpreters who endeavoured to harmonize the ancient case law with the body of apodictic law which had been developing since the time of Moses" (pp. 174–175).

11. W. F. Albright, *New Horizons in Biblical Research* (London: Oxford University Press, 1966), p. 29: "The Lex Talionis (Exodus 21:23–25) 'life for life, eye for eye,' is the oldest known explicit statement of a fundamental legal principle, equal justice for all. Today it may sound harsh, but it was a tremendous improvement over earlier vendetta law or differential penalties depending on the social status of aggressor and victim."

12. Deut. 25:11–12.

was the object of the punishment. Although equivalent sanction
was the principle of the punishment, in actual practice the Rabbis
commuted the punishment to a monetary fine if it was determined
the woman could have saved her husband without the use of force,
otherwise, she would be exempt from the fine.

> Thus the ruling: "Then thou shalt cut off her hand," means only a
> monetary fine . . . for were she unable to save [him] by any other
> means, the resort to force in her case should be considered as if
> exercised by an officer of the Court [in the discharge of his duties]
> and there would be exemption.[13]

Importance of Motives

It is interesting to note that the actual performance of a crime was
not always necessary for one to be guilty, and therefore subject to
the "measure for measure" penalty. Motive was often the decisive
factor in determining guilt. This feature highlights the ethical
ingredient in this principle as it takes into account the thoughts
and intents of the mind. If it could be proven that a person intended to do injury to another, as in the case of a false witness,
then what he intended to do to his fellow was done to him.

> . . . the judges shall inquire diligently, and if the witness is a false
> witness and has accused his brother falsely, then you shall do to him
> as he had meant to do to his brother; so you shall purge the evil
> from the midst of you.[14]

The Rabbis of talmudic times were sensitive to the motiva-
tional element involved when determining the guilt or innocence of
the accused. This ethical consideration entered into their interpretation of many biblical statements, which resulted in their applying
the "measure for measure" rule to such cases; e.g.,

13. B.K. 28a.
14. Deut. 19:18–19.

Resh Laḳish said: He who lifts his hand against his neighbour, even if he did not smite him, is called a wicked man, as it is written, "And he said unto the wicked man, Wherefore wouldst thou smite thy fellow?" (Ex. 2:13) "Wherefore has thou smitten" is not said, but "wherefore wouldst thou smite," shewing that though he had not smitten him yet, he was termed a wicked man.[15]

With the exception of the last example from tractate Sanhedrin, the discussion thus far about the "measure for measure" application of punishment has dealt specifically with the biblical precepts. It was noted that God himself was seen as acting often on this principle. Also, his people lived under the law that required the application of "measure for measure" either exactly or in an equivalent way.[16]

More Lenient Rabbinic View

During the talmudic period one can detect a shift in emphasis with reference to the application of the "measure for measure" principle toward a more lenient view, while at the same time there were some Rabbis who continued to stress the exact application as the most valid. For example:

Why not perhaps say that for eyesight taken away the Divine Law ordered eyesight to be taken away from the offender? For if you will not say this, how could capital punishment be applied in the case of a dwarf killing a giant or a giant killing a dwarf, seeing that the Torah says, "Ye shall have one manner of law," implying that the manner of law should be the same in all cases, unless you say that

15. San. 58b.

16. Theophile J. Meek, *Hebrew Origins* (New York: Harper & Brothers, 1936), p. 68. This author stresses the points of similarity between the Hammurabi code and Hebrew law codes, including the "measure for measure" principle, and says, "Both are the concrete expression of the same general principles of morality and justice, and a spirit of humaneness pervades both codes."

for a life taken away the Divine Law ordered the life of the murderer to be taken away? Why then not similarly say here too that
for eyesight taken away the Divine Law ordered eyesight to be
taken away from the offender?[17]

However, the shift in emphasis persisted, and that shift was in
the direction away from exact retribution. This reorientation was
apparently brought about largely because of practical considerations. One practical consideration with which the Rabbis struggled
was the difficulty, if not impossibility, of actually applying the
"measure for measure" punishment in anything other than murder
cases, i.e., "Whoever strikes a man so that he dies shall be put to
death" (Exod. 21:12). For example: How could the "eye for eye"
procedure be carried out without considerable loss of blood and
other related injuries? How could exact retribution be obtained in
the "tooth for tooth" injunction if the lost tooth had been a loose
baby tooth and the attacker was an adult whose tooth extraction
would involve pain, bruises, and loss of blood?

> The School of Hezekiah taught: "Eye for eye, life for life," (Ex.
> 21:24) but not "life and eye for eye." Now if you assume that actual
> retaliation is meant, it could sometimes happen that eye and life
> would be taken for eye, as while the offender is being blinded, his
> soul might depart from him.[18]

These kinds of problems were frustrating, yet the Rabbis were well
aware of the teaching, "You shall have one law for the sojourner
and for the native; for I am the Lord your God" (Lev. 24:22),
which implied a uniform law applicable to all circumstances.

---

17. B.Ḳ. 83b–84a.
18. B.Ḳ. 84a. However, again it should be noted that the shift away from the
teaching of the literal application of the *lex talionis* was not unanimous among the
Rabbis; e.g., "R. Eliezer said, 'Eye for eye literally refers to the eye' [of the
offender]," loc. cit. R. Eliezer's ultra conservative view reflects the actual practice
of an earlier age.

Compensation for Damages

The question became: How could this "measure for measure" rule be applied in principle without facing the hurdles involved in its literal application? The predominant answer came to be— compensation for damages. In fact, Daube advocates that

> the principle of compensation, in Hebrew Law, goes back to the earliest period of legal history open to inquiry . . . and that the Rabbis only elaborate and put into words what had been a feature of the law all along—the idea that punishment includes restitution, that punishment itself compensates the party wronged for his loss.[19]

Thus, this author argues that even the early practice of *lex talionis* had within it the embryo of positive compensation which was later articulated as monetary compensation.[20]

Once established, the principle of compensation for damages became generally accepted as a judicial norm in rabbincial law. For example:

> Why [pay compensation]? Does the Divine Law not say "Eye for eye"? (Ex. 21:24) Why not take this literally to mean [putting out] the eye [of the offender]?—Let not this enter your mind, since it has been taught: You might think that where he put out his eye, the offender's eye should be put out, or where he cut off his arm, the offender's arm should be cut off, or again where he broke his leg, the offender's leg should be broken. [Not so; for] it is laid down, "He that smiteth any man . . ." "And he that smiteth a beast . . .": (Lev. 24) just as in the case of smiting a beast compensation is to be paid, so also in the case of smiting a man compensation is to be paid. And should this [reason] not satisfy you, note that it is stated, "Moreover ye shall take no ransom for the life of a murderer, that

---

19. David Daube, *Studies in Biblical Law* (New York: KTAV, 1969), pp. 102–153.

20. The replacement of the death penalty by ransom is, in specific cases, provided for in the Mosaic code; cf. Exod. 21:29ff.

is guilty of death," (Num. 35:31) implying that it is only for the life of a murderer that you may not take "satisfaction," whereas you may take "satisfaction" [even] for the principal limbs, though these cannot be restored.[21]

THE FIVEFOLD LIABILITY FOR INFLICTING INJURY. Once the principle of compensation for damages was well established, it was then elaborately articulated and keenly refined to apply to all kinds of damage suits, both large and small. The following excerpt from tractate Baba Ḳamma sets out the elaborate fivefold liability incurred by one who injured his fellow man.

One who injures a fellow man becomes liable to him for five items: For depreciation, for pain, for healing, for loss of time and for degradation. How is it with "depreciation"? If he put out his eye, cut off his arm or broke his leg, the injured person is considered as if he were a slave being sold in the market place, and a valuation is made as to how much he was worth [previously], and how much he is worth [now]. "Pain"—if he burnt him either with a spit or with a nail, even though on his [finger] nail which is a place where no bruise could be made, it has to be calculated how much a man of equal standing would require to be paid to undergo such pain. "Healing"—if he has struck him he is under obligation to pay medical expenses. Should ulcers [meanwhile] arise on his body, if as a result of the wound, the offender would be liable, but if not as a result of the wound, he would be exempt. Where the wound was healed but reopened, healed again but reopened, he would still be under obligation to heal him. If, however, it had completely healed [but had subsequently reopened] he would no more be under obligation to heal him. "Loss of time"—the injured person is considered as if he were a watchman of cucumber beds (n. As even a lame or one-armed person could be employed in this capacity.) [so that the loss of such wages (n. But not of the previous employment on account of the reason which follows.) sustained by him during the period of illness may be reimbursed to him], for there has already been paid to him the value of his hand or the value of his leg [through which deprivation he would no more be able to carry on his previous employment]. "Degradation"—all to be estimated in accordance with the status of the offender and the offended.[22]

COMPENSATION: CIVIL AND PUNITIVE EFFECTS. At this point in the discussion it should be noted that the ethical rationale motivating the Rabbis in the shift from exact retribution to compensation for damages was the desire to apply a practical justice in the spirit, if not the letter, of the "measure for measure" principle. This approach made it possible for them to circumvent the difficulties of the "one standard" while retaining it in essence.

> The equitable application of the "one standard" or "one manner of law" to the stranger as well as the Israelite was based, according to Rabbinic interpretation, upon the phrase כי אני יהוה אלהיכם (Lev. 24:22) which meant to them "The God of all of you," both of the Israelite and the stranger.[23]

It was not their intention to apply a "civil" solution to a "criminal" problem, but rather to establish a workable system which would assure justice in all matters. It is not surprising, then, to note that the compensation for damages was designed to have both a civil and a punitive effect. This is obvious from the fact that one found guilty of injury to another could not have a sentence of payment for damages and also flogging imposed upon him.

> . . . when one person injures another person, in which case there are

22. M. B.Ḳ. VIII, 1.
23. A. Cohen, [ed.], *The Soncino Chumash: The Five Books of Moses with Haphtaroth* (Hindhead, Surrey: Soncino Press, 1947), p. 760.

the payment of money and the punishment of lashes, he pays money and does not receive the lashes? And if you will say that this is only when they did not warn him, but when they warned him, he receives the lashes and does not pay—did not R. Ammi say in the name of R. Joḥanan that, if one person struck another person a blow, for which no *peruṭah* (n. A small coin.) can be claimed as damages, (n. Lit., "in which there is not the value of a *peruṭah*.") he receives the lashes? How shall we imagine this case? If they did not warn him, why does he receive the lashes? Hence it is clear that they warned him, and the reason [why he receives the lashes and does not pay] is because the damages do not amount to a *peruṭah,* but if they amount to a *peruṭah* he pays the money but does not receive the lashes![24]

Since flogging could not be administered in an injury suit where compensatory damages were paid, this meant that payment of damages had the practical effect of being punitive in such cases. One could not be punished both "civilly" and "criminally" for the same offense; and since compensation had a civil element (payment of damages) and a criminal element (punitive) within it, both flogging and payment of compensation could not be required for any one offense.

For it is said in scripture, and yet no harm follow he shall be surely fined etc. Is, however, the deduction (n. That one who suffers the death penalty is exempt from a monetary fine.) made from this text? (Ex. 21:22, cited in our Mishnah.) Is it not in fact made from the following text: "According to the measure of his crime," (Deut. 25:2). [which implies] (n. Since the text makes use of the sing.) you make him liable to a penalty (n. Flogging, spoken of in the text cited.) for one crime, but you cannot make him liable [at the same time] for two crimes? (n. By the imposition of two forms of punishment.)—One [text deals] with [the penalties of] death and money and the other with [the penalties of] flogging and money. And [both texts were] needed.[25]

24. Ket. 32b. [trans. Samuel Daiches].
25. Ket. 37a. [trans. Israel W. Slotki].

So, as time went on, the practice of direct "measure for measure" gave way more and more to equivalent and compensatory sanctions by the courts. This was done without losing sight of the fact that punishment, in principle, should always be measured by the gravity of the crime. Thus, each convicted person was to receive punishment "according to his guilt."

> If there is a dispute between men, and they come into court, and the judges decide between them, acquitting the innocent and condemning the guilty, then if the guilty man deserves to be beaten, the judge shall cause him to lie down and be beaten in his presence with a number of stripes in proportion to his offense.[26]

"Measure for Measure": Retained but Mitigated

While the application of the direct "measure for measure" principle was greatly mitigated by a wider use of the equivalent sanctions mentioned earlier and the judicious concern for payment of compensation for damages, the Rabbis continued to recognize this principle and apply it through the courts. In addition, it was often stressed in the Talmud as the expression of ultimate justice, or the effect of a cause from which one simply could not escape.[27] "In the measure with which a man measures it is meted out to him" is interpreted in the Talmud as a cause-and-effect relationship having its explanation in the divine order of things.

> In the measure with which a man measures it is meted out to him. She adorned herself for a transgression; the Holy One, blessed be He, made her repulsive. She exposed herself for a transgression; the Holy One, blessed be He, held her up for exposure. She began the transgression with the thigh and afterwards with the womb; therefore she is punished first in the thigh and afterwards in the womb, (Num. 5:21 f.) nor does all the body escape.[28]

26. Deut. 25:1–2.
27. Cf. Matt. 7:1–2 for N.T. parallel.
28. M. Soṭ. I, 7.

Summary

Some salient points may be emphasized in summary. It has been shown that the judicial ethics of punishment equal to the crime had its grounding in the very nature of God. Therefore, the Torah was explicit in its laws on this principle. However, it was also pointed out that the application of "measure for measure" did not always require *exact* retribution. In fact, the Torah spoke specifically of equivalent sanctions for the violation of many laws. Further inquiry into the Talmud showed that the Rabbis were, with but few exceptions, seeking to retain the essence of the law while ameliorating its application.[29] They did this by placing a greater emphasis on equivalent and compensatory sanctions than on the direct "measure for measure." This humane concern on the part of the Sages was expressed by a growing corpus of legal literature which provided supervision by the legal authorities through the court system. Thus, the judicial ethics undergirding the "measure for measure" laws were on a high level, and continued to be developed and refined from biblical through talmudic times.

GENESIS 9:6

"Whoever sheds the blood of man, by man shall his blood be shed; for God made man in his own image."[30] Nowhere in the Bible is

---

29. Jacob Neusner, [ed.], *Understanding Rabbinic Judaism from Talmudic to Modern Times* (New York: KTAV, 1974), p. 10: "The rabbi functioned in the Jewish community as judge and administrator. But he lived in a society in some ways quite separate from that of Jewry as a whole. The rabbinical academy was, first, a law school. Some of its graduates served as judges and administrators of the law. . . . one of its functions concerned those parts of the Torah to be applied in everyday life through the judiciary."

30. Gen. 9:6. Gerhard von Rad, *Genesis: A Commentary*, [trans. John H. Marks], (Philadelphia: Westminster Press, 1956), p. 128: ". . . man is God's possession and was created in God's image. The saying in v. 6 is extremely ancient and forceful, masterfully pregnant both in form (exact correspondence of the words in both halves of the statement; talion!) as well as in content. . . . It could

the requirement of the death penalty more forcefully stated. Nowhere in the Bible is the principle of "measure for measure" more clearly enunciated. Nowhere in the Bible is the reason for the death penalty and "measure for measure" more vividly defined. Therefore, after having considered divine punishment, the death penalty, and the "measure for measure" principle, it is logical and profitable to analyze the broad ramifications of Genesis 9:6 for ethical and judicial principles with respect to this kind of punishment.[31]

Ethical Considerations

The ethical considerations for deterrent to murder center around the biblical description of the relationship of God to man. Man is made in the image of God (Gen. 1:27). The life with which man was endowed by God (Gen 2:7) was identified with man's blood.

> For the life of every creature is the blood of it; therefore I have said to the people of Israel, You shall not eat the blood of any creature, for the life of every creature is its blood; whoever eats it shall be cut off.[32]

Therefore, the phrase "sheds the blood of man" is equivalent to "takes the life of man." And since life is identified as the gift of God, the shedding of man's blood, or in other words, the taking of man's life, is not only considered an irreparable injustice against man, but an outrage against God himself.[33]

---

be that it once legally prescribed and limited the exercise of blood vengeance: In the event of a murder the blood vengeance could not be reckless (cf. ch. 4:23); only the murderer (he, and no substitute!) atones with death."

31. Cf. Targum Onkelos on Gen. 9:6, below, pp. 164–165.

32. Lev. 17:14.

33. D. J. McCarthy, "The Symbolism of Blood and Sacrifice," *Journal of Biblical Literature* 88 (1969): 174, 176: ". . . the explicit claim that blood is life and so divine remains isolated to Israel. . . . the evidence from the ancient Semitic and Aegean areas does not show a general belief outside Israel in blood as a divine

Universal Application

It is not surprising, then, to note that the biblical declaration of
retribution against the murderer is of universal application. The
death penalty for murder was not enunciated merely because
murder is a horrible social crime, although no doubt that would
have been sufficient reason, but because murder is seen as striking
at that very likeness of God with which man is stamped. Thus, the
pre-Mosaic pronouncement of Genesis 9:6 applied to all men. The
outraged reaction of God against the first murder was a very personal reaction; i.e., God said:

> What have you done? The voice of your brother's blood is crying to
> me from the ground. And now you are cursed from the ground,
> which has opened its mouth to receive your brother's blood from
> your hand.[34]

The anger of God against the shedder of blood is pictured as a
timeless, universal, personal response on his part. Just as the biblical narrative describes his outrage at murder before the flood, so
after the flood the account of his personal announcement to all
men is given, viz., "Surely I will require your lifeblood; from every
beast I will require it. And from every man, from every man's
brother I will require the life of man" (Gen. 9:5, NASB). Milgrom
presents the thesis that even the biblical legislation concerning
dietary practices

> rests on foundations that are essentially ethical, and ethical in the
> highest sense, [and] that the dietary laws are anchored in an ethical
> foundation was not unknown to the rabbis of the Talmudic age. . . .
> The fathers of Judaism felt so keenly about the ethical primacy of
> the dietary system that they enjoined one of its tenets, the blood

---

element. . . . As far as we know, the reservation of blood to God because it was
life and so divine is specifically Israelite."
    34. Gen. 4:10–11.

prohibition, upon all mankind. . . . The Hebrew Bible, according to its own testimony, was intended for Israel alone—even the Ten Commandments. Only one biblical statute, the blood prohibition, is commanded to all men.[35]

Judicial Emphasis in the Torah

It is, therefore, to be expected that the Torah would place judicial emphasis upon matters related to the shedding of blood. Neither is it surprising that the people took these laws seriously. For example, in view of the expiatory nature of blood in the sacrificial system under which they lived, the Israelites could readily accept the divine imperative for the man's blood to be shed in expiation who had himself polluted the land by shedding his fellow man's blood.

> You shall not thus pollute the land in which you live; for blood pollutes the land, and no expiation can be made for the land, for the blood that is shed in it, except by the blood of him who shed it.[36]

Basically, the judicial sanctions against the one guilty of bloodshed were ultimately viewed as expressions of the divine

35. J. Milgrom, "The Biblical Diet Laws as an Ethical System," *Interpretation* 17 (1963): 291, 294, 300. But cf. the numerous rabbinic legends indicating that the Torah—and certainly the Decalogue—was meant for all mankind, though other nations rejected it when God offered it to them; e.g., Sifre on Deut. 33:2. The divine utterance was heard in seventy languages, according to Shab. 88b [trans. H. Freedman]: "Every single word that went forth from the Omnipotent was split up into seventy languages. (n. The traditional number of the languages of man, i.e., the Torah was given to all humanity.)"

36. Num. 35:33. M. Greenberg, "Bloodguilt," *Interpreter's Dictionary of the Bible,* vol. 1, p. 449: "In Israel . . . bloodguilt was defiling, but it was incurred only through slaying a man who did not deserve to die (נקי דם *dam naki,* 'innocent blood'; Deut. 19:10; Jer. 26:15; Jonah 1:14). Killing in self-defence and the judicial execution of criminals are explicitly exempted (Ex. 22:2—H[eb.] 22:1; Lev. 20:9; etc.)."

wrath, and therefore were incurred as consequences for sin. This punishment for the sin of bloodshed was understood to be of high priority in the eyes of God.

> For behold, the Lord is coming forth out of his place to punish the inhabitants of the earth for their iniquity, and the earth will disclose the blood shed upon her, and will no more cover her slain.[37]

Consequences of Bloodshed

Therefore, the intricate system of various punishments for different kinds of bloodshed was very much a part of the life of Israel in biblical times. If someone took another person's life deliberately, the slayer was to be put to death (Gen. 9:6). If man failed to carry out his responsibilities, God gave his assurance that he would personally require the lifeblood of the guilty (Gen. 9:5). The assurance that the murderer would eventually be punished, if not by man under God's law then by divine wrath, is seen in the type of language used to describe God's action where murder was concerned. Examples are:

> And you shall strike down the house of Ahab your master, that I may avenge on Jezebel the blood of my servants the prophets, and the blood of all the servants of the Lord.[38]

> And the Lord said to him, "Call his name Jezreel; for yet a little while, and I will punish the house of Jehu for the blood of Jezreel, and I will put an end to the kingdom of the house of Israel."[39]

37. Isa. 26:21.
38. II Kings 9:7.
39. Hos. 1:4. John Mauchline, "Hosea," *Interpreter's Bible,* vol. 6, pp. 569–570. With reference to the name "Jezreel," Mauchline holds, "The view of Rashi that the name refers to the exile of Israel and to their being sown or scattered is farfetched." He goes on to say that "The name Jezreel, as borne by Hosea's child, was a reminder of the bloodshed for which punishment was about to come . . ." (ibid.).

Through the crime of bloodshed the Temple was destroyed and the Shechinah departed from Israel, as it is written, "So ye shall not pollute the land wherein ye are; for blood, it polluteth the land. . . . And thou shalt not defile the land which ye inhabit, in the midst of which I dwell": (Num. 35:33–34) hence, if ye do defile it, ye will not inhabit it and I will not dwell in its midst. (n. It may be remarked that the destruction of the Temple is regarded here as synonymous with exile from the country.)[40]

So, the shedding of blood was not only viewed in the Bible as the cause for God's bringing down of dynasties; it was also viewed by the later Rabbis as the reason for the destruction of the Temple.

Bloodshed was also seen by the Sages as a partial reason for exile. "Exile comes to the world for idolatry, for incest and for bloodshed, and for [transgressing the commandment of] the [year of the] release of the land."[41]

The homeowner was warned against becoming the cause of death on his premises at the risk of incurring guilt. "When you build a new house, you shall make a parapet for your roof, that you may not bring the guilt of blood upon your house, if any one fall from it" (Deut. 22:8).[42] Examples are numerous in the Bible as to what constituted a potential or actual demand under law that one pay the price of his own blood for his deed.

Gō'ēl Hadām

Another significant feature in Jewish law was the provision for the

---

40. Shab. 33a [trans. H. Freedman]. Also, cf. Yoma 9b, where it is stated that one of the reasons for the destruction of the first Temple was bloodshed, as follows: "Why was the first Sanctuary destroyed? Because of three [evil] things which prevailed there: idolatry, immorality, bloodshed."

41. M. Ab. V, 9.

42. S. R. Driver, *Deuteronomy,* International Critical Commentary, 3d ed. (1902), p. 251: "This law is peculiar to Dt., but a provision prompted by the same general motive is found in Ex. 21:33 ff. (a pit not to be left open, so that an ox or an ass may fall into it)."

blood-avenger. In view of what has been said earlier in this section in connection with the ethical background and the expiatory nature of sacrificial blood for the sins of the people and of man's blood for the blood he has shed, it is obviously no mere coincidence that the Hebrew term for "blood-avenger" (*gō'ēl hadām*) is applied with equal validity to one who acted as redeemer,[43] e.g.,

> The blood avenger [גאל הדם] himself shall put the murderer to death; he shall put him to death when he meets him. (NASB)

> And now it is true that I am a near kinsman, yet there is a kinsman nearer than I. ["kinsman" = גֹּאֵל][44]

EARLY ACTIVITY OF THE GŌ'ĒL HADĀM. Theoretically, there was a sense in which the blood-avenger was committing a "redemptive" act rather than a "vengeful" act when he put the murderer to death. The murderer had polluted the land and no expiation could be made for the land on account of the blood which had been shed on it except the blood of the murderer (Num. 35:33). Therefore, the act of the avenger was, from the biblical point of view, primarily expiatory in essence, while admittedly often vindictive in practice.

It is a fact that in early times the act of outright simple vengeance in taking life as a satisfaction for a grievance was common practice. In describing Bedouin life among the early Arab clans, Hitti states:

> Blood, according to the primitive law of the desert, calls for blood; no chastisement is recognized other than that of vengeance. The nearest of kin is supposed to assume primary responsibility. A

43. The verb [גאל] means "to redeem," and what one "redeemed" depends on circumstances. It may be a kinsman's house or field—or his blood if he is murdered. The only common factor is the blood relationship, i.e., kinship, between the [גֹּאֵל] and the person on whose behalf he acts.

44. Num. 35:19; Ruth 3:12.

blood feud may last forty years. . . . In all the *ayyam al-'Arab,* those intertribal battles of pre-Islamic days, the chronicles emphasize the blood feud motif.[45]

An early example of the "blood feud motif" in the Bible is seen in Lamech's pronouncement.

> Lamech said to his wives: "Adah and Zillah, hear my voice; you wives of Lamech, hearken to what I say: I have slain a man for wounding me, a young man for striking me. If Cain is avenged sevenfold, truly Lamech seventy-sevenfold."[46]

ROLE GREATLY CURTAILED BY TORAH. However, by the law of the Torah the role of the blood-avenger was sharply curtailed, and as a result of rabbinic elaboration and refinement of the law, further restrictions were imposed. For example, the avenger was not free to seek vengeance unless the murder was premeditated.

> And if he stabbed him from hatred, or hurled at him, lying in wait, so that he died, or in enmity struck him down with his hand, so that he died, then he who struck the blow shall be put to death; he is a murderer; the avenger of blood shall put the murderer to death, when he meets him.[47]

That the murder was indeed committed with malice could be determined by the fact that the murderer carried out his deed with a murder weapon.

> But if he struck him down with an instrument of iron, so that he

---

45. Philip K. Hitti, *History of the Arabs* (London: Macmillan, 1940), p. 26. Also cf. Bernard Lewis, *The Arabs in History* (Tiptree, Essex: Anchor Press, 1950), p. 30. "The chief social limitation of the prevailing anarchy was the custom of blood-vengeance, imposing on the kin of a murdered man the duty of exacting vengeance from the murderer or one of his fellow tribesmen."
46. Gen. 4:23–24.
47. Num. 35:20–21.

died, he is a murderer; the murderer shall be put to death. And if he struck him down with a stone in the hand, by which a man may die, and he died, he is a murderer; the murderer shall be put to death. Or if he struck him down with a weapon of wood in the hand, by which a man may die, and he died, he is a murderer; the murderer shall be put to death.[48]

FURTHER REGULATED BY RABBINIC RULES AND COURTS. As the Rabbis interpreted the Torah and expanded on its principles with reference to the role of the blood-avenger, they eventually brought the courts to a place of greater jurisdiction in certain cases.[49] For example, if the murder victim had no near relative who could serve as blood-avenger, the court appointed one.

> And what is the reference to the "avenger of blood"?—It has been taught: "The avenger of blood shall himself put the murderer to death"; (Num. 35:19) it is [primarily] the duty of the avenger of blood [to slay the murderer]. And whence do we know that, if he [the murdered man] has no avenger of blood, (n. A near kinsman, upon whom devolved the duty of hunting down a murderer to death.) the Beth Din must appoint one? (n. I.e., the Court is always responsible for prosecuting the murderer, whether there is a relative or not.)—From the verse, "When he meeteth him," i.e., in all cases. (n. Thus this verse too shows that the provisions of an avenging kinsman are not limited to the precise statement of the Bible.)[50]

This example is important. It shows that the role of the blood-avenger was not altogether an act of vengeance, as was pointed out earlier, but that under law, the court-appointed avenger was actually serving as a dispassionate executioner of a criminal for the committing of a capital offense. This is again a reminder that the ethics of this practice under Jewish law were higher than the name

48. Num. 35:16–18.
49. J. Blidstein, "Capital Punishment—The Classic Jewish Discussion," Judaism 14, no. 2 (Spring 1965): 169, nn. 4 and 5.
50. San. 45b [trans. Jacob Shachter].

"blood-avenger" may superficially suggest. In fact, the Aramaic rendering of Targum Onkelos on Genesis 9:6 shows that the requirement of witnesses and due judicial process in effect eliminated the action of the blood-avenger independent of the courts, i.e., "He that sheds the blood of man before witness, by the word of the judges shall his blood be shed" = דישוד דמא דאנשא בסהדין על מימר דיניא דמה יתשד.[51]

Cities of Refuge

Another feature of the Torah which showed a compassionate concern for human life was the provision of cities of refuge to which one could flee if he had accidentally slain someone. "These six cities shall be for refuge for the people of Israel, and for the stranger and for the sojourner among them, that any one who kills any person without intent may flee there" (Num. 35:15). Thus, under law, a way was provided for the protection of one who had become a manslayer but who was not guilty of premeditated murder. Interestingly enough, however, von Rad says,

> The institution of the right of asylum serves above all to limit the rights of blood-revenge, which in itself has absolute authority, that is, whenever one of a family is killed the next of kin know they will be called upon to exact vengeance. . . . blood-revenge is not by any means a custom which the lawgiver wishes to abolish. . . . So far as we can see, kingship and the power of the State have no effective influence on legal practice, certainly in the countryside. Hence, in cases of murder in Israel, blood-revenge remained a quite legitimate institution in itself . . .[52]

51. A. M. Silbermann, [ed.], *Pentateuch with Targum Onkelos and Rashi's Commentary: Genesis,* [trans. and annotated by M. Rosenbaum, A. M. Silbermann, A. Blashki, and L. Joseph], (London: Shapiro, Vallentine, 1929), pp. 37–38. Also cf. above, introductory remarks on Gen. 9:6.

52. Gerhard von Rad, *Deuteronomy: A Commentary,* [trans. Dorothea Barton], (Philadelphia: Westminster Press, 1966), pp. 127–128.

Thus, the legal arrangements with respect to this entire subject not only protected the innocent; they also prevented the blood-avenger from acting rashly and prematurely by shedding innocent blood. A practical illustration of this arrangement under law is spelled out in detail in the Torah as follows:

> This is the provision for the manslayer, who by fleeing there may save his life. If any one kills his neighbor unintentionally without having been at enmity with him in time past—as when a man goes into the forest with his neighbor to cut wood, and his hand swings the axe to cut down a tree, and the head slips from the handle and strikes his neighbor so that he dies—he may flee to one of these cities and save his life; lest the avenger of blood in hot anger pursue the manslayer and overtake him, because the way is long, and wound him mortally, though the man did not deserve to die, since he was not at enmity with this neighbor in time past.[53]

Another curtailment of the blood-avenger's scope of action had to do with cases where there was doubt as to whether the one who had shed blood was guilty of involuntary manslaughter or murder. In such cases the manslayer had the assurance of a public trial. ". . . then the congregation shall judge between the slayer and the blood avenger according to these ordinances" (Num. 35:24, NASB). Under this legal procedure the manslayer was given every consideration possible. First, the cities of refuge were a true haven for him if he had accidentally killed someone.[54] The "hot anger" of the blood-avenger could not touch him there. Second, if there was doubt as to whether he had taken life with murderous intent, the blood-avenger was held at bay while he received a public trial.

---

53. Deut. 19:4–6.

54. Emanuel Rackman, "Talmudic Insights on Human Rights," *Judaism* 1, no. 2 (April 1952): 160: "Rabbi Isaac explained the significance of the verse, 'and that fleeing unto one of these cities he might live' (Deut. 4:42). This implies, 'provide the means for a livelihood' (B. Makkot 10a). If the refugee was a scholar, he was even to be provided with a college for the continuous practice of his calling (J. Makkot 6)."

Third, he was assured he would not be turned over to the avenger unless he was proven guilty of murder by the due process of law. "The cities shall be for you a refuge from the avenger, that the manslayer may not die until he stands before the congregation for judgment" (Num. 35:12).

Summary

The judicial ethics of punishment equal to the crime committed have been analyzed in this chapter. The "measure for measure" principle was rooted in the nature of God, who often operates on this principle in a personal, direct manner. Man's use of this principle as a judicial procedure was regulated by the Torah. In the Torah there was legislation to guide the people with respect to exact retribution and equivalent sanctions for crimes committed. The Talmud indicates that the Rabbis were attempting to mitigate the harshness of this principle when they developed a system of monetary compensation for damages resulting from law violations.

The evidence from the sources shows that ethical considerations for deterrence of murder center around the relationship of God to man. God's wrath is stirred when man sheds man's blood because man is made in God's image and man's life is "in the blood." Therefore, God often acted directly against the offender. He also supplied in the Torah the legislation by which man was regulated in his desire for revenge against the shedder of blood. The early pre-Mosaic practice of personal revenge for injustice suffered was channeled by the Torah into a judicial framework whereby the blood-avenger was a redeemer as well as an avenger. Also, protection was provided in the cities of refuge for the manslayer who had taken life inadvertently. The Sages, in their conviction that actions in the matter of "blood for blood" should be governed by law and not motivated by personal vengeance, brought these matters more fully under the jurisdiction of the courts.

CHAPTER VI

ETHICS OF GOVERNMENT IN WAR AND PEACE

INTRODUCTION

It is impossible to comprehend the ethics of government espoused by the Israelites during times of war unless one is very careful to analyze the convictions, motives, and perspectives of the Hebrew nation that was so often engaged in war.[1] It does not contribute to an understanding of the subject of warfare in the Hebrew Scriptures to try to superimpose upon those Scriptures a twentieth-century view of man or war which has been shaped by naturalism and the nuclear age. This approach distorts the clarity of the biblical record. This record portrays an ancient people governed by leaders in both war and peace who were convinced they were under Divine Providence. This trust in divine leadership applied as much to warfare as to peacetime, and was rooted and grounded in Torah.

This section of the chapter examines the question of the governmental ethics of the Israelites during time of war and from

1. Roland de Vaux, *Ancient Israel: Its Life and Institutions,* [trans. John McHugh], (New York: McGraw-Hill, 1961). Cf. chap. 4, "War," esp. pp. 247–250, for a "short military history of Israel."

the standpoint of their types of wars, their theological attitudes toward war, the "war ethic" of the war leaders, their ethical standards during wartime, the presence of unethical actions by their military leaders, the unethical actions of kings during wartime, and the ethics of government with reference to kingship in war and peace.

The second section of the chapter is concerned with the subject of peace and deals with the biblical emphasis on peace, the talmudical emphasis on peace, peace as the "third pillar" of Judaism, the theological foundations of peace, the quest of the Israelites for peace during biblical times and in postbiblical Judaism, legislation having peace as its motive, and the prophetic promise of peace.

RULES FOR WAR: THE PEOPLE, THE ARMY, THE KING

Types of Warfare

An examination of selected events recorded in the law (Deuteronomy) gives ample evidence of the ethical principles of leadership during times of war and the people's response to their leaders.[2]

JUSTIFIED WAR. The first example may be described as the justified war. Moses recounted the history of how the people had been led by the Lord from the wilderness in their march northward toward the Promised Land.[3] When opposition was encountered from the forces of Sihon, king of Heshbon, after overtures of peace had been made,[4] Moses said, "The Lord our God delivered him over to us; and we defeated him . . . " (Deut. 2:33). They were victorious

2. Ibid. Cf. pp. 250–254 for "the conduct of war."
3. Patrick D. Miller, Jr., *The Divine Warrior in Early Israel* (Cambridge, Mass.: Harvard University Press, 1973), p. 160: "The journey of the Israelites into the land of Canaan appears to have been viewed throughout Israel's history from a very early time as the holy war or Yahweh war *par excellence.*"
4. Num. 21:21–22; Deut. 2:26–29.

in battle against those who opposed them. This caused Moses to encourage Joshua with the following words:

> Your eyes have seen all that the Lord your God has done. . . . so will the Lord do to all the kingdoms into which you are going over. You shall not fear them; *for it is the Lord your God who fights for you.*[5]

Thus, the leaders and the people were convinced that as long as they followed the instructions of the Lord, the wars they fought would be justified and their victories would be assured.[6]

PURGING WAR. The second example may be correctly termed the purging war. According to Scripture, if an entire city became idolatrous, the army was to march against that city, and, in the words of Moses, "you shall surely put the inhabitants of that city to the sword, destroying it utterly, all who are in it and its cattle, with the edge of the sword" (Deut. 13:15). They were to offer up the booty of the destroyed city in a great burnt offering to the Lord God. These regulations against idolatry were meant to serve as a solemn warning to the people. Actually, there is no evidence that such a destruction of an entire city ever took place in this way.[7]

REGULATED WAR. The third example offered is one concerning regulated war.[8] When the army went out to fight against superior

5. Deut. 3:21–22 (emphasis added).

6. Miller, *Divine Warrior,* p. 133: "The overall theme of this book is that the nation believed that Yahweh, as Israel's 'Divine Warrior,' fought with and for them. Therefore the phrase 'fear not' is a familiar word of encouragement and battle cry of holy war (Ex. 14:13; Josh. 8:1; 10:8, 25; 11:6)."

7. According to San. 71a, such an event never happened and could not happen.

8. The example of a regulated war is a composite account drawn from Deut. 20; M. Soṭ. VIII, 1–7; and Maimonides' *Code,* bk. XIV ("The Book of Judges"), treatise V, chap. vii, pars. 1–5 [trans. Abraham M. Hershman] in: Yale Judaica Series, vol. 3 [New Haven: Yale University Press, 1949], pp. 224–227). It should be noted that these sources cover a span of almost two thousand years.

numbers who had horses and chariots, they were to be encouraged by the priest who was with them. He would remind them they were not fighting against their kinsmen, who might be compassionate with them if they were defeated, but they were fighting with an enemy who would have no mercy on them. Since God was with them, however, they need not be afraid, "for the Lord your God is he that goes with you, to fight for you against your enemies, to give you the victory" (Deut. 20:4). They were urged not to fear the horses or swords, clashing of shields or rushing of feet, sound of trumpets or shouting. They were to remember that the enemy was merely flesh and blood while the Israelites fought in the strength of the Almighty. Then the officers would excuse from battle those soldiers who met the following exemption requirements: (1) one who had built a new house but had not dedicated it; (2) one who had become betrothed but had not married; (3) one who had planted a vineyard but had not enjoyed any of its fruit; (4) any who were afraid or fainthearted. These were instructed by the priest to return home and provide water and food and repair roads. Following this, the officers put the people under commanders who placed guards at the front and rear of each company with orders to break the legs of any soldiers who tried to escape and avoid the battle. As the armed forces came against the city of the enemy they were to offer terms of peace. If the city chose to fight, the Israelite army was told, " . . . when the Lord your God gives it into your hand you shall put all its males to the sword" (Deut. 20:13). The women and children were to be spared if the city was not a part of the Israelite inheritance. However, if it was a city of the nearby nations, all the people in it were to be slain. During the siege of the city the fruit trees roundabout were to be spared.[9] Other trees could be cut down for siegeworks. The army

---

9. Gerhard von Rad, *Deuteronomy: A Commentary,* [trans. Dorothea Barton], (Philadelphia: Westminster Press, 1966), p. 133. Speaking of "the theoretical nature of Deuteronomy which is easily inclined to be doctrinaire," von Rad says, "The fact that Deuteronomy contains in the contexts of its laws concerning war a rule to protect fruit-growing is probably unique in the history of the growth of a

was under the leadership of stern military commanders who were subject to regulations and specific rules which were often quite humane. Also, the entire expedition of a regulated war was encouraged by the presence of a priest, who admonished them and assured them of God's blessings and victory.

HOLY WAR. In this fourth example the emphasis is the concept of holy war.[10] As Miller remarks,

> At the center of Israel's warfare was the unyielding conviction that victory was the result of a fusion of divine and human activity. . . . Yahweh fought for Israel even as Israel fought for Yahweh (Josh. 10:14; Judg. 7:20–22; and so on); the battles were Yahweh's battles (I Sam. 18:17; 25:28).[11]

The army was instructed in the following words, "When you go forth against your enemies and are in camp, then you shall keep yourself from every evil thing" (Deut. 23:9).[12] The state of purity for battle was to be maintained at all costs. If uncleanness did occur within the camp, the unclean person was to leave the camp until the proper purification rites had been performed.[13] This call

---

humane outlook in ancient times. Deuteronomy is really concerned to restrain the vandalism of war and not with considerations of utility."

10. Frank Moore Cross, "The Early History of the Qumran Community," in *New Directions in Biblical Archaeology*, [eds. David Noel Freedman and Jonas C. Greenfield], (Garden City, N.Y.: Doubleday, 1969), p. 71: "As Israel in the desert was mustered into army ranks in preparation for the Holy War of conquest, so the Essenes marshaled their community in battle array, and wrote liturgies of the Holy Warfare of Armageddon, living for the day of the Second Conquest when they would march with their Messianic leaders to Zion. Meanwhile they kept the laws of purity laid down in Scripture for soldiers of Holy Warfare, an ascetic regimen which at the same time anticipated life with the holy angels before the throne of God, a situation requiring a similar ritual purity."

11. Miller, *Divine Warrior,* p. 156.

12. de Vaux, *Ancient Israel,* pp. 258–260.

13. von Rad, *Deuteronomy,* p. 15: "A particularly characteristic part of the material peculiar to Deuteronomy is the so-called code of laws concerning war,

for purity included maintaining proper hygienic conditions about the camp, but it is significant that the rules of sanitation were to be obeyed for reasons of holiness: "Because the Lord your God walks in the midst of your camp . . . therefore your camp must be holy" (Deut. 23:14a).[14]

Theological Attitudes Toward War

These four examples of justified, purging, regulated, and holy wars show that the conflicts in which the Israelites were engaged were governed by a set of principles which applied to both officers and soldiers.[15] These principles reflect an unusual degree of ethical awareness and moral courage and were implemented by leadership provided by both priest and commander. The literature on this subject shows an army convinced it would be victorious if it remained obedient, courageous, and pure.[16]

When the army did remain obedient, courageous, and pure, it

---

namely regulations about release from military service (20:1–9), two about the siege of cities (20:10–20), and one about keeping the camp clean (23:9–14)."

14. Maimonides, chap. vi, pars. 14–15 (Sif. Deut. 23:13–14, p. 93a [185]), pp. 223–224.

15. It should be noted that the sources indicate that the idealized concepts of the Israelites' approach to war were basically theological. Cf. *The First Book of Maccabees*, [trans. Sidney Tedesche], (New York: Harper & Brothers, 1950), pp. 103–105. "When he [Judah] saw how strong the expedition was [Lysias and his army of 65,000 men], he prayed and said, 'Blessed art Thou, O Savior of Israel, who staved off the charge of the mighty man by the hand of Thy servant David. . . . In the same way be in this camp by the hand of Thy people Israel, and let them be put to shame in spite of their army and their horsemen. Make them cowardly. Melt the boldness of their strength. Let them quake at their destruction. Cast them down with the sword of those that love Thee, and let all who know Thy name praise Thee with hymns.'" For other prayers for victory, cf. I Macc. 4:30–33, 9:44–46; II Macc. 15:21–24.

16. E.g., cf. G. R. Driver, *The Judean Scrolls: The Problem and a Solution* (Oxford: Basil Blackwell, 1965), pp. 170–171. In speaking of the inscriptions on the standards carried by God's people (*'am 'ēl*), when they went out to war as described in the War Scroll, Driver quotes from (W III 13–IV 14) as follows:

was victorious in battle. When these features were lacking, the army was defeated. These moral prerequisites for victory were in harmony with the Israelites' overall concept of warfare. Their approach to war was basically theological. The "master plan" for consummating the promises of God with respect to their inheritance in the land of Canaan was largely a military operation carried out with theologically grounded motives and actions.[17] God had given them the "master plan" through Moses as follows:

> When you cross over the Jordan into the land of Canaan, then you shall drive out all the inhabitants of the land from before you, . . . and you shall take possession of the land and live in it, for I have given the land to you to possess it. . . . But if you do not drive out the inhabitants of the land from before you . . . it shall come about that *as I plan to do to them,* so I will do to you.[18]

These describe the units as God's when they march out and announce on *engaging the enemy* and on *returning to camp*

"God's War"	"God's Deliverance"
"God's Vengeance"	"God's Victory"
"God's Strife"	"God's Succour"
"God's Revenge"	"God's Support"
"God's Power"	"God's Joy"
"Recompense from God"	"Thanksgiving to God"
"God's Prowess"	"Praise to God"
"God's Destruction"	"God's Peace"

Although, as Driver states (p. 179), "The unreality, if not the absurdity, of these battles is apparent," such a description does reflect the theological perspective of the Qumran scribe as he contemplates the final victory of the Sons of Light over the Sons of Darkness.

17. von Rad, *Deuteronomy.* For extensive interpretative remarks concerning Israel's "holy war" perspectives as reflected in Deuteronomy, cf. von Rad's comments on 6:18 ff., 7:1 ff., 11:23 ff., 12:29, 19:1, 20:1–20, 23:9–14, esp. pp. 24–26, 67, 69, where such key phrases as "the warlike spirit of Deuteronomy," "militant piety," "old traditions concerning holy wars," and "revived ideas of holy war" occur.

18. Num. 33:50–56 (NASB; emphasis added).

Thus, ideally at least, their obedience was not merely obedience
to captains, but obedience to God, their Ultimate Leader. Their
courage was supposed to be not merely the grit of good soldiers,
but faith in the Lord of Hosts. Their purity was meant to be not
merely the purity of sanitation, but a purity of holiness emulating
the holiness of Him in their midst. Subsequent discussions will
throw light on the question of how well the Israelites actually
adhered to the ideal regulations of war as set out in the biblical and
rabbinic discussions.

The theological perspective of war held by the Israelites is the
key to understanding their actions in war.[19] Also, the theological
framework out of which the rules of war were articulated supplies
the rationale for those rules. The people's trust in God during time
of war was meant to be rooted and grounded in what they were
taught through Torah. Therefore, examples from the law (Pentateuch) will illustrate the theological attitude of the Israelites
toward war.

RESTRICTED WARFARE. The first example shows that the Israelites
were restricted in war. As they traveled north from Mount Seir on
their journey from the wilderness to Canaan, they were instructed
by the Lord to be careful not to provoke or attack the Edomites,
Moabites, or Ammonites. These people were their "relatives"
whom the Lord had promised a possesion which the Israelites were
not to molest (Deut. 2:4–5, 9, 19). Therefore, when they came into
the area of Edom, they tried to negotiate for passage through
Edomite territory. However, the king of Edom would not permit
it.[20]

19. M. San. I, 5; M. Soṭ. VIII, 7, speak of a distinction between a war for a
religious cause, or obligatory war, and an optional war. However, the ethical
principles governing the leadership in both types of wars were basically identical.

20. Nelson Glueck, *Rivers in the Desert: A History of the Negev* (New York:
Farrar, Straus & Cudahy, 1959), p. 10. The point is made that at the time of this
confrontation between Edom and Israel, Edom and Moab were so strong mili-
tarily that Israel's "enfeebled forces would have been overwhelmed by the armies
of these two entrenched kingdoms" (ibid.).

But he said, "You shall not pass through." And Edom came out against them with many men, and with a strong force. Thus Edom refused to give Israel passage through his territory; so Israel turned away from him.[21]

This incident illustrates the limitations of conquest placed upon the Israelites. They were not to fight for mere exploitation of the enemy. They were not to fight merely because negotiations with the enemy failed. They were made to realize that their warfare was guided by higher principles than these and that they could not engage in battle without divine sanction.

JUST WAR. The second example shows the response of the army when they knew they were to fight a just war. While the Israelites were still in Trans-Jordan on their northward trek, they came to the territory of Bashan. They were confronted by Og, king of Bashan, and his army. However, they did not "turn away from him" as they had turned from Edom. Rather, they "smote him until no survivor was left to him" (Deut. 3:3). The difference in these two incidents is that while God forbade them to fight the Edomites, he said with regard to Og, "Do not fear him; for I have given him and all his people and his land into your hand . . ." (Deut. 3:2a). The people were convinced that if the Lord justified the battle, that was tantamount to victory.

WAR OF DIVINE WRATH. The third example concerns the war of divine wrath.[22] The Israelites came in contact with the Midianites while en route to Canaan, and some of them were ensnared in idolatrous and vile practices (Num. 25:1–8). As a result, "the Lord

21. Num. 20:20–21.
22. Miller, *Divine Warrior*. This author points out many times that the concept of "holy war" was universal in the ancient Near East, and that while the Israelite nation was similar to neighboring nations, it also was markedly different in many respects, e.g., cf. p. 81 for the role of Yahweh *vis-à-vis* that of Mesopotamian Enlil.

said to Moses, 'Harass the Midianites, and smite them . . . '"
(Num. 25:16–17). Later, a full-scale war was waged against the
five kings who ruled in Midian. This was a war of divine wrath.

> The Lord said to Moses, "Avenge the people of Israel on the
> Midianites . . . " And Moses said to the people, "Arm men from
> among you for the war, that they may go against Midian, to execute
> the Lord's vengeance on Midian." . . . They warred against
> Midian, as the Lord commanded Moses, and slew every male.[23]

This war was waged as a regulated war. There was the personal
encouragement by Phinehas the son of Eleazar the priest, who
went to war with them as a visible sign of God's blessings.[24] There
were the purification rites which were required for those who had
become impure for any reason. And there was the sharing of the
booty, including a tax which was levied for the Lord to be
presented at the tent of meeting as a memorial (Num. 31:6, 20, 28,
54).[25]

TOTAL WAR. The fourth example is the picture of total war. The
"master plan" mentioned earlier specifically said with regard to

23. Num. 31:1–7.
24. G. Ernest Wright, "The Book of Deuteronomy," *Interpreter's Bible,* vol.
2. Cf. pp. 390–391 for discussion of the "holy war" concept in ancient Israel,
where, among other things, Wright says, "The institution of holy war in early
Israel was derived from the knowledge that the history of the nation was under
God's direction and that with this elect nation God was doing a special work."
25. John Marsh, "The Book of Numbers," *Interpreter's Bible,* vol. 2, pp.
283–285. Marsh holds that in this episode "we have the essence of a holy war,
viz., that nothing shall survive that is known to be offensive to Yahweh. . . . The
lessons that are taught, then, are not that wars of extermination are ordered by
Yahweh and therefore justified, but rather that since victory in war belongs to
Yahweh as his gift, any booty belongs to him, and must be divided in accordance
with his will; and further, that the activity of killing in war is something that
defiles a man and renders it necessary for him to be purified before he can resume
his rightful place in a divinely based society."

the fulfillment of God's promises to his people for an inheritance in Canaan, "When you pass over the Jordan into the land of Canaan, then you shall drive out all the inhabitants of the land before you . . . " (Num. 33:51–52a). Yet, when the Israelites at last reached the point in their journey from which they could plan to cross over the Jordan into Canaan, the tribes of Gad and Reuben, and the half-tribe of Manasseh, requested permission from Moses to receive their possession east of the Jordan. Moses rebuked them, asking, "Shall your brethren go to war while you sit here?" (Num. 32:6). He then reminded them that their actions would stir the anger of the Lord just as the actions of the ten spies had earlier caused the Lord's anger to burn. Moses called Gad and Reuben "a brood of sinful men, to increase still more the fierce anger of the Lord against Israel!" (Num. 32:14). After these tribes agreed to cross over the Jordan and fight with the remainder of Israel until the land was secure before returning to their inheritance, Moses warned them, " . . . if you will not do so, behold, you have sinned against the Lord; and be sure your sin will find you out" (Num. 32:23). From this episode it is clear that anything short of total mobilization of Israel for the conquest of Canaan was out of the question. It is also clear that a failure to muster for war in totality was a sin against the Lord, not merely a poor military strategy. There was the call for equality of sacrifice. All were called to fight in order to inherit the land. Total participation in war by God's people for the express purpose of carrying out his "master plan" was an absolute necessity if they were to receive the benefits of that plan. Kaufmann makes the point that

> before Moses' death, God appears in a cloud to charge Joshua with leading the invasion of Canaan (Deut. 31:14 f., 23). By virtue of this unbroken succession, the early "kingdom of God" was able to succeed in its primary undertaking, the conquest of the land.
>
> It is the accepted view that Canaan was conquered gradually, in several unrelated stages, by individual tribes or tribal bands. The evidence, however, argues for the unified conquest of Canaan by a

confederation of tribes that fought to carry out a national plan of conquest.[26]

The eight examples from the Pentateuch which have been briefly treated in the foregoing pages show that the Israelites held a theological view of warfare that led them into regulated, holy wars. Their obedience to the call of war was inspired by their faith in the Lord of Hosts, leading them to commit themselves to the struggle in all purity. Because they were restricted in war, they were not expected to press for personal gain.[27] However, when called by their leaders to what they thought to be a just war under God, they often fought the battle as an expression of the divine wrath, and, when called to total mobilization under Moses, they fought to carry out the "master plan" of YHWH.

"War Ethic" of War Leaders

The above résumé of the theological view of war as a method by which the divine will was implemented in carrying out the plan for God's elect helps one to keep the ethical behavior of some of the leaders in proper perspective. It also helps to explain why some of the actions taken during time of war, especially by the leaders, were considered ethical even though they no doubt would not have been considered so under other circumstances.[28] The following examples are given to illustrate the "war ethic" exercised by the war leaders of the Israelites, which was itself an integral part of their theological perspective of war.

---

26. Yehezkel Kaufmann, *The Religion of Israel,* [trans. and abridged by Moshe Greenberg], (Chicago: University of Chicago Press, 1960), p. 245.

27. In these considerations it should be noted that reality did not always conform to the ideal. Cf., e.g., I Sam. 15. There, as well as in the case of the capture of Jericho, the people who were captured and the spoils were חֵרֶם *ḥerem*—devoted to God and consigned to destruction. Achan in Jericho and Saul in the Amalekite war transgressed this command.

28. de Vaux, *Ancient Israel.* Cf. pp. 254–257 for "the Consequences of War" in Israel's history.

SUMMARY EXECUTION OF ENEMY WAR LEADER. The first example
is the summary execution of the enemy war leader. When Joshua
and the army had successfully conquered and sacked the city of Ai,
"the king of Ai they took alive, and brought him to Joshua.
. . . And he hanged the king of Ai on a tree until evening . . ."
(Josh. 8:23, 29). This kind of action could hardly be regarded as
ethical under ordinary circumstances, but as an expedient of war it
was in compliance with faith in a divine directive; and, being a
normal contemporary method of warfare, was not considered
cruel or exceptional. Joshua had been reminded that he himself
was subordinate to "the captain of the Lord's host" (Josh.
5:13–15). He was therefore completely receptive to the following
command of the Lord:

> Do not fear or be dismayed; take all the fighting men with you, and
> arise, go up to Ai; see, I have given into your hand the king of Ai,
> and his people, his city, and his land; and you shall do to Ai and its
> king as you did to Jericho and its king . . . [29]

Thus, there was no question in the mind of Joshua but that this
action was ethical under the circumstances because it was done by
divine imperative.

RETALIATION AGAINST THE ENEMY WAR LEADER. The second
example shows that retaliation against the enemy war leader was
not only practiced by the Israelites, but was viewed by him, as well
as by the Israelites, as the act of God through the victor. When the
tribes of Judah and Simeon went up to fight against the Canaanites
and the Perizzites, they were successful in their mission. Among
their captives was Adoni-bezek, whom they took and cut off his
thumbs and big toes. Again, such action out of its war context
could hardly be called ethical, but Adoni-bezek viewed it as the
expected act of God in retribution for his actions. He said,

29. Josh. 8:1–2a.

"Seventy kings with their thumbs and their great toes cut off used to pick up scraps under my table; as I have done, so God has requited me" (Judg. 1:7).

PRAISEWORTHY TO KILL THE ENEMY WAR LEADER. The third example occurred during the tenure of Israel's female judge, Deborah, and shows how it was viewed as worthy of praise to kill the enemy war leader. The people had been under the yoke of Jabin, king of Canaan, for twenty years when God instructed Deborah to send Barak with an army to go against the army of Jabin, which was under the command of Sisera.[30] When it became obvious to Sisera during the heat of battle that the Israelites were winning, he fled on foot and hid in the tent of Jael, a Kenite. Since peace existed between the Kenites and Jabin, Sisera assumed he would be safe in Jael's tent. However, Jael covered him up, then stealthily took a hammer and tent peg and drove the peg through Sisera's temple into the ground (Judg. 4:1–21). In peacetime this would, no doubt, have been considered by the judge at the time, Deborah, as murder in cold blood. However, since it was the result of the exigencies of war, this action received praise from Deborah in her victory song.[31] She also offered a eulogy to Jael as the "most blessed of women." In this song she praised Jael by describing how she subdued the enemy.

30. de Vaux, *Ancient Israel,* "In reality, then, this was a holy war" (p. 261).
31. William F. Albright, *Samuel and the Beginnings of the Prophetic Movement* (Cincinnati: Hebrew Union College Press, 1961), pp. 21–22. In advocating an early date for this poem, Albright states, "During the past twenty years I have become increasingly confident that the minimal dating of Israelite poetry by the Wellhausen school is generally quite erroneous. This is particularly true of the earliest Hebrew verse. . . . Thanks to the discovery and decipherment since 1929 of early Northwest-Semitic epics at Ugarit in northern Canaan, it is now possible to place the Song of Miriam (Exodus 15) at the beginning of Israelite verse, since it is consistently closer to Ugaritic style than any other poem of any length in the Bible. The Song of Miriam is followed in stylistic sequence dating by the Song of Deborah and the Oracles of Balaam, both from the twelfth century."

She put her hand to the tent peg and her right hand to the work-
men's mallet; she struck Sisera a blow, she crushed his head, she
shattered and pierced his temple.[32]

She concludes her song by saying, "Thus let all Thine enemies
perish, O Lord; but let those who love Him be like the rising of the
sun in its might" (Judg. 5:31, NASB).[33]

DISOBEDIENCE TO "DIVINE DIRECTIVE" = INSUBORDINATION. The
fourth example involves Saul and Samuel and illustrates how even
a king of Israel's refusal to kill the enemy war leader was considered as rebellion against God and intolerable insubordination.
Under orders from the Lord of Hosts, Samuel the judge commis-
sioned Saul the king to lead the army in a battle of utter destruc-
tions (חרם lit., "devoted" [viz., to God]) against the Amalekites.[34]
They won the battle but brought back some booty for sacrifice and
Agag, king of Amalek.[35] This failure to follow exactly the divine
commission led Samuel to say to Saul,

Has the Lord as great delight in burnt offerings and sacrifices, as in
obeying the voice of the Lord? Behold, to obey is better than sacri-

32. Judg. 5:26.
33. The killing of an enemy war leader has often been viewed as praiseworthy,
e.g., the hanging of Mussolini in 1945. Also, refugees from Czarist oppression,
even anti-Communists, did not regard the murder of the Czar and his family as a
crime.
34. Maimonides, chap. i, par. 2 (Sif. Deut. 17:14, p. 81b [162]; Tos. San. 4:3),
p. 207. "The appointment of a king was to precede the war with Amalek (I Sam.
15:1, 3). . . . The destruction of the seed of Amalek was to precede the erection of
the sanctuary (II Sam. 7:1–2)."
35. C. G. Montefiore and H. Loewe, *A Rabbinic Anthology* (London: Macmillan, 1938), pp. 654–655. Montefiore gives a discourse on this incident, citing
some difficulties pertaining to its historicity in the modern sense, e.g., vv. 8 and 9
in light of 30:1, and lays the difficulty at the feet of the scribe. However, with
respect to Samuel's actions, Montefiore says, "Agag was judicially executed for
wholesale murder (I Sam. 15:33) . . . "

fice, and to hearken than the fat of rams. For rebellion is as the sin
of divination, and stubbornness is as inquity and idolatry. Because
you have rejected the word of the Lord, he has also rejected you
from being king.[36]

These four examples include men, women, military commanders, judges, and kings. They illustrate a "war ethic" which,
because of its foundations in theological convictions, viewed certain actions in wartime as either approved or demanded by God.
They were therefore considered ethical.

This ethical-theological rationale may be seen, e.g., when
Samuel justifies the killing of Agag on the grounds of his own
murderous career (I Sam. 15:32–33); and when the Israelites act
under the conviction that God is driving out the inhabitants of the
land before them because of their abominable wickedness (Gen.
15:16, Deut. 9:4–5, 12:31), and that they themselves are God's
instrument by which this purging is to occur (Num. 33:55). As
Wright says in this connection:

> He (God) does what he does in the first place because of the
> wickedness of the Canaanite civilization. In the economy of God
> this evil had to go, and Israel was his chosen instrument to effect its
> punishment. . . . In the second place, God does what he does, not
> because of the righteousness of Israel, but to confirm his promises
> to the patriarchs, i.e., to fulfill his own redemptive plan to be effec-
> tuated through the mediation of Israel.[37]

36. I Sam. 15:22–23. Samuel G. Broude, "Civil Disobedience and the Jewish
Tradition," in *Judaism and Ethics,* [ed. Daniel Jeremy Silver], (New York: KTAV,
1970), p. 233: "The king must constantly be reminded that he is under God's rule,
and that God's law must be administered by him, irrespective of the response of
the people. . . . There is one issue only: is God's agent in power, the king, living
up to his commission or is he not? It is the prophet's task to decide and to act on
his judgment. If this means opposing the king, then so be it."
37. Wright, "Book of Deuteronomy," p. 392; cf. Deut. 7:7 ff.

Wartime Ethical Standards

Although the Israelites knew that a state of war did not justify every kind of action, there is evidence of mixed ethical awareness during wartime conditions.

SIEGE REGULATIONS. There were times when the Israelite army acted in utter disregard of regulations. The injunction was clear that fruit-bearing trees were not to be cut down and used for timber to build siegeworks when a city was attacked (Deut. 20:19–20). This injunction was, according to von Rad, "to restrain the vandalism of war" (cf. note 9, p. 173). Yet in spite of this plain order, when the Israelites overthrew the Moabites, they

> rose and attacked the Moabites, till they fled before them; and they went forward, slaughtering the Moabites as they went. And they overthrew the cities, and on every good piece of land every man threw a stone, until it was covered; they stopped every spring of water, and felled all the good trees . . . [38]

WOMEN AND CHILDREN. Instructions concerning the treatment of women and children seized in war are found in Deuteronomy 20. They applied to those ancient nations who inhabited the land into which the Israelites came. With the passing of those nations out of the history of the Near East, the rules of warfare applying to them were no longer applicable. The later rabbinic discussions of these laws were academic and theoretical. The general regulation was to spare the women and children of conquered cities which were not a part of the territory the Israelites were obtaining (Deut. 20:16–17). Various examples indicate that, generally speaking, there was

---

38. II Kings 3:24b–25. But they did this by order of the prophet Elisha, speaking in the name of God (II Kings 3:19). Either this was an exceptional case or one must regard it as a prediction rather than a command.

broad destruction as the people fought under the conviction of divine mandate.[39] However, the accounts of warfare by the Israelites in their later history contain instances where more humane consideration is extended to prisoners of war generally.

TREATMENT OF CAPTURED WOMEN AS PROSPECTIVE WIVES. A female prisoner of war taken as a prospective wife by an Israelite was extended humane care, proper treatment, protection, a reasonable period of readjustment—all before the marriage could be consummated.[40] The law also stated that in the event the marriage was not pleasing, the man could neither enslave nor sell her. He was required to let her go free (Deut. 21:10–14).

TREATMENT OF PRISONERS OF WAR. There are some interesting examples of the treatment of prisoners of war. Although the incident of Samuel's execution of Agag, king of the Amalekites, is well known, it should be noted that a stated justification for this action was the application of the "measure for measure" principle. Samuel said to Agag before executing him, "As your sword has made women childless, so shall your mother be childless among women" (I Sam. 15:33).

Another example of prisoner of war treatment concerns Ahab, king of Israel, and Benhadad, king of Syria. Benhadad attacked Israel, and, according to the account found in I Kings 20, God delivered the Syrians into the hands of the Israelite army. However, following a dramatic gesture of obeisance, the surrender of cities, and other concessions by Benhadad, Ahab "made a covenant with him and let him go" (I Kings 20:34). It is interesting to note that Benhadad was motivated to plead for his life before Ahab because his servants who advised him had "heard that the kings of the house of Israel are merciful kings" (I Kings 20:31a).

Mercy to prisoners of war was not forthcoming from the kings

---

39. Deut. 2:34, 3:6; Josh. 8:24–26.
40. Maimonides, chap. iii, pars. 2 and 6, pp. 228–229.

of Israel only. The prophet Elisha also extended mercy to captives. When Syrian soldiers found themselves prisoners in the city of Samaria due to Elisha's activity, the king of Israel asked Elisha, "My father, shall I slay them? Shall I slay them?" (II Kings 6:21b).

> He answered, "You shall not slay them. Would you slay those whom you have taken captive with your sword and with your bow? Set bread and water before them, that they may eat and drink and go to their master." So he prepared for them a great feast; and when they had eaten and drunk, he sent them away, and they went to their master.[41]

Elisha's rhetorical question, "Would you slay those whom you have taken captive with your sword and with your bow?" implies that there was a generally understood practice of mercy toward war prisoners.[42]

However, it should be noted that when the Israelites felt they were engaging in warfare under divine directive, they did not always extend mercy to war captives.[43]

HONOR TO LEGITIMATE RULER. Another example of deliberate restraint based on an ethical concern is seen in the way David spared the life of king Saul on two different occasions. Once, when Saul and his men were searching for David in the wilderness of Engedi, David caught Saul while asleep and cut off the edge of his robe. He also persuaded his men to do Saul no harm. After estab-

---

41. II Kings 6:22–23a.

42. This reading and its implication is according to the Massoretic Text. However, some scholars suggest that the text should be amended, following Lucian's recension of the Septuagint, to read, "Would you strike down him whom you have *not* taken with sword and bow?" This would suggest that the right to slay prisoners was restricted to the one who had personally captured them. Cf. C. F. Burney, *Notes on the Hebrew Text of the Books of Kings* (Oxford: Clarendon Press, 1903), p. 287, and John Gray, *I & II Kings: A Commentary*, 2d rev. ed. (London: SCM Press, 1970), p. 515 + note.

43. Deut. 3:3; Josh. 8:22, etc.

lishing some distance between himself and Saul he called to him, saying,

> See, my father, see the skirt of your robe in my hand; for by the fact that I cut off the skirt of your robe, and did not kill you, you may know and see that there is no wrong or treason in my hands. I have not sinned against you, though you hunt my life to take it.[44]

RECOGNITION OF THE "LORD'S ANOINTED." Again, David came upon Saul's camp and took his spear and jug of water. He called to Saul and said, " . . . the Lord delivered you into my hand today, but I refused to stretch out my hand against the Lord's anointed" (I Sam. 26:23b). Thus, one may detect in David's behavior toward Saul two motivating principles. First, there was a lofty ethic with a religious foundation which caused him to exercise restraint in sparing Saul's life. Second, there was the desire to insure his own succession to the kingship and safeguard his own position when he would be the crowned "anointed of the Lord."

After David became king he was eventually challenged by his son Absalom. When David acted to quell the rebellion he sent out his army (II Sam. 18:1–5) with orders to take Absalom alive. When Absalom was killed, David mourned for him (II Sam. 18:5, 33). Yet David acknowledged that Absalom had done harm to the kingdom (II Sam. 20:6). Thus, one sees David's recognition that unauthorized rebellion against God's "anointed" could not be tolerated. This was a matter of grave ethical concern.[45] David would not engage in it; neither would he tolerate it.

CURBING UNRESTRAINED SLAUGHTER OF THE INNOCENT. The unrestrained slaughter of innocent human beings during time of rebellion was not generally practiced. For example, when Joab caught up with a rebel against David at the city of Bethmaacah, he

44. I Sam. 24:11.
45. Maimonides, chap. iii, par. 8 (San. 49a), p. 213, "The king is empowered to put to death anyone who rebels against him."

besieged the city.[46] When a plea for mercy was made by one of the inhabitants, Joab said, "Sheba the son of Bichri by name, has lifted up his hand against king David. Only hand him over, and I will depart from the city." After the death of the rebel, Joab left the city unharmed and returned to Jerusalem.

The preceding examples illustrate some of the "rules of warfare" which were based on ethical principles. Prospective wives who were prisoners of war were supposed to receive considerate, humane treatment. The opportunity to take Saul's life and engage in unlawful rebellion against constituted authority was considered unethical as well as inexpedient by David. Uprisings against David as the legitimate king of Israel were crushed by him with a conviction that he was doing God's will as his anointed. In the heat of Absalom's rebellion David said, concerning his relationship to God,

> If I find favor in the eyes of the Lord, he will bring me back and let me see both it [the ark] and his habitation; but if he says, "I have no pleasure in you," behold, here I am, let him do to me what seems good to him.[47]

Finally, wholesale slaughter was not supposed to be practiced upon innocent people during these rebellions.

Unethical Actions by War Leaders

The state of warfare and rebellion did not justify every kind of action. An ethical consciousness is evident in these examples. However, there were times when ethical standards were neglected.

46. Ibid., chap. vi, par. 7, p. 222. Rabbinic theory proscribed unrestrained slaughter by the following rule, which was probably never followed in real life: "When siege is laid to a city for the purpose of capture, it may not be surrounded on all four sides but only on three in order to give opportunity for escape to those who would flee to save their lives . . . "
47. II Sam. 15:25b–26.

DURING ERA OF THE JUDGES. A profound lack of reason and a disposition to act in an unethical, retaliatory fashion is found in the precipitous action of the men of Ephraim against Jephthah and his forces after he had led his army successfully against the Ammonites. After the battle, the men of Ephraim asked Jephthah why he had not enlisted their aid in the battle, and concluded with the threat, "We will burn your house down on you." Jephthah explained that he had summoned them but had received no response.[48] In his attempt to reason with them he asked, "Why then have you come up to me this day, to fight against me?" Their answer, "You are fugitives of Ephraim, O Gileadites, in the midst of Ephraim and in the midst of Manasseh,"[49] seems to be a thinly disguised expression of contempt, envy, and hatred for this son of a harlot (Judg. 11:1) who had come to prominence in Gilead (Judg. 11:11) and won fame in Ammon (Judg. 11:32–33). At any rate, in the civil war that ensued Ephraim lost some 42,000 men.[50] The horror of this unrestrained and ill-motivated provocation to civil war by Ephraim stands out in bold contrast to the careful avoidance of civil war as negotiated by the Trans-Jordanian tribes of Reuben, Gad, and the half-tribe of Manasseh with the remainder of Israel. In this instance civil strife was avoided by open communication, mutual understanding, a conviction that all parties involved were conscientiously trying to act ethically, and a common commitment to God. As a result, "the sons of Israel blessed God; and they did not speak of going up against them in war, to destroy the land in which the sons of Reuben and the sons of Gad were living."[51]

---

48. Robert G. Boling, "Judges," *Anchor Bible,* vol. 6a (Garden City, N.Y.: Doubleday, 1975). The author makes the point that the Ephraimites took a similar stance against Gideon (Judg. 8:1 ff.) and Jephthah (Judg. 12:1 ff.), pp. 150–151. However, the result in each case was drastically different. Gideon's diplomatic prowess averted the impending civil war; Jephthah's lack of persuasive finesse was a contributing factor to the war which broke out between his forces and Ephraim.
49. Judg. 12:4.
50. Cf. Judg. 10:17–12:7 for this complete episode of tragic civil war.
51. Josh. 22; quote from v. 33 (NASB).

DURING ERA OF THE KINGS. The two preceding examples of unethical conduct during time of war occurred during the era of the judges. However, unethical conduct of leaders in Israel was certainly not limited to this period of history. After the period of kingship was inaugurated, one frequently finds many of the kings acting in a manner quite contrary to that which was prescribed for them in the law. The law specifically instructed that when the Israelites possessed Canaan and desired to set a king over them, they would appoint one whom the Lord God chose from among them.[52] He was not to multiply horses, wives, or wealth for himself. The king was to be governed by the law as he led the people.[53]

However, it is easy to find examples of kings failing to provide the high ethical standards of leadership which were obviously required of them by law. The two examples which follow show different kings acting unethically by abusing their power in the areas of military and governmental tactics, respectively.

DAVID'S ETHICAL LAPSE. While his armies were away at war, David became involved in an affair with Bathsheba, wife of one of his Hittite mercenary soldiers whose name was Uriah. When his plan to have Uriah united with Bathsheba in order to cover up the fact that she was already pregnant by him had failed, he ordered Joab, captain of his forces, to place Uriah in a battle where he would certainly be killed. This sordid tale is infamous as an

52. Maimonides, chap. i, par. 2 (Sif. Deut. 17:14, p. 81b [162]; Tos. San. 4:3), p. 207. The position of Maimonides is that although the people had been commanded to appoint a king over them upon entering Palestine, God was not pleased with their request of Samuel for a king "because they asked it in a querulous spirit. Their request was prompted not by a desire to fulfill the commandment but by a desire to rid themselves of Samuel the prophet (I Sam. 8:7)." Other views are expressed in the Talmud, e.g., San. 20b, "It has been taught: R. Eliezer said; The elders of the generation made a fit request, as it is written, 'Give us a king to judge us.' But the am ha-areẓ acted unworthily, as it is written, 'That we also may be like all the nations and that our king may judge us and go before us.'"

53. Ibid., chap. iii, pars. 1–4 (M. San. II, 4; San. 21a–b), pp. 212–213, for amplification of these and related principles.

example of intrigue, adultery, and murder (II Sam. 11). It is also a
glaring example of the basest sort of ethics and of the crude abuse
of royal power. It had dire consequences for David.[54]

SOLOMON'S ETHICAL LAPSE. Solomon's hasty coronation was to
avert a seizure of the throne by Adonijah, his older half-brother.[55]
When Adonijah saw that his strategy had failed, he begged Solomon for mercy. Solomon said, "If he prove to be a worthy man,
not one of his hairs shall fall to the earth; but if wickedness is
found in him, he shall die" (I Kings 1:52). Yet, Solomon had
Adonijah put to death (I Kings 2:25). Also, there was a man of
Bahurim in the land of Benjamin whose name was Shimei. Shimei
had cursed king David during Absalom's rebellion (II Sam.
16:6–7). However, after the death of Absalom, Shimei pleaded
with David to spare his life, and David swore before God that he
would not kill him.[56] But upon his deathbed David asked Solomon
to kill him (I Kings 2:9). This Solomon did, utilizing a technicality
to accomplish his purpose (I Kings 2:36–46a). These slayings,
together with the summary execution of Joab, the captain of the
army, who had sided with Adonijah in his aborted attempt to seize
the throne, brought it about that "the kingdom was established in
the hands of Solomon" (I Kings 2:46b).[57] With the possible exception of the death of Joab,[58] these slayings raise grave ethical ques-

54. II Sam. 12:9–10a.
55. II Sam. 3:4, 12:24; I Kings 1:5, 38–39.
56. II Sam. 19:18–23; I Kings 2:8.
57. James A. Montgomery, *The Book of Kings,* International Critical Commentary (Edinburgh: T & T Clark, 1951), p. 101. The observation is made that
almost the exact terminology is used here as in I Kings 2:12b, where Solomon is
pictured as the reigning monarch over an established kingdom. Therefore, the
conclusion is drawn that in the verse under consideration the "kingdom was
established in the hand of Solomon" in that "the confirmation of his power is
illustrated by his proud marriage (I Kings. 3:1)" (ibid., p. 102).
58. John Peter Lange, *Commentary on the Holy Scripture: Kings* (Grand
Rapids, Mich.: Zondervan, n.d.). "Joab was the most formidable opponent,
because of his position as head of the entire army, and his well-known military
roughness and unscrupulousness. . . . Besides this, the guilt of a double murder

tions with respect to the king and his abuse of power. Although it is true that there was a rabbinical ruling based on Joshua 1:18 that the king had the legitimate power to put to death anyone who rebelled against him,[59] it is also true that the king was supposed to be humble,[60] and watch over his people as a shepherd does a flock.[61] Since Shimei had not rebelled against Solomon, and Adonijah had been put on probation, it appears that Solomon, by removing all possible opposition in a violent and highly unethical manner, started his reign by abusing his royal power. From Solomon's point of view, however, as Lange remarks,

> The vital point was to establish the kingdom. . . . As to Adonijah, the whole East knew but one punishment for such plans as he cherished, viz., death. Had his enterprise succeeded he would doubtless have destroyed Solomon and his principal adherents, in accordance with the usual practice hitherto.[62]

Ethics of Monarchial Government

Apart from individual examples of kings in their various roles as described in the previous pages, there was a large body of law which applied to kingship in Israel. It was rooted in pentateuchal foundations and developed historically in the life of Israel. Robinson presents a practical picture of the working of judicial matters in this connection.

---

rested on him, and should be washed out" (p. 37). Also cf. Norman H. Snaith, "I Kings," *Interpreter's Bible,* vol. 3, p. 36: "The bloodguilt for the murders of Abner and Amasa can be removed from David's house only by the blood of him who was responsible for the murders, i.e., of Joab, who had actually done the deeds, or of David and his kin, who were ultimately responsible." San. 49a describes the court inquiry of Joab before Solomon, as imagined by the Rabbis, who could not conceive of unhalakhic behavior by biblical heroes.

59. Maimonides, chap. iii, par. 8, p. 213.
60. Deut. 17:20; Ps. 109:22.
61. Maimonides, chap. iii, par. 6, p. 212.
62. Lange, loc. cit.

When we turn to the judiciary we have even less direct information than on other points. . . . We may suppose that the old
methods of settling disputes still maintained themselves, and that
the general organization of the village and city communities had
undergone little, if any, change. Justice seems to have been still a
local matter, as we may see from the story told by the Tekoan
woman in 2 Sam. xiv. 5–7, where the whole community rises up and
demands the penalty for fratricide. But there was one novel feature.
This same story shows that an appeal lay to the king, and that he
had the right to set aside even the immemorial tradition and custom
of the land, cancel the sentence of a lower court, pardon the condemned criminal—act, in a word, as the final court. His position
and duties are brought out clearly also in the story of Absalom's
revolt, for the young rebel's method of winning himself a party is to
condole the suitors who meet with delay or with an adverse decision, and assure them that if only he had control, they would have
far more reason to be satisfied.[63]

Not only were such principles grounded in biblical back-
grounds, they were also expanded and developed in rabbinical
literature. The biblical and rabbinical literature reveals that the
king was vested with great power in the judicial and executive
areas, with special consideration given to his war powers.[64] A brief
survey of some of this material helps one to evaluate better the
ethics of government in Israel from the standpoint of biblical

63. Theodore H. Robinson, *A History of Israel,* vol. 1 (Oxford: Clarendon
Press, 1932), p. 232.

64. Martin Noth, *The Laws of the Pentateuch and Other Studies* (Philadelphia:
Fortress Press, 1967), p. 18. However, Noth makes the following observation:
" . . . the laws preserved in the Pentateuch . . . do not presuppose monarchy. . . .
In these law-codes the word 'king' occurs only in one single passage—in the so-
called 'law of the king' in Deuteronomy (Deut. xvii. 14–20). . . . In this 'law of
the king' it is not the rights and duties of the monarchy which are specified, but
rather all manner of general limitations which are laid upon the king's freedom of
action. . . . This unusual 'king's right' is mainly formulated in prohibitions; on
the positive side there is only the duty laid upon the king of punctually obeying
the deuteronomic law—which does not otherwise mention him" (ibid.).

teaching and later rabbinic theory with reference to kingship, both in war and in peace.

BIBLICAL PASSAGES. A key passage of Scripture on this theme is I Samuel 8. Bright deals with the complexity of this account in the following way:

> The account of Saul's election comes to us in two (probably originally three) parallel narratives, one tacitly favorable to the monarchy, the other bitterly hostile. The first (I Sam. 9:1 to 10:16) tells how Saul was privately anointed by Samuel in Ramah; it is continued in ch. 13:3b, 4b–15. Woven with this narrative is the originally separate account (ch. 11) of Saul's victory over Ammon and his subsequent acclamation by the people at Gilgal. The other strand (chs. 8; 10:17–27; 12) has Samuel, having yielded with angry protests to popular demand, presiding over Saul's election at Mizpah.[65]

Although there may be some justifiable grounds for taking this chapter as a warning to the people in regard to the consequences of having a king reign over them,[66] it has long been viewed by some of the Rabbis,[67] including Maimonides, as a catalogue of the prerog-

65. John Bright, *A History of Israel* (London: SCM Press, 1960), pp. 166–167.

66. D. B. Redford, "Studies in Relations Between Palestine and Egypt During the First Millenium B.C.," in: *Studies on the Ancient Palestinian World,* [eds. J. W. Wevers and D. B. Redford], (Toronto: University of Toronto Press, 1972). With reference to the levy mentioned in this chapter, it has been noted that "perhaps the most striking innovation of the United Monarchy, usually ascribed to Solomon, [was] the taxation system [which] proved new and intolerable to the rustic Israelites" (pp. 144, 156). Also, cf. I Kings 12 for some disastrous results for the United Monarchy due to the excesses of the monarch in applying heavy taxes on the people.

67. San. 20b: "Rab Judah said in Samuel's name: All that is set out in the chapter [dealing with the actions] of a king (I Sam. VIII), he is permitted to do. Rab said: That chapter was intended only to inspire them with awe, for it is written, 'Thou in anywise set him king over thee'; (Deut. XVII, 15) [i.e.] his awe should be over thee."

atives of the king and stipulations of the duties of the people toward him. Another passage in the kingship literature is found in Deuteronomy 17:14–20, which is concerned primarily with the duties and conduct of the king. By utilizing these and other Scriptures, together with the amplification of the king's law found in Maimonides' *Code,* the ethics of monarchial government in Israel, according to rabbinic theory, is made clearer. The next paragraphs use this method to examine some rabbinic theories of kingship during wartime.

RABBINIC THEORIES OF KINGSHIP IN WARTIME. The first inquiry concerns the role of the king during wartime. It was said that the chief purpose of appointing a king in Israel was that he wage war and execute judgment (I Sam. 8:20). Rabbinic theory applied retrospectively to kingship and the war powers of the king, and was engaged in as an academic and theoretical exercise by which the Rabbis often described an ideal situation as they thought it should have been. Thus, it was understood that many instructions concerning war were no longer applicable; e.g., with reference to the "seven nations,"

> R. Akiva declared . . . "that since Sennacherib came and confused all the peoples" it was no longer possible to identify any of the ancient nations. Hence, the special laws of the Torah which prescribed a course of conduct towards certain ancient peoples were deemed to have lapsed as early as Biblical times and to have become of no force and effect long before the Rabbis declared them obsolete.[68]

Therefore, an examination of rabbinic theories pertaining to the subject under consideration serves not so much as a means of ascertaining the historical events as they actually occurred, but,

---

68. George Horowitz, *The Spirit of Jewish Law* (New York: Central Book Co., 1953), p. 148.

more specifically, as a way of understanding the ethical insight of the Rabbis as they set down their understanding of how things "ought to have been."

If a war waged by the king was religious in nature (cf. above esp. pp. 173 and 177), he did not need the sanction of the court. However, religious wars would include any defensive war. If the war was an optional (nonreligious) war, he did need the sanction of the court of seventy-one.[69] If the king fought in accordance with the decision of the court, the lands conquered became a part of Israel if they were annexed after Palestine had been reconquered. The king was required to carry a scroll of the law with him when he went to battle. He could levy taxes for war purposes.[70] He could also claim the royal treasuries of kingdoms in war, as well as half of the booty plundered from the land. The other half was distributed equally among those who fought and supported the army. All lands he conquered belonged to him. He could give them away or keep them as he chose. Peace offers were to be made before the king waged war (Deut. 20:10). If the inhabitants of the city accepted the terms, they had to agree to follow the seven commandments given to the descendants of Noah: the prohibition of idolatry, blasphemy, murder, adultery, and robbery, the command to establish courts of justice, and the prohibition of eating a limb from a living animal. They also agreed to become tributary (Deut. 20:11), and in their bondage they were to serve the king with both their bodies and their money. If a city about to be attacked sued for peace, they not only had to agree to the above seven commands and servitude; they also had to give up the worship of idols.[71] If

69. M. San. I, 5; San. 16a–b; Maimonides, *Code,* Hilkoth Melakim V, 2. It is doubtful if any of this was ever realized in practice.

70. Deut. 20:11; I Sam. 8:17.

71. The above summary of rabbinic theories concerning war regulations for the Israelites is found in Maimonides' *Code,* treatise V, chap. iii, par. 1, pp. 212, 214; chap. iv, pars. 9–10, p. 215; chap. v, pars. 1–2, 6, pp. 217–218; chap. vi, pars. 1–2, p. 220; chap. viii, par. 9, p. 230; chap. ix, par. 1, pp. 230–231.

they did not, they were to be put to death if they came under
Israelite control.[72]

These rules of war and kingship in Israel were, again, academic
in character and were formulated long after kingship, including
the Herodian rulers, had ceased. They describe an ideal kingship,
not one that ever existed in reality. Baron's comments reflect a
more historical and realistic view of the role of kings in Israel.

> Theoretically the king was not even a lawgiver. The legislative
> power remained wholly in the domain of God himself; and God
> acted either through the people as a whole or through the teachers
> of the Torah. Whenever great legislative reforms were to be enact-
> ed, the kings had to conclude public covenants with the people. The
> levitical teachers expounded whatever laws tradition accepted, as
> revealed by God through Moses. The king could issue ordinances,
> but these had validity only insofar as they were reconcilable with
> the "divine" laws and thus acceptable to public opinion.[73]

Thus, there was the high religio-ethical demand on the king,
not only from a rabbinic theoretical point of view, but also from
the judicial and practical point of view, that reminded him that he,

72. Jacob Z. Lauterbach, *Studies in Jewish Law, Custom and Folklore* (New
York: KTAV, 1970), p. 191: " . . . these laws have been . . . abrogated by all
Jewish authorities in that they have been unanimously interpreted to have been
intended or directed only against the idolatrous nations of antiquity, especially
the morally corrupt Canaanitic peoples or the so-called 'seven Canaanitic
nations,' who, in the course of time, have entirely disappeared from the scene of
history."

73. Salo W. Baron, *A Social and Religious History of the Jews,* vol. 1, rev. ed.
(New York: Columbia University Press, 1952), p. 74. Also, cf. I Kings 12:18 for
the stoning of Adoram, Rehoboam's tax collector, by the people.

But cf. U. Cassuto, *A Commentary on the Book of Exodus,* [trans. Israel
Abrahams], 1st English ed. (Jerusalem: Magnes Press, 1967), p. 260. "Clear indi-
cations of the existence of secular law among the Israelites are to be found in the
Bible—In I Sam. xxx 24–25 it is related that David established a rule for the division of the spoils of war, and it is stated there: 'And from that day forward he
made it a statute and an ordinance for Israel to this day.'"

too, was under a King who required of him service and honor. Maimonides expressed the ideal in these words:

> Whatever he does should be done by him for the sake of Heaven. His sole aim and thought should be to uplift the true religion, to fill the world with righteousness, to break the arm of the wicked, and to fight the battles of the Lord.[74]

PEACE: A DOMINANT THEME IN THE BIBLE AND TALMUD

The Hebrew Scriptures literally abound with references to peace. In fact, in reading these Scriptures, one comes across the word *shālōm* (שלום) 249 times.[75] The wide range of meaning of *shālōm*, as indicated by the many different ways it is used, shows that peace is, indeed, a dominant theme in the Bible.

Biblical Passages

In its different contextual usages *shālōm* is seen to mean: (1) general well-being and life in the form of inquiry (ויאמר להם השלום לו ויאמרו שלום);[76] (2) disputes settled (Exod. 18:23); (3) protection of land or life from beasts and the sword (Lev. 26:6); (4) general prosperity (Isa. 60:17); (5) the absence of curses and destruction (Ezek. 7:25); (6) justice and truth (II Kings 20:19); (7) the opposite of war (Ps. 120:6); (8) national welfare (Esth. 10:2); (9) the absence of war (I Sam. 7:14); (10) tranquillity (I Chron. 22:9); (11) the nature of God's covenant (Isa. 54:10); (12) characteristic of God

---

74. Maimonides, chap. iv, par. 10, p. 216.
75. *Biblia Hebraica,* [eds. R. Kittel, P. Kahle, A. Alt, and O. Eissfeldt, 7th ed.], (New York: American Bible Society, 1951). All Hebrew words, phrases, and sentences are from this source.
76. Gen. 29:6. Hebrew phrases are given only in those references where the English of the Revised Standard Version does not contain the word "peace."

(Job 25:2); (13) God's plan for his people (כי אנכי ידעתי את המחשבת

[77](אשר אנכי חשב עליכם נאם יהוה מחשבות שלום ולא לרעה לתת לכם אחרית ותקוה)
(14) gift of God (Hag. 2:9).[78]

This array of citations from the Law, Prophets, and Hagiographa indicates that the theme of peace permeated the life of the Jews in Bible times. It was a part of their thinking all the way from a personal greeting to the concept and reality of God. One would hardly think that the emphasis on peace could be put any stronger than the Bible presentation. However, the writings of the Sages in the Talmud stress the subject of peace with equal, if not stronger, force. The following examples illustrate the central place of peace in the talmudical literature, and, like the biblical examples, show the broadness of the spectrum of thought concerning peace.

Passages from the Mishnah

The Mishnah points out that: (1) one should love and pursue peace;[79] (2) poor Gentiles could glean in the fields in the interest of peace;[80] (3) pray for the welfare of the government;[81] (4) greetings may be given to Gentiles in the interest of peace;[82] (5) the world is sustained by truth, judgment, and peace;[83] (6) being a peacemaker between a man and his fellow has rewards in this world and the world to come;[84] (7) for the sake of peace the cistern nearest a water channel is filled first;[85] (8) Gentiles may be encouraged when working in their fields, even in the Seventh Year.[86]

77. Jer. 29:11.
78. M. Wald, *Jewish Teachings on Peace* (New York: Bloch, 1944). Cf. pp. 22–24 for additional biblical references on peace.
79. M. Ab. I, 12.
80. M. Giṭ. V, 8.
81. M. Ab. III, 2.
82. M. Sheb. IV, 3.
83. M. Ab. I, 18.
84. M. Pe'ah I, 1.
85. M. Giṭ. V, 8.
86. M. Giṭ. V, 9.

Passages from the Gemara

In the Gemara the Rabbis elaborated at great length on the subject of peace. (1) God's blessings of love, fellowship, peace, and friendliness were invoked during the changing of the guard at the Temple.[87] (2) One must extend peace to his fellow countrymen, relatives, and all men to be approved above and popular below.[88] (3) Generous and loving deeds are peacemakers with God.[89]

Other Talmudic References

Other passages that emphasize the theme of peace are numerous. Note:

> Aaron loved peace and pursued peace and made peace between man and man.[90]

> Surely where there is strict justice there is no peace, and where there is peace, there is no strict justice![91]

> If, for the purpose of establishing harmony between man and wife, the Torah said, "Let my name that was written in sanctity be blotted out by the water," how much more so may it be done in order to establish peace in the world![92]

> May the descendants of the heathen, who do the work of Aaron, arrive in peace, but the descendant of Aaron, who does not do the work of Aaron, he shall not come in peace.[93]

> These are the things which a man performs and enjoys their fruits in this world, while the principal remains for him for the

87. Ber. 12a.
88. Ber. 17a.
89. B.B. 10a.
90. San. 6b.
91. Ibid.
92. Suk. 53b.
93. Yoma 71b.

world to come, viz.: honoring one's parents, the practice of loving deeds, and making peace between man and his fellow . . . [94]

Secondary References from Sefer Ha-Aggadah

Also, the haggadic writings present a wide range of comments on peace. Although this genre of literature is not legal in nature, the subject of peace is prominently treated. A few quotations are given to show that a yearning for peace is noticeable. Its great value is stressed, and ethical considerations are attached to the rabbinic treatment of this subject. Examples are:

> . . . the Lord, blessed be He, did not find any vessel that would hold blessing for Israel but peace, as it is said: "May the Lord give strength to his people! May the Lord bless his people with peace" (Ps. 29:11).[95]

> Beware that you say not, "Here is food; here is drink. If there is no peace, there is nothing . . . "[96]

> Peace is great, for the prophets put in the mouths of all the people nothing but peace.[97]

> . . . peace, what is said of it? "Seek peace and pursue it" (Ps. 34:15 [Eng. 34:14]).[98]

> Resh Lakish said, "Chastisement leads to peace." His stated opin-

94. Shab. 127a.

95. Ḥayyim Naḥman Bialik and Joshua Chana Ravnitzky, *Sefer Ha-Aggadah* (Tel-Aviv: Dvir, 1947), p. 538 = ,"דביר" :תל אביב) **ספר האגדה** ,רבניצקי .ח .י ביאליק .נ .ח (תש"ח), תקלח. *Note:* The quotations cited from this source are this writer's translations, since the work is not available in English. The original is carried in each footnote.

לא מצא הקדוש ברוך הוא כלי מחזיק ברכה לישראל אלא השלום, שנאמר: "יי עז לעמו יתן, יי יברך את עמו בשלום".

96. Ibid., שמא תאמרו: 'הרי מאכל, הרי משתה,' אם אין שלום אין כלום.

97. Ibid., p. 539. גדול הוא השלום, שלא נטעו הנביאים בפי כל הבריות אלא שלום.

98. Ibid., ". . . השלום, מה נאמר בו? — בקש שלום ורדפהו."

ion is, "Any peace which is not accompanied with chastisement is not peace."[99]

The above representative samples concerning peace from the Bible and rabbinic literature are enough to make it clear that peace was an integral part of the aspirations and literature of the Jews.

Peace as the "Third Pillar" of Judaism

R. Simeon ben Gamaliel saw peace as the third pillar of the social world, along with justice and truth,[100] and utilized the following biblical injunction to motivate the practice of peace: "These are the things that you shall do: Speak the truth to one another, render in your gates judgments that are true and make for peace . . . " (Zech. 8:16). Thus, in the Bible and the Talmud peace is called for on every hand.

> For the individual it is welfare of every kind, sound health, prosperity, security, contentment, and the like. In the relations of men to their fellows it is that harmony without which the welfare of the individual or the community is impossible; aggression, enmity, strife, are destructive of welfare, as external and internal peace, in our sense, is its fundamental condition.[101]

The people were taught to "judge with truth and judgment for peace in your gates," and "in the relations of men to their fellows" to seek "that harmony without which the welfare of the individual or the community is impossible." A large body of the judicial material within the Pentateuch laid great stress on laws which were

99. Ibid., p. 541. אמר ריש לקיש, "תוכחה מביאה לידי שלום." היא דעתו שאמר, "כל שלום "שאין עמו תוכחה אינו שלום."

100. M. Ab. I, 18.

101. George Foot Moore, *Judaism in the First Centuries of the Christian Era: The Age of the Tannaim,* vol. 2 (Cambridge: Harvard University Press, 1927), p. 195.

designed to produce peace within the nation of Israel, between Israel and aliens, and between God and Israel. One of the outstanding features of most of this material was the humanitarianism which it advocated. For example, justice was not to be perverted in a dispute with a poor man. There was to be no false charge. No illegal executions were to be sanctioned. The receiving of bribes in the subverting of the causes of the just was not to be condoned. Neither were the Israelites to oppress a stranger in their midst. Rather, they should sympathize with him since they had also been strangers in Egypt (Exod. 23:6–9). Adherence to laws of this kind would result in greater justice, equity, and peace in the land.

Theological Foundations of Peace

Biblical Hebrew law raises the principles of justice, fairness, equity, humaneness, and honesty above mere motives for the acquisition of peace; the law holds these challenging standards out to God's people because these are his traits. He wants his people to be like him. The acquiring and practicing of these traits will produce peace, and he is the God of peace whose very name is Peace (Judg. 6:24). So, in refusing bribes, showing no partiality, practicing justice, caring for orphans and widows, and loving the alien, the people were not merely obeying laws, they were being Godlike.

> For the Lord your God is God of gods and Lord of lords, the great, the mighty, and the terrible God, who is not partial and takes no bribe. He executes justice for the fatherless and the widow, and loves the sojourner, giving him food and clothing. Love the sojourner therefore; for you were sojourners in the land of Egypt. You shall fear the Lord your God; you shall serve him and cleave to him, and by his name you shall swear.[102]

102. Deut. 10:17 20.

Rabbinic Theories for Peace in the Land

Many of the talmudic statements with reference to peace are made in the form of rabbinic theories which describe events ideally, i.e., as they ought to have been. For example, rabbinic theory has it that when Joshua was ready to lead the army and the people into Canaan, he sent out the following message to the inhabitants. "Whoever wants to emigrate, let him emigrate. Whoever wishes to make peace, let him do so. Whoever wants war may have war."[103] Thus, options for peace were to be available. War was to be the move of last resort. If a nation sued for peace, it was neither destroyed nor stripped of all its possessions. Its people could either surrender half their money or land and keep chattel property, or vice versa.[104]

People of the conquered lands were to function under a system of judges set up in assigned districts whose responsibility it was to apply the Noahide commandments.[105] When the people of the conquered land became resident aliens, the Jewish court was duty-bound to provide them with either Gentile or Jewish judges to render decisions in accord with the Noahide laws. All of this was "so moral order not be destroyed."[106] These details indicate that there was a theory that the Israelites made a serious effort to promote peace in the land when they came into Canaan and to preserve peace through established judicial procedures after they were settled.

Rabbinic Theories of Kingship in Peacetime

Teachings with reference to the king and his role in peacetime

---

103. Maimonides, ibid., chap. vi, par. 5, p. 221; T.Y. Sheb. VI, 5; Midrash Lev. R., chap. 17 end.
104. Maimonides, ibid., chap. vi, par. 2, p. 220.
105. Ibid., chap. ix, par. 14, p. 234.
106. Ibid., chap. x, par. 11, p. 237.

included the following rules. According to Maimonides, when a new dynasty began, the king had to be appointed by a prophet and a court of seventy-one. No woman could be the lawful king in Israel. A prophet could appoint a king from other than the tribe of Judah; and, if he ruled well and fought the Lord's battles, all the rules of kingship were to apply to him (I Kings 11:36, 38). However, the kings from the house of David would endure (II Sam. 7:16), while kings from other tribes would not. The king was to be accorded great honor. However, in private meetings the king was also to pay honor to members of the Sanhedrin as students of the Torah in that he rose before them and had them seated in his presence. The king was not to drink to the point of being drunk (Prov. 31:4), but rather to devote himself to the study of law (Deut. 17:19). He was to refrain from sexual excess (Deut. 17:17; Prov. 31:3).[107] The kings of Judah could be judged and testified against; however, the kings of Israel could not. The rabbis ruled that because they were so arrogant they would have to be treated as commoners in court and this would make the cause of religion suffer.[108] A rare exception to obedience to a king's command was when one disobeyed in order to perform a religious decree. The king could levy taxes for his own needs.

Rabbinic Theories Concerning the King and Criminal Law

The special wartime prerogatives and powers of the king have already been discussed in the first section of this chapter. Also, with reference to the theme of peace, it is interesting to note that Maimonides developed an elaborate theory, based in part on talmudic statements, with reference to the king and his exceptional authority in the realm of criminal law. For example, the king could

---

107. Cf. San. 21a, where the number of wives permitted to the king is limited to eighteen!

108. The historical background out of which this ruling came was Herod's arrogance in court. Cf. Josephus, *Jewish Antiquities,* bk. XIV, ix, 4 (Loeb Classical Library ed., vol. 7, pp. 539–543), and San. 19a–b.

execute an individual who had killed another, even though the evidence was not clear, *if* the circumstances of the time demanded it to maintain a stable social order; in other words, if it was necessary for peace to prevail. Also, contrary to the usual legal procedures, he could hang several criminals in one day and allow their corpses to hang for a long time in order to put fear in the hearts of the wicked.[109]

Historically speaking, however, there is hardly any evidence that the ancient Israelite kings acted in accordance with this or any other theory of kingship. Horowitz's observation concerning kingship in Israel is appropriate at this point.

> . . . whenever a Hebrew king committed an act of tyranny or ruled like an "oriental despot," he was a law-breaker. He was not above, but subject to, the law. Prophets, priests, elders and even the humblest persons were not "oriental subjects," completely under the king's power. By fundamental law, elders, priests and prophets exercised certain functions and had rights independent of royal authority; and could call the king to account for crimes, acts of oppression, usurpation of power, and even for idolatry.[110]

The Quest for Peace

The reign of peace which the Bible speaks of as prevailing during the time of Solomon (I Kings 4:24–25) was, in prospect, something of an ideal to which Israel had looked forward for centuries; in retrospect, it was certainly idealized as the golden time when Israel had enjoyed the support of her three great pillars: justice, truth, and peace.[111]

---

109. The above summary of rabbinic theories concerning kingship in peacetime and the king and criminal law is taken from Maimonides' *Code,* ibid., treatise V, chap. i, pars. 4, 5, 8–9, pp. 207–209; chap. ii, pars. 1, 5, pp. 210–211; chap. iii, pars. 5–7, 9–10, pp. 212–214; chap. iv, par. 1, p. 214.

110. Horowitz, *Spirit of Jewish Law,* pp. 71–72.

111. Robinson, *History of Israel.* However, according to Robinson, Solomon's reign was "marked by tyrannical oppression. He was selfish, ostentatious,

DURING BIBLE TIMES. At any rate, it was apparent to Solomon during his reign that his father, David, had not been able to accomplish all that he desired for the name of the Lord his God because of the incessant warfare in which he was obliged to engage. Solomon expressed this awareness to Hiram, king of Tyre, as follows, "You know that David my father could not build a house for the name of the Lord his God because of the warfare with which his enemies surrounded him . . . "[112]

The conviction continued to grow among the Sages that the pursuit of peace was worth the effort of a lifetime, while warfare was to be avoided. This was a logical path to take, since the biblical literature showed that "war to the lawgiver, prophets, and historians was only a result of the evil passions of the human heart and the failure of man to live up to the laws of God."[113] A good example of this perspective of the cause of war comes from the reformation period of king Asa of Judah. He was told by the prophet Azariah that Israel had been without the true God, a teaching priest, and law for a long time. As a result, Azariah said, "They were broken in pieces, nation against nation and city against city, for God troubled them with every sort of distress" (II Chron. 15:6). In other words, war resulted when people turned away from God. This view of war and its causes provided the most powerful motivation for developing an aversion to armed conflict and for steadfastly refusing to become a nation that glorified war.

> While a war of defence in a case of well-established aggression is considered a moral obligation, yet, in the upward trend of peace, it

and extravagant. . . . He had little or no regard for the feelings of his people, and his reign was one of tyrannous oppression . . . he wasted the resources of the land, both in material goods and in manpower, and gave opportunity for the growth of jealousy which frittered away what strength the country had left in petty local struggles. If he did not actually destroy the national edifice erected by David, he did at least undermine its foundations" (pp. 239, 242–243).

112. I Kings 5:3.

113. Meyer Waxman, *A Handbook of Judaism* (New York: Bloch, 1947), p. 175.

is a transitory phase, for the ideal goal, according to the Jewish teachings, is the complete abolition and outlawry of war.[114]

DURING TALMUDIC TIMES. In view of this stress on the actualizing of peace in the world, the Sages were eventually able to say,

A man may not go out [i.e., on the Sabbath] with a sword or a bow or a shield or a club or a spear; and if he went out [with the like of these] he is liable to a Sin-offering. . . . the Sages say: "They are naught save a reproach, for it is written . . . " (Isa. 2:4).[115]

Peace, then, remained a cardinal theme in the thinking, writing, and aspirations of the Jewish nation. This emphasis on peace has continued to be reflected in Jewish literature into modern times. Hirsch wrote:

No steel may have touched a stone out of which you wish to build your altar, no steel may touch any stone out of which you have built your altar. The stone over which you have swung your steel becomes desecrated thereby for the altar of God. Not destruction, not sacrifice, nor giving up life, is the meaning and purpose of the altar, and the sword, the instrument of force and violence can not get any consecration at the Jewish altar, right and humanity must build the altar, and the realm of rights and humaneness, not the mastery of the sword, is to spread from it. In the "Hall of Stone" adjoining the altar of stone, Jewish Right had its permanent citadel

114. Wald, *Jewish Teachings on Peace,* p. 178.
115. M. Shab. VI, 4 (trans. H. Freedman). Rabbinic rules prohibited the carrying of burdens on the Sabbath, unless, with some exceptions, they were ornaments. Thus, R. Eliezer held weapons of war could be worn on the Sabbath on ornamental grounds, while the Sages held, "When war will be abolished, the instruments of war will not be ornamental. Now, however, that they may be needed, they are also ornamental." R. Eliezer's "hawkish" view is based on Ps. 45:4. I. Epstein, [ed.], *The Babylonian Talmud,* vol. 1, Seder Mo'ed, [trans. H. Freedman], Shabbath, p. 295, note.

(the Sanhedrin was housed there) and not the sword, the altar is the symbol of Jewish Justice.[116]

Although these remarks are in reality a commentary on Exodus 20:22 ff., the elaboration on the subject of peace implies a strong conviction of its great worth.

Establishing peace among men was seen as a prime reason for God's gift of the Torah. "The whole Torah was given for the sake of peace; as it is said, 'Her ways are ways of pleasantness, and all her paths are peace' (Prov. 3:17)."[117] Although this verse from Proverbs speaks of wisdom, "the teachers of the Talmud always identified the wisdom spoken of in the Book of Proverbs with the Torah."[118]

Legislation Having Peace as Its Motive

A good illustration of how this principle was utilized for the establishment and promulgation of peace is seen in the juridical interpretation of law by the *Amoraim*. The "ways of pleasantness" and "paths of peace" reflected by Torah were viewed by the *Amoraim* as basic to biblical law and became the basis of their rejection of any juridical interpretation of established enactments which would jeopardize peace or cause injury. Therefore, their discussions are frequently interlaced with references to the peaceful purposes of Torah as the basic reason for a particular ruling. For example, in an attempt to resolve the complexities of the rulings of Beth Shammai and Beth Hillel with reference to the marriages of rivals in Israel with the least possible amount of unpleasantness for the parties concerned, R. Naḥman b. Isaac said,

116. Samson Raphael Hirsch, *The Pentateuch,* (1867–78), vol. 2, *Exodus,* [trans. Isaac Levy], 2d ed. rev. (London: Isaac Levy, 1960), p. 285. Cf. Jacob Z. Lauterbach, [ed.], *Mekilta (de-Rabbi Ishmael),* vol. 2 (Philadelphia: Jewish Publication Society, 1933), commentary on Exod. 20:22. Also, cf. below, pp. 212–213.
117. Giṭ. 59b.
118. Waxman, *Handbook of Judaism,* p. 175.

How shall we, according to Beth Shammai, proceed with those rivals [who married (n. Strangers, previously performing the *ḥaliẓah*.) in accordance with the rulings] of Beth Hillel? Should they be asked to perform the *ḥaliẓah,* they would become despised by their husbands; and should you say, "Let them be despised," [it could be retorted], "Her ways are ways of pleasantness and all her paths are peace." (n. Prov. 3:17. The ways of the law must lead to no unpleasantness for the innocent.)[119]

Even before the *Amoraim* did their juridical interpretative work along the lines described above, the *Tannaim* had been busy with enactments and adjustments to existing law in an effort to promulgate peace, especially in the area of social legislation. In many respects this type of legislation reflects some of the highest ethical standards in all of Jewish law because it is an attempt to bring within the scope of legal enforcement the type of behavior that is already morally desirable. The following is an admirable statement of the unique function of Jewish law in this regard.

In every civilised society governed by a definite legal system there is the consciousness of a certain gap, more or less wide, sometimes existing between the law as actually enforced by the courts and the categoric imperative of ethical duty. . . . This inevitable shortcoming is tacitly recognised, but generally speaking, legal codes and rules pass over in silence the ethical aspect when it might be introduced to supplement the law as enforced by the courts. This is regarded as outside of their province. And here Jewish law, to an appreciable extent, offers an exception. This peculiarity of Jewish law is due, in no small measure, to its specifically religious character. In Judaism what would generally be described as civil law is an integral part of the Jewish religion.[120]

The *Tannaim* were especially sensitive to this type of problem

119. Yeb. 14b–15a [trans. Israel W. Slotki].
120. Isaac Herzog, *The Main Institutions of Jewish Law,* vol. 1 (London: Soncino Press, 1936), p. 381.

and attempted solutions by legalizing a situation of fairness which already existed in society, or by extending legal rights to persons or situations that had not been covered previously. All of this was done to keep down conflict and promote the interests of peace. An example of this type of legislation is seen in the excerpts from the following Mishnah.

> The following rules were laid down in the interests of peace. A priest is called up first to read the law and after him a Levite and then a lay Israelite, in the interests of Peace. [The taking of] beasts, birds and fishes from snares [set by others] is reckoned as a kind of robbery, in the interests of peace. [To take away] anything found by a deaf-mute, an idiot or a minor is reckoned as a kind of robbery, (n. Although these cannot legally acquire ownership.) in the interests of peace.[121]

The Prophetic Promise of Peace

This section has pointed out that the Jewish nation had a very high regard for peace as a religious, legal, and moral principle, and sought to implement peace in communal, national, and international life. R. Johanan b. Zakkai brought this point out clearly by way of analogy in his commentary on Exodus 20:21–22 and Deuteronomy 27:6. In his remarks concerning the type of stones to be used for building the altar, he said,

> They shall be stones that establish peace. . . . The stones for the altar do not see nor hear nor speak. Yet because they serve to establish peace between Israel and their Father in heaven the Holy One, blessed be He, said: "Thou shalt lift up no iron tool against them" (*ibid.,* v. 5). How much more then should he who establishes peace between man and his fellow-man, between husband and wife, between city and city, between nation and nation, between family

121. M. Giṭ. V, 8 [trans. Maurice Simon].

and family, between government and government, be protected so that no harm should come to him.[122]

It seems an irony of history that a nation so dedicated to peace had relatively few opportunities to enjoy it throughout her long history. Out of the turmoil of her biblical history, the voice of the prophets spoke of a new era in which the blessing of peace would be realized.[123] The Rabbis continued to extol the principles of peace. In their rulings, laws, and interpretations, they produced some of the most exalted and ethically demanding legislation when they were working directly "in the interests of peace." It seems appropriate that the entire work of the Mishnah should literally conclude with a Bible quotation which extols the blessing of peace:

The Holy One, blessed is he, found no vessel that could hold Israel's blessing excepting Peace, for it is written, "The Lord will give strength unto his people; the Lord will bless his people in peace" (Ps. 29:11).[124]

122. Lauterbach, *Mekilta,* p. 290. Cf. above, p. 210.
123. Isa. 2:1–4; Mic. 4:1–4; Isa. 11:6–9, 52:7–10, 65:17–25; Zech. 9:9–10; Hos. 2:18–20; etc.
124. M. 'Uk. III, 12.

CHAPTER VII

CONCLUSION

SUMMARY

Chapter I, First Section
The Bible and the Law of Government

The concept of law in the Bible was examined in order to establish a foundation for a more specific diagnosis of the ethics of government in this literature. The examination showed that from its very inception the Hebrew nation was governed by *tōrōth* (instructions) from God. They were his elect people. A covenant relationship existed between God and Israel.

When the Torah was received by the Israelites, they recognized this law as being divine in origin. Therefore, the idea of law in the Bible was essentially a theological concept. The law was viewed by the Israelites as being God's expressed will for them. It had as basic premises the reality of God, the significance of each individual, and the need for harmony between God and his people, which could be achieved only through Israel's observance of the law.

The formative impact of the law reached into every facet of life. The order of government, by its very nature, reflected legal, moral, ethical, religious, and social characteristics. After Moses, the law was transmitted to the people by prophet, priest, judge, and king.[1] Although its mode of expression varied from time to time, it continued to be viewed as a unique revelation from God possessing supreme authority.

Chapter I, Second Section
Postbiblical and Talmudic Concepts of the Law of Government

The concept of law in the Talmud was examined from the historical point of view and analyzed with regard to the evolution of Jewish law from the time of Ezra to the redaction of the Talmud. The purpose of this inquiry was to lay a foundation upon which a meaningful study could subsequently be made with respect to the ethics of government as reflected in the Talmud. This analysis of the concept of law in the Talmud showed that the Jews never lost sight of the Torah as God's law of government for them. However, the concept of Torah broadened to include all the Hebrew Scriptures; and, in addition, the "Traditions of the Elders," or Oral Law, was at last written down and preserved in the Mishnah. The Rabbis saw the continuity of this Tradition as going all the way back to Moses at Sinai, and therefore viewed it as authoritative in nature.

Although the Mishnah was viewed as an authoritative text after it was compiled at the close of the tannaitic era, the evolutionary character of Jewish law continued to unfold in the halakhic work of the *Amoraim* and *Savoraim*. These Sages, working under a strong feeling of commitment to divine mandate, were concerned that every rule or regulation added to the body of legal literature should reflect, either directly or indirectly, its divine origin, the written Torah. Eventually, they brought the Mishnah and Gemara together in redacted form to produce the Talmud.

---

1. However, only in rare instances did the king fill this role, as in the case of David, who was also endowed with prophetic qualities. The king was the executive officer of the law, not its transmitter.

From about the beginning of the seventh century C.E. the Babylonian Talmud, for all practical purposes, became for the Jews the infallible source of the *halākhāh,* the law of government.

Chapter II, First Section
Legal Ethics in Judaism

In order to illustrate the rationale behind specific laws in the Talmud and to show the method by which these laws were enacted, some attention was given to the process and role of legislation in producing the law of government in Judaism.

The Sages continued to practice the continuity of *halākhāh* in regard to legislation by inaugurating laws in areas where none had existed before, by circumventing laws which were no longer tenable, and by altering existing laws so as to cope more adequately with the circumstances of the times. This process for reaching legislative goals was implemented largely by *takkanah* or *gezerah.* The *Tannaim* saw the *takkanah* (enactment) method reflected in Scripture as far back as pre-Sinaitic times. The *gezerah* (decree) technique was utilized for preventive measures, usually with the idea of "making a fence around the Torah." Before the destruction of the Temple such rulings were usually anonymous because they came from the Great Sanhedrin. After the Temple's destruction, rulings by a *Nasi* and the Beth Din became an established procedure.

The *Amoraim* expanded the legislative scope of the earlier Sages, especially in social and economic matters, by supplementing the existing laws for greater justice on the principle of "you shall do what is right and good" (Deut. 6:18), and the deducted principle of "arise and do" (Ezra 10:8). This philosophy of legislation allowed the Rabbis to enact *takkanoth* which in effect (never directly) set aside Torah law to insure justice and equity. In criminal legislation the motive for many of the laws was to maintain good order in society.

Also, often the Sages recognized the valid place of established custom and the will of the people in their legislative deliberations,

based upon the rabbinic interpretation of Exodus 23:2. Thus, the
majority opinion or prevailing custom was often translated into
law by way of the majority rulings of the courts.

Chapter II, Second Section
Ethics of Judaism in Penal Legislation

A study of the governmental legal system in Judaism showed that
ethical considerations carried heavy weight with the Rabbis as
they continued their work in this field. They produced the
halākhāh, the legal side of Judaism, from the Written Law, the
Oral Law, traditions handed down in the form of commandments
or requirements infrequently found here and there in the Prophets
and Hagiographa, the teachings of the Sages, and custom.

The inherent ethical quality prevading the governmental legal
system in Judaism was seen in the way the Rabbis attempted to
establish and retain in legal form appropriate expressions of ethical behavior. They did this in their rulings by comparing unethical
to illegal behavior on the one hand, and ethical to legal behavior
on the other; likening a criminal offense to one much more serious,
attaching the "worthy of death" pronouncement to a crime which
was not actually a capital offense; ruling that failure to comply
with the spirit of the law would result in divine retribution if not
legal punishment; encouraging compliance with a particular ruling
to retain their esteem; showing their displeasure in their ruling
toward those who would not comply with it on the grounds there
was no legal sanction involved; urging ethical conduct even
beyond the letter of the law; incorporating into law by enactment
what had earlier been an ethical concern; pressing for a display of
proper attitude by persons involved in legal problems or situations; and requiring ethical actions on legal grounds by invoking
the principle, "you shall do what is right and good."

These techniques utilized by the Rabbis show that they thought
in terms of legal-ethical relationships. The result of their work was
a governmental legal system in Judaism highlighted by its ethical
concerns.

Penal legislation was examined to show the high quality of ethics in the governmental legal system of Judaism. This rich resource indicated that the basic ethical nature of talmudic law pointed to the high goal of justice.

Care and caution were key themes in penal legislation. Generally speaking, for penal purposes an act was not criminal unless it was a violation of a negative biblical command. This meant there was a close link between negative injunctions and penal legislation. However, if the Rabbis felt that the Torah had to be safeguarded, they did not hesitate to apply penal sanctions even though there had been no violation of a negative command.

The ethical awareness of the Rabbis in penal legislation was noted in the following ways. They gave the accused the benefit of all reasonable doubt. A crime committed by someone through another individual implicated both parties, if not legally, at least morally.[2] Ordinarily, an illegal act had to be actually performed before guilt accrued. However, in the cases of enticement to idolatry, intent to strike another, and unsuccessful false testimony, the mere intent to do wrong, if proven, was construed as guilt. An act done inadvertently did not carry liability. Additionally, an act had to be done willingly to incur guilt. Furthermore, even if done willingly, guilt could be avoided if there were extenuating circumstances. Incompetents were exempt from guilt. Taking of life in defense of person or property was to act without guilt, even though the person or property being protected might not be one's own.

Rulings of this kind strengthen the contention that the supreme motive of talmudic law was basically ethical in nature because of the obvious concern for justice. The law remained a standard for the people. However, its application was flexible, and took into account the different circumstances and conditions involved. This

2. M. B.Ḳ. VI, 4. "If a man sent out something burning through a deaf mute, an idiot, or a minor [and damage resulted] he would be exempt from the judgments of man, but liable in accordance with the judgments of heaven. But if he sent [it] through a normal person, the normal person would be liable." Also, cf. Ḳid. 42b.

flexibility, taking into account the nature of the offense, shows an ethical strain in the law in Judaism which adapted the law to man's needs. Because of the retention of ethical principles within penal legislation, the goal of justice in the governmental legal system of Judaism remained a practical goal.

Chapter III, First Section
Recognition of Authority

The governmental ethics in Judaism were grounded in the conviction that the Torah was of divine origin and had been given to govern Israel. Therefore, the Sages were concerned that the Torah, and the laws which they subsequently developed out of Torah, be administered equitably. For governmental ethics to be enforced, there had to be a general recognition of valid authority, the establishment of a court system functioning on a high ethical plane, capable leadership, and the just administration of law.

God was the source of authority in Judaism. The Rabbis agreed that Moses had received a Written Law and an Oral Law from God at Sinai. The articulation of the Written Torah and the transmission and development of the Oral Law through the ages by the rabbinic scholars enabled them to continue to develop principles of law which were accepted as divinely authorized. This meant that while God was the ultimate source of authority in Judaism, the interpretation of the Torah had been left to the Rabbis, whose majority decisions, whether right or wrong, had divine authority. This conviction was rooted in the Torah, e.g., Deuteronomy 17:11.

Chapter III, Second Section
Establishment of the Court System

The implementing of the law interpreted and developed through the authoritative channel of the rabbinical scholars required the establishment of an equitable court system if the enforcement of governmental ethics in Judaism was to be a reality. The court system which functioned in postbiblical Judaism had its foundations in biblical history from the time of Moses, who had said, "You shall appoint for yourselves judges and officers in all your towns . . . " (Deut. 16:18). The court system which evolved in Judaism was historical evidence of a prolonged determination to attain the highest degree of judicial ethics possible.

Organizationally speaking, there was the court of seventy-one (Great Sanhedrin), which functioned as the "supreme" court until restricted and then eliminated by foreign rulers. Small Sanhedrins located throughout Israel consisted of twenty-three members. Small courts of three men could be called together by the mutual consent of the parties in a case.

The judges who served on the larger courts dealing with capital cases had to be highly qualified. Their conduct not only had to be above reproach, it had to avoid the very appearance of misconduct. They were regulated by strict judicial rules of procedure when the court was convened in order to insure a fair trial for all parties. This court system in Judaism was one of the key factors in enforcing judicial and governmental ethics within the nation.

ETHICAL LEADERSHIP. Men of high caliber and dedication, coupled with the efficient organization found in the court system in Judaism, were major contributing elements in maintaining an ethical system of government. Although the authority of the Rabbis was usually confined to judicial and religious matters, their influence through the courts and their religious leadership usually had a wholesome impact on the people.

Their ethical leadership was not merely a matter of law; it grew out of the heritage, biblical examples, and teachings through the ages. From the time of Moses, an outstanding leader of the people had been referred to as *Nāsī*. This same term, although in Moses' time designating a tribal chief distinguished for military leadership, was used for the leaders of the Sanhedrin during much of its history, indicating that the Jewish nation looked with respect to the office of leadership over the Great Sanhedrin. The authority which the *Nāsī* had as head of the Great Sanhedrin, and the justice which he represented as chief of the highest court, was reflected through the entire court system. Theoretically, though not always in practice, this high view of law and legal leadership made it easier to enforce governmental ethics in Judaism.

Chapter III, Third Section
The Law and Morality

Another reason why it was possible to enforce a high governmental ethic in Judaism was the close relationship between law and morality. Law in Judaism was not a mere legal entity regulating the affairs of men; it was also designed to relate men to God properly. This meant that Jewish law and morality sprang from the same source, viz., the Written Law and the Oral Law. There was no ambiguity between law and morality. God was the origin of both. This "holy" view of law made it easier to enforce a high legal ethic. Obedience was both a civic duty and a God-given responsibility for the Jews.

This religious view also accounts for some of the most enlightened features found in the law. Since God was merciful, it was understood by the Pharisees and the Rabbis, though not by the Sadducees, that the law which originated from him should be interpreted and applied mercifully. Under this principle, morality was enhanced by the practice of going beyond the letter of the law out of concern for one's neighbor.

Under a legal system which was so closely allied to morality, the authoritative stance of the Rabbis as religious figures as well as judges was relatively easy to maintain. Since Jewish law was a matter of faith, having its ultimate origin in divine revelation, it was natural for the people to look to those scholars as the means by which the law was interpreted, expanded, vitalized, and applied. For the people, obedience to the law thus presented was a matter of morals, and this morality of obedience was closely tied to religious conviction.

Chapter IV, First Section
Divine Reward and Punishment for Rulers and Subjects

The principle of reward and punishment was a prominent feature in the biblical and postbiblical government of the Jews. Reward was an inducement to obedience; punishment was a deterrent to lawlessness.

Rewards as well as punishments were viewed as either administered directly by God, or indirectly by him through the application of his law. This divine regulation applied to the leaders of Israel as well as to the common people. The promises, instruction, and encouragement found in the Torah were incentives for keeping the law, as were the love, mercy, and holiness of God which were reflected in the Scriptures. However, God's divine justice required that violators of his law be punished, and this punishment usually came through the judicial channels of the courts.

The death penalty was the extreme sentence required by law. It was regulated by specific judicial procedures and carefully defined rules of application, especially in the talmudic period.[3] This extreme penalty covered a wide variety of offenses ranging from criminal and religious to social and domestic areas. There was little, if any, distinction between religious and criminal violations so far as the death penalty for capital offenses was concerned.

Chapter IV, Second Section
The Death Penalty

An ethical feature of the death penalty was seen in one of its chief motives. It was utilized to put away the evil, and not primarily for the purpose of putting away the evil person. Ethically speaking, this elevated the practice above mere retaliation or simple ven-

3. For the biblical period the evidence is very scanty indeed. For a rare example, cf. II Kings 14:5–6.

geance, and also reminded the people that one of its benefits was as a deterrent to further crime.

The judicial forms of capital punishment in the Bible were burning and stoning. Hanging was often a superimposed action on a criminal after execution, no doubt as a reminder to others that crime did not pay.

During the rabbinical period many of the severe features of the criminal law found in the Torah were either modified or eliminated. This was due, in part, to the search of the Rabbis for more humane ways of applying sanctions against crime. Other reasons included the domination of Palestine by foreign rulers, the destruction of the Temple, and the disbanding of the Great Sanhedrin.

Three major ethical principles motivating the Rabbis in their postbiblical application of the death penalty were: love (Lev. 19:18), which required the most humane death permissible under law; nonmutilation as God's way of terminating life; and death achieved by strangulation if the form of punishment was not specified. As noted above, this form of punishment for capital offenders was seen as a purging of sin from the land rather than an act of mere vengeance upon the sinner. Eventually, in their attempt to reduce to an absolute minimum the application of the death penalty, the Jewish courts developed judicial procedures which made it virtually impossible to carry out a death sentence. Consequently, the laws relating to capital punishment were then classed with the laws relating to sacrifices; that is, they were worthy of study because learning has its own merit. However, they were not to be applied.

Chapter V, First Section
"Measure for Measure"

One of the major principles standing out in the Torah was the "measure for measure" sanction against many kinds of law violations. This biblical principle was made viable by the ethical demand for administration of justice commensurate with the crime. The law which called for the "measure for measure" sanction and the court system through which this punishment was applied were both accepted as having a divine origin. Therefore, the application of the law in this area was the actualizing of religious convictions within legal categories.

Sometimes the "measure for measure" principle called for punishment identical with the crime. Some crimes were punishable by measures which were equivalent but not identical. In some instances the motives of the accused were the determining factor of guilt even though the deed was not actually done. In such cases, the punishment was commensurate with what the criminal had intended to do.

The talmudic era ushered in a more lenient implementation of the "measure for measure" sanctions. The "one standard" (Lev. 24:22) was retained in principle while the literal application of this type of punishment gave way in appropriate cases to a settlement involving compensation for damages. Elaborate degrees of damages developed, including depreciation, pain, healing, loss of time, and disgrace (or shame) of blemished appearance. In legal cases compensation for damages was designed to have both a civil and punitive effect.

Thus, as history moved from Torah to Talmud, one sees a continuing effort to retain the essence of the "measure for measure" principle while ameliorating its application.

Chapter V, Second Section
Genesis 9:6

Genesis 9:6 provides a biblical source for the death penalty, a statement of the "measure for measure" principle as a valid procedure in punishment for crime, and a theological foundation for these sanctions. The ethical considerations for deterring murder were, in the final analysis, religiously grounded. Thus, the one who shed man's blood committed an outrage against God, in whose image man was made.

The biblical sources showed that God often acted directly against the murderer. However, man's tendency to move in unilateral action when blood had been shed was carefully regulated by legislation found in the Torah. The law provided a judicial framework in which the blood-avenger's action was regulated.

The cities of refuge were designated for the one who had inadvertently taken the life of another. This legal arrangement not only protected the manslayer but also hindered the blood-avenger from shedding innocent blood. If there was doubt as to whether the one who fled to a city of refuge had committed involuntary manslaughter or murder, he had the assurance of a public trial; he was protected from the blood-avenger; he was not turned over to him unless proven guilty.

During talmudic times the Rabbis brought these matters more completely under court jurisdiction. Under their supervision, if one who was murdered had no relative to serve as blood-avenger, one was assigned by the court. The court-appointed blood-avenger was, in effect, a dispassionate executioner of a criminal who had committed a capital offense.

Chapter VI, First Section
Rules for War: The People, the Army, the King

The Israelites and their leaders saw themselves acting under Divine Providence during the course of their long history. This divine leadership was as active in wartime as in peacetime. Therefore, the ethics of government during times of war were as firmly grounded in theological foundations as they were during times of peace. Thus, the biblical history of the Hebrews, and the later interpretations of that history by rabbinical scholars, are punctuated with example after example of wars which were fought under the impetus of divine fiat. Such were the justified, purging, regulated, holy, and defensive/preventive wars. These wars were engaged in as part of a divinely inspired "master plan" for Israel in respect to their taking and securing the Promised Land.

Within this framework of divine guidance, the Israelites were sometimes restricted in war activity. On the other hand, they were encouraged by YHWH to fight his just wars. These wars were often the expression of his divine wrath; and, in view of God's "master plan" for his people, they were required to wage total war in taking Canaan. In the course of these wars, the Israelites were expected to retaliate against the enemy war leaders and put them to death if they were captured. Refusal to do so was viewed by God as an act of disobedience.

This "war ethic" was based on the Torah. Therefore, it had theological foundations and was not devoid of humanitarian principles. Deliberate restraint for the preservation or dignity of human life was required under specifically prescribed guidelines in many war situations. There was also the regard for the Lord's "anointed" as illustrated by David's dealings with king Saul. Also, the rabbinical teaching that the citizens of a besieged city were allowed to escape with their lives indicates an element of war perceived with a humanitarian ethic.

Unfortunately, through the long history of Israel there were many times when war conditions highlighted actions which were clearly unethical. Since these actions were usually those of leaders, they illustrate a lapse in the ethics of government in Israel when they occurred. The civil war of Ephraim against Jephthah is an example of this type of ethical lapse.

However, perhaps the most vivid examples of unethical government and abuse of power came during the period of kingship. David displayed poor moral, ethical, and military behavior in connection with his murder of Uriah; Solomon abused his kingly power by ruthlessly removing all possible opposition to the throne in a violent and highly unethical manner; and, later, by imposing an oppressive slave labor system upon his subjects.

The power of the king was enormous. However, there was a very large body of law which applied to kingship in Israel. It was rooted in pentateuchal foundations and expanded in rabbinical writings. Key passages from Scripture on this point are I Samuel 8 and Deuteronomy 17:14–20. A definitive exposition from rabbinical literature giving theories of kingship is Maimonides' *Code,* book XIV, treatise V, "The Laws of the Kings." Although his powers as prescribed by law were great, the king could be called to account for flagrant abuses. And, in the final analysis, it was expected that "whatever he does should be done by him for the sake of Heaven."

Chapter VI, Second Section
Peace: A Dominant Theme in the Bible and Talmud

In spite of the fact that the history of the Hebrews was often marked by war, peace is one of the major themes in biblical and rabbinical literature. The idea of peace permeated the whole fabric of Jewish life, as indicated by the large number of meanings attached to *shālōm* in the Bible, Mishnah, and Gemara.

Peace was, indeed, viewed as the "third pillar" in the social world, along with justice and truth. Therefore, much of the judicial material in the Pentateuch stressed laws designed to produce peace in Israel, between Israel and foreigners, and between God and Israel. Most of the laws in this context designed for the regulation of human relationships were humanitarian in emphasis. When obeyed, the result was not only greater justice and equity in the land, but also a social climate in which peace could flourish.

There was a strong theological connection between Israel's quest for peace and the ethical humanitarianism reflected in these laws. In many cases, the motive for obedience to a particular law of this kind was to be God-like and to win God's blessing. Thus, peace was not only established between men, but also between God and Israel.

The Tradition stresses this concern for peace during the time of judges and the period of kings which followed. The reign of Solomon was idealized in biblical and rabbinic literature as an extended period of peace although other features of that period were far from ideal. God's refusal to allow David to build the Temple because he had "waged great wars" became a sort of turning point upon which the Rabbis later built the conclusion that anything other than a defensive/preventive war was to be avoided, and that war "was only a result of the evil passions of the human heart and the failure of man to live up to the laws of God."[4]

The Sages taught that peace was the primary reason for God's gift of the Torah, and cited Proverbs 3:17 to bolster this teaching. The *Tannaim* devoted much of their energies to enacting laws and adjusting existing laws in the interest of peace. In fact, they produced some of the most ethical legislation in Judaism because they sought to bring morally acceptable behavior into the corpus of law with their enactments. The later *Amoraim* rejected any judicial interpretation of established enactments which would jeopardize peace in any way, and related many of their own rulings to the peaceful purposes of the Torah.

Thus, as time passed, postbiblical Judaism showed a very high regard for peace as an ethical, religious, legal, and moral principle. Much of the work of the Sages continued to be dedicated to implementing peace in communal, national, and international life.

CONCLUSIONS

The Task

A study which encompasses over two thousand years of Hebrew history, and attempts to probe the literature produced by the Jews in the Bible and Talmud, is an undertaking of considerable magnitude. The limitation of this inquiry to the specific consideration of judicial and governmental ethics has not eliminated the necessity of providing a continuing context within which such a study would be meaningful. This context has been provided by a historical backdrop. This historical perspective has been by design, and has kept the major theses of this work from unfolding in a vacuum, so to speak.

4. Meyer Waxman, *A Handbook of Judaism* (New York: Bloch, 1947), p. 175.

Case Law

By relating the ethics of government enunciated in the Bible and
the Talmud to real-life situations, this study has utilized the case
law methodology so prominent in this vast literature.[5] This
approach has enabled the inquiry to come to grips with the subject
at hand in a specific way, and has been the chief motive for the
consistent emphasis upon the primary literary sources. The analysis of these sources, with additional insights gleaned from many
competent scholars, has produced the foregoing chapters. Although many principles of judicial and governmental ethics have
become self-evident throughout this study, and are spelled out in
the various chapters, the following conclusions need to be stressed.

Ethical Questions Answered

So far as the Hebrews were concerned, many of the basic ethical
questions of life were directly related to the ethics of government.
For example, the system of government under which the Hebrews
lived presupposed an affirmative answer to the highly ethical question, "Does man have a freedom of choice in his actions?"
Another ethical question which the Hebrews had no difficulty
answering was, "What is man's source of knowledge of the highest
good?" Every Jew knew this to be the law itself, the Torah. Again,
"What is the final authority for right and wrong?" was answered
by recourse to the rulings of the Rabbis, the judicial work of the
courts, and the interpretations of the law. All of these procedures
implied a reliance upon an ultimate authority which was first
revealed at Sinai.

---

5. Hermann Kleinknecht and W. Gutbrod, "Law," in: *Bible Key Words from
Gerhard Kittel's 'Theologisches Worterbuch zum Neuen Testament,'* [trans.
Dorothea M. Barton; ed. P. R. Ackroyd], (London: A. & C. Black, 1962), p. 77.
"The fact that life depends on fulfilling the Torah makes it a very important con-
cern that the law should be developed in the direction of case-law."

Judicial and Governmental Ethics Theocentric in Nature

Thus, the judicial and governmental ethics in Judaism were, in fact, expressions of a system of government which was theocentric. This was more pronounced in biblical times due to the revelatory nature of the Torah. However, the theocentric aspect remained prominent in postbiblical times in the continuing amplification of the Torah, the growing body of Oral Tradition, and the vast work of the Sages in the Talmud. This theocentric characteristic found in the judicial and governmental ethics of Judaism illustrates a prime reason for the close relationship between the ethical, legal, moral, and religious fabric of Jewish life. The strands of this fabric were woven together on the same loom, so to speak, and they all went together to make a composite whole.

Continuity of Tradition Gave Stability

Another conclusion that emerges is that the maintenance of continuity within the halakhic tradition was one of the vitalizing forces which supported the authority of law and jurisprudence in Judaism through the centuries. This built-in method of keeping the law on a continuously contemporary basis, while at the same time retaining the support of the Torah and Tradition, provided each generation of Jews with a legal framework of reference that offered stability and equity on an authoritative basis.

Torah as Foundation of Law

A close corollary to the principle of continuity of Tradition was the persistent esteem for the Torah as a foundation of law and government in Judaism. Upon this bedrock the Jews built their convictions concerning ethical government and structured the judicial procedures for implementing the laws. As Steinberg has said,

> Law is an element in Judaism ... because of the intense Jewish
> preoccupation with ethics, and because of the historic Jewish insis-
> tence that ideals need to be put to work.[6]

The governmental and judicial ethics found in Judaism are clues to
the high ethical ideals present in that system of law which was
rooted and grounded in the Torah.

Rabbis as Judicial Figures

It is easy to conclude that the Rabbis played an indispensable role
and filled an essential place in implementing the judicial system in
Judaism and in maintaining the ethics characteristic of that system. Their presence was so pervading and their judicial authority
was so strong that it is safe to say the court system in Judaism
could not have continued for so many centuries without them.

A Shift Toward Leniency

Finally, this study has adduced accumulative evidence to show
that in postbiblical Judaism there was a rather consistent effort on
the part of the Sages to mitigate some of the harsh features of the
law found in the Bible. This was accomplished by reinterpretation
or regulation of existing laws, or by the passage of new laws. For
example, by the introduction of complicated judicial procedures in
later Judaism, it became virtually impossible to inflict the death
penalty for any offense.

The Challenge

The governmental and judicial ethics found in the Hebrew Scriptures and in postbiblical rabbinic literature stand out as highlights

---

6. Milton Steinberg, *Basic Judaism* (New York. Harcourt, Brace & World,
1947), p. 145.

of civilization from the ancient world. It is true, there were occasional ethical lapses by individual rulers in the long course of Hebrew government and law, just as there were occasional laws which did not measure up to the generally high ethical standard of the legal system as a whole. However, taken as a complete system, and evaluated in totality on the basis of the legal and ethical principles involved, the governmental and judicial ethics which have been the subject of this study still present some of the greatest challenges to a modern world tending toward a permissive society and anarchy.

EXCURSUS I

POLITICAL POWER IN ISRAEL

INTRODUCTION

As one examines the sources, one finds that royal law was not identical with religious law in the ancient Near East. After surveying the Sumerian and Akkadian laws of Babylonia, the Assyrian laws, and the Hittite laws,[1] Cassuto states, "In all the aforementioned codes we observe that the law does not emanate from the will of the gods."[2] For example, Cassuto points out that the early conclusion that Hammurabi, on the so-called stele of Hammurabi, is receiving a code of laws from the god Shamash is now recognized to be wrong thanks to a more careful analysis of the prologue and epilogue of the code, and that, in actuality, "it is clear that it is Hammurabi who enacts the laws."[3] As a matter of fact, the conclusion is reached that "the legal tradition of the Ancient East was, in all its branches, secular, not religious. The sources of law were on the one hand usage . . . and on the other, the king's will."[4]

---

1. Cf. above, pp. 12–20.
2. U. Cassuto, *A Commentary on the Book of Exodus,* [trans. Israel Abrahams], (Jerusalem: Magnes Press, 1951), p. 260.
3. Ibid.
4. Ibid., pp. 259–260.

Against this background[5] Cassuto makes some observations with reference to Israel. He states:

> Now it is possible to show that also among the Israelites, during the whole period preceding the destruction of the First Temple, the sources of the official law were the secular statutes of the ruling authorities and accepted usage; whereas the Torah laws were regarded as religious and ethical requirements directed to the collective and individual conscience.[6]

Cassuto cites several examples from the Bible to indicate the existence of secular law among the Israelites. Two are: David's rule concerning the distribution of the spoils of war,[7] and Isaiah's "woe" upon "those who decree iniquitous decrees, and the writers who keep writing oppression" (Isa. 10:1), which can only mean that the oppressors were within their legal rights. Other references of Scripture indicate the existence of recognized legal usage, e.g., the bride money (Exod. 22:16), the "custom in former times in Israel" (Ruth 4:7), and Joab's flight for safety to the horns of the altar (I Kings 2:28 ff.).[8]

Finally, Cassuto sees Israel's law as a part of the general legal tradition in the ancient Near East. However, the qualification he states in the following passage is significant.

> The statutes of the Torah are not to be identified with Israel's secular legislation. Only in the time of Ezra were the laws of the Torah accepted as the laws of the country, by the consent of the people and its leaders. When we come to compare the Pentateuchal statutes with those of the neighbouring peoples, we must not forget . . . the difference in character between them: the laws of the neighbouring peoples were not decreed on behalf of the gods, but on behalf of the kings; whereas the laws of the Torah were not promulgated in

---

5. Ibid., pp. 257–259.
6. Ibid., p. 260.
7. I Sam. 30:24–25.
8. Cassuto, *Commentary on the Book of Exodus,* pp. 260–261.

the name of the monarchy, nor even in the name of Moses as the leader of Israel, but are religious and ethical instructions in judicial matters ordained in the name of the God of Israel.[9]

One may conclude from the above introduction that in ancient Israel, up to the time of Ezra, there was a distinction between secular and religious law; yet, at the same time, there was a very close relationship between the two in the day-to-day affairs of the people. A close examination of biblical sources indicates the practical way in which political power was expressed in Israel. Sometimes this power was with law and sometimes contrary to it.

POLITICAL ROLE OF KINGS IN ISRAEL

A study of kingship in Israel brings one to a better insight into the role of the king with all of its political ramifications for the people. A. R. Johnson speaks of three aspects of the theory and practice of the king's function in Israel.

> 1. For the Hebrews an important, if not the most important, aspect of the king's function was that of being a leader in war (I Sam. 8:19–20; II Sam. 8:2, 14, etc.).
>
> 2. Another and equally important aspect of the Hebrew view of kingship is that of being responsible for the administration of justice within the realm (I Kings. 3:16–28; II Kings. 8:1–6, etc.).
>
> 3. A third aspect of the prevailing Hebrew conception of kingship which stands out clearly in the Old Testament records is that which centers in the king's relations, not with his subjects, but with Yahweh as the national god; for in the last resort that which bound together the confederation of tribes which went to the making of the Israelite nation was a common loyalty to Yahweh (I Sam. 16:13; 24:6; II Sam. 23:1–5, etc.).[10]

9. Ibid., p. 262.
10. A. R. Johnson. "Hebrew Concepts of Kingship," in: *Myth, Ritual, and Kingship,* [ed. S. H. Hooks], (Oxford: Clarendon Press, 1958), pp. 205–207.

In this connection, Johnson points out that disasters on a national scale could be attributed to the fact that the king had overstepped the mark and offended Yahweh.[11]

It is now appropriate to examine specific biblical texts in determining more exactly the political role of kings in Israel, and to relate their activity to the law as it was observed at the time.

The King and Secular Power

Abimelech, Gideon's son by his concubine, acted in a completely unrestrained manner in his move to become king, killing seventy of his brothers in order to remove all opposition to his usurpation of power.[12] The infamy of Abimelech, as an example of what a king should not be, remained in the memory of the Israelites, as indicated by the insightful message sent by Joab to David at the time of Uriah's murder.[13] Samuel's opposition to kingship, assuming that it does not reflect a later period, may have been influenced in part by the experience of Abimelech's bloody attempt to establish a monarchy.

An episode in the life of king Saul illustrates his possession of secular power and his use of it. After a striking victory against the Ammonites under Saul's leadership, his followers were ready to put those to death who had earlier questioned Saul's capability.[14] They said to Samuel:

> Who is it that said, "Shall Saul reign over us?" Bring the men, that we may put them to death. But Saul said, "Not a man shall be put to death this day, for today the Lord has wrought deliverance in Israel."[15]

11. Ibid., p. 211. Also, cf. II Sam. 24:10–25; Jer. 15:4.
12. Judg. 9:1–9.
13. II Sam. 11:19–21.
14. I Sam. 10:26–27.
15. I Sam. 11:12–13.

Clearly, the law of the Torah did not permit a king to put to death people who had peacefully objected to his assumption of royal power. Saul's ability to impose the death penalty on dissidents was purely secular law and custom.

The fact that Saul, as king, had the power to put others to death is illustrated by the oath that he pronounced against anyone who stopped to eat during the battle against the Philistines.[16] When Jonathan, his son, unknowingly violated the oath, Saul pronounced the death sentence upon him.[17] The fact that the people had to ransom Jonathan to prevent the execution indicates the awesome reality of Saul's power over the lives of his subjects.[18]

Even before Saul, one is startled to find that Jephthah had the undisputed right to sacrifice his daughter because of an ill-advised vow.[19]

It was to limit the power of the father to put his children to death at will that the deuteronomic law concerning "the stubborn and rebellious son" was introduced (Deut. 21:18–21). Henceforth, such a delinquent could be put to death only after a proper trial before an authorized court.[20]

16. I Sam. 14:24.
17. I Sam. 14:43–44.
18. I Sam. 14:45.
19. Judg. 11:30–31, 34–35, 39.
20. T.B. San. 71a contains rabbinic debate concerning this law. With regard to actually applying it, one view was, "It never happened and never will happen." But R. Jonathan said, "I saw him [a rebellious son who was executed at his parents' demand] and sat on his grave," indicating that the law was still alive in his time.

Apparently this law was still in use at the time of Herod, who cited it to justify his charges against his sons Alexander and Aristobulus. Cf. Josephus, *Jewish Antiquities,* XVI, xi, 2, 361–366 [trans. Ralph Marcus, Loeb Classical Library ed., vol. 8, pp. 355–357]. "He said that both by nature and by Caesar's grant he himself had authority to act, but he added that there was also a law in his country that provided that if a man's parents, after accusing him, placed their hands on his head, the bystanders were bound to stone him and to kill him in this way. This, he said, he was prepared to do in his own country and realm . . . "

Again, the power of life and death that the king could exercise is seen in the relationship of Saul and David. On several occasions, Saul made direct attempts to kill David.[21] There was no one who questioned Saul's legal power to do so. Furthermore, Saul's execution of the eighty-five priests of Nob, plus the entire population of the city,[22] went unchallenged.

During this period of Israel's history there was no power to restrain the king, or even a claimant to the throne. This point is well illustrated in the account of David's reaction to Nabal's refusal to let him have any provisions. Replying to Abigail, Nabal's wife, who had managed to appease him, David said,

> Blessed be your discretion, and blessed be you, who have kept me this day from bloodguilt and from avenging myself with my own hand! For as surely as the Lord the God of Israel lives, who has restrained me from hurting you, unless you had made haste and come to meet me, truly by morning there had not been left to Nabal so much as one male.[23]

Clearly, no religious law could have justified David's threats, which, in view of his oath ("For as surely as the Lord the God of Israel lives . . . "), he undoubtedly intended to put into action.

These examples indicate the secular power that rested with the king. It is obvious that he could, without fear, exercise this power, even to the extent of execution. It is also interesting to note that long after the monarchy had ceased, the rabbinic view does not include a general condemnation of kingship as such,[24] merely an occasional denunciation of individual kings.[25]

---

21. I Sam. 19:9–10, etc.
22. I Sam. 22:18–19.
23. I Sam. 25:32–34.
24. M. San. II, 2–5.
25. Cf., e.g., M. San. X, 2; also, for another view of kingship, cf. Aristotle, *Politics,* bk. III, chap. 16, in: *The Basic Works of Aristotle,* [ed. Richard McKeon], (New York: Random House, 1941), p. 1202. "He who bids the law rule may be deemed to bid God and Reason alone rule, but he who bids man rule adds

In view of the virtually unlimited authority wielded by various kings as indicated in the examples described above, it is not surprising that king David did not hesitate to kill on the spot a man who had confessed to slaying Saul.[26]

SOME ARBITRARY RULINGS BY KING DAVID. The first case is that concerning Mephibosheth and Ziba. Mephibosheth was Saul's grandson. David, as king, wanted to extend a kindness to one of the house of Saul for the sake of Jonathan.[27] Therefore, David had Jonathan's son, Mephibosheth, brought to the royal court with this pronouncement,

> "I will restore to you all the land of Saul your father; and you shall eat at my table always . . ." Then the king called Ziba, Saul's servant, and said to him, "All that belonged to Saul and to all his house I have given to your master's son. And you and your sons and your servants shall till the land for him, and shall bring in the produce, that your master's son may have bread to eat; but Mephibosheth your master's son shall always eat at my table."[28]

However, in spite of this royal decree, David, upon hearing of possible disloyalty on Mephibosheth's part, awarded to Ziba all the property he had originally given to Mephibosheth,[29] making no

an element of the beast; for desire is a wild beast, and passion perverts the mind of rulers, even when they are the best of men. The law is reason unaffected by desire."

26. II Sam. 1:5–16.

27. Theodore H. Robinson, *A History of Israel,* vol. 1 (Oxford: Clarendon Press, 1932), p. 224. "One representative of the family is left, a lame son of Jonathan, who David takes into his own household. He has no reason to fear Meribaal (Mephibosheth), partly because of his physical weakness, and partly because the king is so sure of the devotion of Israel, and gives him a position of honour at court." Cf. also William McKane, *I & II Samuel* (London: SCM Press, 1963), p. 225, where McKane points out the political sagacity as well as the kindness of David in bringing Jonathan's son under the shadow of his watchful eye.

28. II. Sam. 9:7, 9–10.

29. II Sam. 16:1–4.

attempt to listen to Mephibosheth's explanation. Then, in yet
another arbitrary ruling, after being assured by Mephibosheth of
his loyalty to the king, David states, "I have decided you and Ziba
shall divide the land."[30] Neither biblical nor rabbinic law justified
such arbitrary procedures.[31] That considerable property was
involved in the three different rulings by king David indicates the
great secular power the king wielded.

The second case goes even further in illustrating the power of
the king because it involves the ritual execution of innocent citizens by the vengeful Gibeonites, who sought vengeance for the ill-
treatment they had received at the hand of Saul. When David
hears that their request is that they be given seven sons of Saul for
public hanging, David agrees to do so.[32] In addition, David shows
favoritism in the grim task of selecting the victims by sparing
Mephibosheth, the son of Saul's son Jonathan.[33] This action was
taken in the face of the law of Moses which states, "The fathers
shall not be put to death for the children, nor shall the children be
put to death for the fathers; every man shall be put to death for his
own sin."[34] Also, this action by David was in contrast to the action
of a later king, Amaziah, who spared the children of the murderers
of his father on the basis of the same law.[35]

DAVID AND SOLOMON COOPERATE IN EXERCISING ROYAL POWER.
The first case involves Joab's execution. Joab, David's military
commander, had engaged in a series of bloody deeds. He had

30. II Sam. 19:24–30, esp. v. 29.

31. Cf. Shab. 56a–b, where the rabbinic debate over David's action in this
matter includes, among other points, a rebuke against him, i.e., "Had not David
paid heed to slander, the kingdom of the house of David would not have been
divided."

32. II Sam. 21:6.

33. II Sam. 21:7.

34. Deut. 24:16.

35. II Kings 14:5–6.

killed Abner,[36] who had been the captain of Saul's army,[37] because Abner had killed his brother Asahel,[38] even though this had been against king David's will.[39] Joab had also slain Amasa,[40] David's commander.[41] David chose not to exercise his option to bring Joab to trial for his deeds; however, he does request Solomon to execute him.[42] Solomon is not slow in carrying out his father's request,[43] apparently because Joab had supported the opposition party upon Solomon's ascension to the throne.[44]

The second case involves Shimei's execution. Shimei had cursed David during the civil war with Absalom.[45] But David exercised his option and spared his life, saying, "You shall not die."[46] Although this was obviously an example of *lèse-majesté*, it was certainly not a crime which had a legal death penalty attached. However, at David's request,[47] Solomon also had Shimei put to death.[48] Since no legal reason existed for this execution, it is another example of political power in the hands of the kings of Israel at this time.

SOME ARBITRARY RULINGS BY KING SOLOMON. The first case is that concerning Abiathar, the priest. While impressing on him that the execution had not been ruled out and that he was lucky to have been spared, Solomon said, ". . . you deserve death. But I will not

36. II Sam. 3:26–27.
37. II Sam. 2:8.
38. II Sam. 3:30, 2:22–23.
39. II Sam. 3:37–38.
40. II Sam. 20:8–10.
41. II Sam. 20:4.
42. I Kings 2:5–6.
43. I Kings 2:29–34.
44. I Kings 1:7, 2:28.
45. II Sam. 16:5–14.
46. II Sam. 19:16–23, esp. v. 23.
47. I Kings 2:8–9.
48. I Kings 2:36–46.

at this time put you to death . . . "[49] This expulsion was apparently because Abiathar had supported Adonijah in his abortive attempt to seize the throne.[50]

The second case concerns Adonijah. Solomon murdered Adonijah[51] after Adonijah had requested Abishag the Shunammite for a wife,[52] apparently because of his coup attempt,[53] although he had already given him conditional amnesty.[54] This kind of unilateral action, involving banishing and executing persons at will, illustrates the immense power that the king possessed. These were not legal executions, of course; rather, they were acts of political expediency for which the king was not called to account.

REHOBOAM AND HIS "SCORPIONS." After the death of Solomon, Rehoboam, his son, came to the throne. Solomon had imposed an oppressive system of forced labor and high taxes; Rehoboam, threatening to be even worse, told the people,

> And now, whereas my father laid upon you a heavy yoke, I will add to your yoke. My father chastised you with whips, but I will chastise you with scorpions.[55]

There was, of course, no recorded law for such "chastisement," and, apparently, no recourse against such action by the king short of actual rebellion. On this occasion the people did take that extreme step, and in doing so stoned to death Adoram, Rehoboam's taskmaster over the forced labor.[56]

---

49. I Kings 2:26–27.
50. I Kings 1:7.
51. I Kings 2:24–25.
52. I Kings 2:13–21.
53. I Kings 1:5–7, 2:22–23.
54. I Kings 1:49–53.
55. I Kings 12:11.
56. I Kings 12:16–19.

Limitations on Royal Power

The case of Rehoboam's harshness and the consequent rebellion by the people represents the practical limits beyond which even the king could not go without disastrous results. However, there were some formal attempts to limit the royal power of the king. Although, as has been illustrated, there were few, if any, formal restraints against the power of the king, as a matter of record the following texts under consideration do indicate that some attempt was made to deal with this problem.

The first example was provided by Samuel, who "told the people the rights and duties of the kingship; and he wrote them in a book and laid it up before the Lord."[57] The Hebrew of this statement includes וידבר שמואל אל העם את משפט המלכה. Although there are differences among scholars as to the exact meaning of this text, the use of *mishpāṭ* has led some to interpret this verse as Samuel's attempt to place limitations on the king's power.[58]

---

57. I Sam. 10:25.

58. S. Goldman, *Samuel* (London: Soncino Press, 1951), p. 58. "Samuel not only chose the king, but laid down the constitution for the new form of government which was now inaugurated." Cf. also McKane, *I & II Samuel*, p. 79. "It refers to a 'law of the king,' the hedging of the monarchy with constitutional safeguards. . . . it may reflect an early if unsuccessful attempt to preserve the social values of amphictyony by limiting the monarchy . . . " Cf. John Mauchline, "I & II Samuel," in: *New Century Bible*, [ed. Ronald E. Clements and Matthew Black], (London: Oliphants, 1971), p. 103, where this author states, "25 describes the *rights and duties* (same word in Hebrew, mišpāṭ) of royal rule. Therefore 25 is concerned with the rights and duties of an anointed king united with Yahweh and his people in covenantal obligation." However, *contra* see above; cf. Henry Preserved Smith, *A Critical and Exegetical Commentary on the Books of Samuel*, in: International Critical Commentary (New York: Charles Scribner's Sons, 1902), p. 74, where Smith writes of the text in question, ". . . it seems impossible to understand this of anything else than the *custom of the king* already cited in 8:9—18. This was threatened as the penalty of the people's choice. . . . The document is laid up before Yahweh as a testimony, so that when they complain of tyranny they can be pointed to the fact that they have brought it upon themselves."

The second example reads as follows:

> When you saw that Nahash the king of the Ammonites came
> against you, you said to me, "No, but a king shall reign over us,"
> when the Lord your God was your king. And now behold the king
> whom you have chosen, for whom you have asked; behold, the
> Lord has set a king over you. If you will fear the Lord and serve him
> and hearken to his voice and not rebel against the commandment of
> the Lord, and if both you and the king who reigns over you will fol-
> low the Lord your God, it will be well; but if you will not hearken to
> the voice of the Lord, but rebel against the commandment of the
> Lord, then the hand of the Lord will be against you and your king
> [Heb. = "fathers"].[59]

This address to the people is, in effect, a call to the king as well as
the people to submit to basic religious law or be destroyed. Provided this "condition" for maintaining the well-being of the kingdom was met, it would, of course, assure the proper attitude and
behavior of the king toward his subjects.

However, when one recalls the several examples which have
already been discussed in which the blatant and often ruthless display of raw power by different kings is seen, one realizes that
Samuel's attempts at formal or religious control of the king were
hardly successful.

The third and final text to be considered in this connection is
Deuteronomy 17:16 ff., where royal excesses are enumerated. In
this passage Charles Foster Kent finds that the king must be a
native Israelite, avoid the crimes of Solomon, and rule in accord
with the deuteronomic laws. He states concerning this text,

> These laws seek primarily to regulate those abuses which became
> most glaringly apparent in the reigns of Solomon and Ahab, cf. I
> Kings. 10:14–11:13. They aim to maintain the original, simple,
> democratic ideal of the Hebrew kingship against the seductive and

59. I Sam. 12:12–15.

subversive influence which came in from the neighbouring despot-isms. In effect these regulations make the king a constitutional ruler, who stands in striking contrast to the tyrants who ruled in all the neighbouring states. They also assume that primitive Hebrew conception of the king, as Jehovah's representative, responsible for all his acts to the Divine Sovereign, which was the historical and abiding basal idea of the theocracy.[60]

If Kent is right in his analysis of this passage, this means that this text has as its motive the regulation of kingship in Israel, and therefore is intended to serve the same purpose as the other two which have been considered, viz., to place formal restrictions on the royal power of the king.

PROPHETIC ETHICS VIS-À-VIS THE KING

In the history of the Israelites there are some enlightening examples of the political role the prophets played, especially in their confrontations with contemporary kings.

Restraining Influence of Prophets on Kings

Although it is clear from the above analysis of their activities that kings in Israel were not inclined to restraint in their use of power, it is equally clear that they were often brought to restraint by the counterbalance of power and influence that many of the prophets possessed.

Samuel was such a prophet. On one occasion Saul was waiting for Samuel to arrive and offer the burnt offering before going into battle against the Philistines. After Samuel's unusually long delay, Saul saw that his army was beginning to scatter so he offered the

60. Charles Foster Kent, *Israel's Laws and Legal Precedents* (New York: Charles Scribner's Sons, 1907), p. 80.

burnt offering himself. When Samuel arrived and saw what had occurred, he said to Saul,

> You have done foolishly; you have not kept the commandment of the Lord your God, which he commanded you; for now the Lord would have established your kingdom over Israel for ever. But now your kingdom shall not continue; the Lord has sought out a man after his own heart; and the Lord has appointed him prince over his people, because you have not kept what the Lord commanded you.[61]

Samuel's influence is apparent in that although he called Saul to account and predicted his downfall, Saul did not imprison him or put him to death.

The influential role of Samuel with regard to king Saul is seen even more dramatically when he denounces Saul for not carrying out orders in his battle against the Amalekites. Again he tells Saul that he has been rejected from being king, saying, "The Lord has torn the kingdom of Israel from you this day, and has given it to a neighbor of yours, who is better than you."[62] Upon hearing this, Saul responded in a way that dramatically illustrates the influence that Samuel had among the people, which no doubt was the reason why Saul did not raise his hand against him. Saul said to Samuel, "I have sinned; yet honor me now before the elders of my people and before Israel, and return with me, that I may worship the Lord your God."[63]

After the death of Solomon and the division of the kingdom, it was Rehoboam's plan to fight a civil war against the Northern Kingdom and regain those tribes for his own rule. He mustered the forces of Judah and Benjamin, some 180,000 fighting men, and was prepared to carry out his plan. However, the prophet She-maiah opposed him, saying, "Thus says the Lord, 'You shall not

---

61. I Sam. 13:13–14.
62. I Sam. 15:26.
63. I Sam. 15:30.

go up or fight against your kinsmen the people of Israel. Return every man to his home, for this thing is from me.' "[64] The people went home and Rehoboam was not able to carry out his plan; yet the record is silent as to any repressive action brought by him on Shemaiah. This is another clear illustration of the restraining influence of a prophet on a king, at least temporarily.[65]

Again, when Jeroboam became king of the Northern Kingdom, he built an altar for worship at Dan in the north and at Bethel near his southern border. Once, when Jeroboam was preparing to worship at the altar at Bethel, a prophet from Judah arrived and predicted its destruction along with its idolatrous priesthood. Jeroboam attempted to have the prophet seized and was stricken. When the altar was destroyed before his eyes, he entreated the prophet for help.[66] In this instance the king was literally forced to respect the prophet.

Political Involvement of the Prophets

The prophets were often engaged in political affairs, and not infrequently they played a crucial role in determining or predicting the destiny of nations. For example, before the division of the kingdom, Ahijah the Shilonite announced its division to Jeroboam and assured him of kingship over the Northern Kingdom.[67] Later, Ahijah predicts the destruction of Jeroboam's house, and is not harmed by him.[68]

Likewise, Jehu the prophet, son of Hanani, speaks out against

64. I Kings 12:24.
65. I Kings 14:30.
66. I Kings 13:6.
67. I Kings 11:29–35. Cf. San. 102a [trans. H. Freedman], for Rabbi Jose's comment on Ahijah's action, viz., "[That time was] a time predestined for punishment. (n. On that occasion Ahijah prophesied the division of the kingdom as a punishment for Solomon's backsliding.)"
68. I Kings 14:7–16; cf. also I Kings 15:27–30 for the end of Jeroboam's house.

king Baasha, predicting destruction against his house in a manner similar to Ahijah's pronouncement against Jeroboam.[69]

It is easy to see the prophets as significant figures in the politics of the period of monarchy. For the most part, they must be recognized as powerful influences exercising a great weight in the affairs of state. The fact that many of them could "tell off" the king and not be harmed is evidence of their power, especially when one remembers the actions of the kings, as analyzed above, when they were not under restraint.

The influence of a prophet is seen to extend even to the battlefield. In Ahab's war against Syria, a prophet encourages Ahab in the battle, and even goes so far as to direct some of the battle strategy.[70] When the war was resumed the following spring, Ahab is again encouraged by a prophet on the battlefield.[71] However, when Ahab comes to peace terms with Benhadad, his enemy, and does not destroy him, Ahab's doom is announced publicly by one of the "sons of the prophets."[72] Even though this was a battlefield setting and the exigencies of war often allow actions which would be unwarranted at other times, king Ahab does no harm to this prophet. Rather, "the king of Israel went to his house resentful and sullen, and came to Samaria."[73] This episode is a vivid example of the involvement and influence of "the sons of the prophets" in military affairs, even to the extent of rebuffing the "commander in chief," all without retaliation against them.

ELIJAH'S POLITICAL INVOLVEMENT. Elijah confronted Ahab and forcefully denounced him for his wickedness and predicted his downfall and the end of his dynasty, comparing his end to that of Jeroboam and Baasha.[74] Yet, instead of becoming angry and seiz-

69. I Kings 16:1–4.
70. I Kings 20:13, 22.
71. I Kings 20:28.
72. I Kings 20:35, 42.
73. I Kings 20:43.
74. I Kings 21:20–24.

ing Elijah, it is said of Ahab, "When Ahab heard those words, he rent his clothes, and put sackcloth upon his flesh, and fasted and lay in sackcloth, and went about dejectedly."[75]

Elijah's confrontation with king Ahaziah is another example of Elijah's power. After rebuking Ahaziah for seeking aid from idols, Elijah informs him that he will not recover from his sickness. When Ahaziah sends a contingent of soldiers after Elijah to "bring him in," Elijah deliberately and repeatedly disobeys the king's order to surrender.[76]

ELISHA'S POLITICAL INVOLVEMENT. Elisha was a prophet who had not only local influence but international significance. The kings of Israel, Judah, and Edom formed a coalition to fight against Moab, who had rebelled against Israel. En route to war on Moab they became desperate in the desert for lack of water. When it became known that Elisha was on the expedition, "the king of Israel and Jehoshaphat and the king of Edom went down to him."[77]

> And Elisha said to the king of Israel, "What have I to do with you? Go to the prophets of your father and the prophets of your mother." But the king of Israel [Jehoram the son of Ahab] said, "No; it is the Lord who has called these three kings to give them into the hand of Moab." And Elisha said, "As the Lord of hosts lives, whom I serve, were it not that I have regard for Jehoshaphat the king of Judah, I would neither look at you, nor see you."[78]

This insult to Jehoram, in openness before them all, was an invitation to disaster. However, the king did not raise his hand against him, indicating the extent of his influence, even among kings.

While the above incident was certainly not very diplomatic, to say the least, Elisha did fill a diplomatic role in curing Naaman,

75. I Kings 21:27.
76. II Kings 1:1–16.
77. II Kings 3:12.
78. II Kings 3:13–14.

commander of the army of the king of Syria, of his leprosy.[79]

The continuing activity of Elisha in international matters between Aram and Israel is again illustrated as Elisha kept warning the king of Israel of Syrian raids being planned into Israelite territory.[80]

Furthermore, Elisha pursued a consistent foreign policy toward Aram as he tried to transform that nation into a friend instead of an enemy, which involved a rebuke against the king of Israel and the return of Syrian captives to their homeland.[81]

Later, when the city of Samaria came under extended siege by the army of Syria, and the people became so desperate for food that they reached the point of cannibalism, Jehoram bitterly blamed Elisha for their difficulties and threatened his life.[82] However, the king did not carry out his threat.

Finally, Elisha continued to exercise a political role by predicting that Hazael would be the king who was to follow Benhadad in Syria,[83] and by selecting Jehu to be king in Israel and commissioning him to wipe out the house of Ahab.[84] In view of Elisha's intimate involvement in the politics of Israel, and his frequent confrontations with kings, it is a tribute to his power and influence as a man of God that he eventually died of natural causes.[85]

JEREMIAH. Jeremiah was another prophet who was deeply involved in the tragic political developments of his time. For example, he gave implied support to Josiah's cultic reforms[86] with the words, "Weep not for him who is dead, nor bemoan him . . ."[87] but

79. II Kings 5:1–14.
80. II Kings 6:8–10.
81. II Kings 6:18–23.
82. II Kings 6:24–31, quote v. 31.
83. II Kings 8:7–15.
84. II Kings 9:1–13.
85. II Kings 13:14, 20.
86. II Kings 22:18–23:25.
87. Jer. 22:10a.

described the fate of Jehoahaz (Shallum) saying, "Weep bitterly for him who goes away, for he shall return no more to see his native land."[88]

He spoke out strongly during the reign of Jehoiakim against the evil practices of the people which were leading them to disaster.[89] This forthright proclamation brought him face to face with death. However, after a public hearing in which both priests and false prophets testified against him, his life was spared when it was recalled that Hezekiah, in earlier times, had spared the faithful prophet Micah, who had ventured to warn of the coming overthrow of Judah.[90]

Jehoiakim, who did not hesitate to cut up and burn a scroll containing the word of God dictated to Baruch, Jeremiah's scribe,[91] received Jeremiah's condemnation and scathing forecast, "With the burial of an ass he shall be buried."[92]

Jeremiah also expressed his opposition to the policies and practices of Jehoiachin (Coniah), and made the dire prediction concerning him that "none of his offspring shall succeed in sitting on the throne of David, and ruling again in Judah."[93]

Zedekiah refused to take Jeremiah's counsel, no doubt because he was a weak king and under strong pressure from his anti-Babylonian nobles.[94] Hence, "He did not humble himself before Jeremiah the prophet . . . "[95] Jeremiah predicted Zedekiah's capture by Nebuchadrezzar,[96] and said to him, "You shall be delivered into the hand of the king of Babylon."[97]

88. Jer. 22:10b–12.
89. Jer. 26:4–6.
90. Jer. 26:10–19.
91. Jer. 36:23 ff.
92. Jer. 22:13–19, quote v. 19.
93. Jer. 22:24–30, quote v. 30.
94. James Philip Hyatt, "Jeremiah," in: *Interpreter's Bible,* vol. 5, pp. 1070–1072.
95. II Chron. 36:11–13, quote v. 12.
96. Jer. 21:3–7.
97. Jer. 37:17.

After the capture of Jerusalem, Jeremiah was treated well by king Nebuchadrezzar.[98]

Persecuted Prophets Who Were Defenseless

There are two instances in Hebrew Scripture where the power and ruthlessness of the kings involved were so great that the prophets were actually put to death. These two examples point up in a vivid manner the fact that political expediency, together with unrestrained power, was often the motivation upon which the kings acted.

The first example occurred during the reign of king Joash. Zechariah spoke to the people and said, "Thus says God, 'Why do you transgress the commandments of the Lord, so that you cannot prosper? Because you have forsaken the Lord, he has forsaken you.'"[99] This rebuke against the people caused them to conspire against him, and, by order of the king, he was murdered.[100]

The second example concerns the prophet Uriah, son of Shemaiah, who spoke out against Jerusalem and the people during the reign of king Jehoiakim. When the king tried to kill him, he escaped to Egypt. Eventually, however, the king obtained his extradition and executed him in Judah.[101] Ironically, Uriah's contemporary, Jeremiah, who had prophesied essentially the same message, was able to escape death, undoubtedly because he was held in higher esteem by the people.[102]

A third example involves the wrath of a king against a prophet which was checked short of the death sentence. However, it, too, is a clear instance of excessive use of power by the king without anyone calling it into question. During his reign Ahab entered into league with Jehoshaphat of Judah to move against the Syrians and

98. Jer. 39:11–14.
99. II Chron. 24:20.
100. II Chron. 24:21.
101. Jer. 26:20–23.
102. Jer. 26:16, 20, 24.

capture Ramoth-gilead. At Jehoshaphat's request, Ahab called together his prophets, about four hundred in number, to seek word as to how the battle might go. They unanimously predicted a great victory for the Israelites. Jehoshaphat, apparently suspicious of such striking unanimity from so many prophets, called for further confirmation. Reluctantly, Ahab summoned Micaiah, who predicted defeat for the expedition and Ahab's death in battle. Upon hearing this, Ahab said,

> Seize Micaiah, and take him back to Amon the governor of the city and to Joash the king's son; and say, "Thus says the king, 'Put this fellow in prison, and feed him with scant fare of bread and water, until I come in peace.'"[103]

In all these cases, we see a clear distinction between powerful prophets, who could speak their mind with impunity, and weaker prophets, who lacked political support and were therefore liable to be punished for any "dangerous" prophecies.

Political Cooperation Between Prophet and King

Of course, there were times in the history of the Israelites when the relationship between king and prophet was that of cooperation. Interestingly enough, the only reference in the Hebrew Scriptures to the prophet Jonah outside of the book by that name is a statement indicating that Jonah heralded the reconquest of Israel's lost territories by king Jeroboam, son of Joash, implying his loyalty and cooperation, at any rate with that particular governmental enterprise.[104]

A more striking example of political cooperation between king and prophet may be seen in the actions of the prophet Isaiah. Although Ahaz was not above reproach as a king,[105] Isaiah stood

103. I Kings 22:1–28, quote v. 27.
104. II Kings 14:25.
105. II Kings 16:1–4.

with him during the trying times of the Israelite-Syrian coalition against Judah.[106]

Again, Isaiah was a great strength to king Hezekiah when the Assyrians were threatening to take Jerusalem. The "critical support" Isaiah offered was enough to give Hezekiah the courage he needed to stand against the enemy.[107] However, Isaiah strongly opposed the subsequent attempt at an anti-Assyrian alliance Hezekiah formed with Merodach-baladan, king of Babylon.[108]

In all of this, Isaiah is seen as counselor and advisor to the court. He had great political influence with royalty, and he used that influence to help shape the foreign policy of the Kingdom of Judah during some of the most critical years of its history.

106. Isa. 7:1–4. But cf. also prophetic criticism of the king, Isaiah 7:13 ff. Cf. also San. 104a for a rabbinic view of Isaiah's influence on king Ahaz.

107. II Kings 18:13–20:11; Isa. 37–38.

108. II Kings 20:12–19; Isa. 39. Cf. San. 26a for a rabbinic description of Isaiah's encouragement of king Hezekiah.

EXCURSUS II

JUDICIAL AND GOVERNMENTAL ETHICS IN THE BIBLE AND THE TALMUD: A COMPARATIVE EVALUATION FROM SELECTED ILLUSTRATIONS

INTRODUCTION

The preceding study has dealt with numerous facets of the judicial and governmental ethics reflected in the Hebrew Scriptures and rabbinic literature. The many varying contexts within which the subject has been analyzed have tended to spread the inquiry over a wide variety of literature and a vast expanse of history. This procedure did not allow for a systematic comparison and evaluation of the judicial and governmental ethics adduced from the two primary sources—the Bible and the Talmud. Therefore, this excursus aims to bring these matters into sharp focus by the use of selected illustrations.

Attempts to Eliminate the Death Penalty

The Scriptures are replete with calls for the death penalty for a number of offenses.[1] The Rabbis did not reject the principle of

1. Deut. 17:5, 21:22; 22:21; Lev. 20:10–16, etc.

capital punishment—indeed, they could not abolish it outright since this would have contradicted the divinely instituted laws of the Torah. However, in many ways, they tried to hedge it round with restrictions which rendered it virtually inapplicable. One way was to utilize complicated judicial procedures.[2] Another was to establish judicial rules which favored the defendant during trial.[3] Thus, circumstantial evidence was not accepted. Two reliable witnesses had to testify not only that they had seen the crime in question, but that they had repeatedly warned the accused before he committed his act. There is also abundant evidence that most Rabbis had a strong aversion to the death penalty,[4] some going so far as to declare that, had they been members of the Sanhedrin, no person would ever have been put to death.[5]

Application of the Death Penalty

According to the Torah, the death penalty was to be applied by burning or stoning.[6] Since hanging was done after execution,[7] and burning was restricted to only two offenses,[8] that meant stoning was the common biblical mode of execution for capital crimes. Very little is said about the method of carrying out this punishment.

The Rabbis attempted to make the application of the death penalty as humane as circumstances would permit. They advocated a method which involved as little suffering and humiliation for the criminal as possible.[9] They tried to devise procedures of execution which would cause a minimum of mutilation to the

2. M. San. V, 1–2; M. Ab. I, 9.
3. San. 37b; M. San. III, 3–4; IV, 1; V, 5–VI, 1.
4. San. 8b, 17a.
5. M. Mak, I, 10.
6. Lev. 20:14, 24:16, etc.
7. Deut. 21:22–23.
8. Lev. 20:14, 21:9.
9. M. San. VI, 3; San. 45a.

body.[10] They restricted the role of the general public in the execution and also regulated the activity of the witnesses,[11] all in an attempt to make it as easy on the condemned person as possible. Some Rabbis maintained that a woman was not hung after stoning.[12] Others held that hanging, in any case, was merely for a moment.[13] Strangulation was utilized as the method of execution in cases where the Torah did not specify the mode of death.[14] This, too, was done because it was thought to be a less stringent death than the other methods.[15]

In most of these cases there were differences of opinion among the Rabbis. At times it was even acknowledged that decapitation was a valid mode of legal execution.[16] However, the general trend was toward reducing the death sentence to an absolute minimum, and, where capital punishment was to be applied, to mitigating the harshness of death as much as possible. This points toward a humane attitude on criminals—a basic approach that is lacking in the Torah.

Conditions for the Establishment of Guilt

The Scriptures speak of applying the death sentence to those who were only obliquely involved in some kind of serious violation, e.g., the stoning of the entire household of Achan,[17] and the slaying of all the inhabitants of an idolatrous city.[18]

In contrast, most Rabbis taught not only that there never had been a case of a condemned city, but that it would never happen.[19]

10. M. San. VII, 2.
11. M. San. VI, 4.
12. Ibid.
13. San. 46b.
14. M. San. VII, 3.
15. San. 52b.
16. M. San. VII, 3.
17. Josh. 7:24–25.
18. Deut. 13:12–15.
19. San. 71a.

They also laid down conditions which had to be satisfied before guilt could be established. Some of these conditions were: (1) intention was necessary before one was guilty of a crime,[20] although mere intention was not, with some exceptions, enough to make one culpable;[21] (2) the illegal act performed had to be intentional beyond reasonable doubt before the accused could be held to have been criminally guilty.[22] Again, although these conditions were not always unanimously agreed upon, the general trend was to safeguard the rights of individuals when they were charged with major crimes.

Lex Talionis

The Hebrew Scriptures show the *lex talionis* being applied in an enlightened way when compared to its use generally in the ancient Near East; i.e., with equal justice for all without regard to social status or economic level. With but few possible exceptions,[23] however, there could be no substitution of punishment for one upon whom the "measure for measure" verdict was pronounced.[24]

The Rabbis, generally speaking, were more lenient in their interpretative rulings on this matter. In the first place, the impracticability of exactly applying the law was stressed.[25] In the second place, punishment was often commuted to a monetary fine,[26] and compensation for damages became the general rule.[27] Also, if one was found guilty of injury to another, he could not have both a "civil" and a "criminal" sentence (such as flogging and payment of compensation) applied against him.[28] All of this indicates a distinct

20. A.Z. 54a.
21. Kid. 39b.
22. M. B.K. V, 6.
23. Exod. 21:29 ff.
24. Exod. 21:22–25; Deut. 25:11–12.
25. B.K. 84a.
26. B.K. 28a.
27. M. B.K. VIII, 1.
28. Ket. 32b.

shift toward leniency by the majority of the Rabbis in their rulings concerning the "measure for measure" principle.

Safeguards Against Killing Out of Vengeance

The Torah made provision for the role of the blood-avenger.[29] There were also some provisions in the law to curtail his unwarranted or hasty action when life had been taken, e.g., the cities of refuge,[30] the demand that it be premeditated murder,[31] and the requirement of a trial in cases where there was a question of involuntary manslaughter or murder.[32] All of this biblical provision, while set in the context of the "blood feud" mentality of the ancient Near East, did show a concern for ethical principles where the blood-avenger was involved.

The Rabbis went further. They denied the right of the avenger of blood to take the law into his own hands, and the culprit could be put to death only if there were two witnesses who saw the murder, and only if the court duly sentenced him.[33] The rabbinic position in effect eliminated the action of the blood-avenger separate and apart from the courts. Additionally, according to Rabbi Isaac's interpretation of Deuteronomy 4:42, the cities of refuge were to provide a livelihood for the manslayer;[34] and, if he was a scholar, he should have access to a school.[35] These rulings are a perfect example of the refinement of biblical law by the Rabbis.

Witnesses: Legal Safeguards

The Talmud elaborates on the role of witnesses in capital cases,

29. Num. 35:33, etc.
30. Deut. 19:4–6.
31. Num. 35:16–18.
32. Num. 35:24.
33. Cf. T.O. on Gen. 9:6.
34. Mak. 10a.
35. J. Mak. 6.

and, in most cases, shows a concern for their welfare. For example, a false witness ordinarily received a severe sentence according to both the Bible and the Talmud.[36] However, according to rabbinic interpretation, he was acquitted if the false testimony was given in ignorance.[37] There was also a rabbinic rule which prevented relatives from testifying against each other, or a witness from testifying regarding himself.[38] All this was designed to guard against possible self-incrimination.

Again, although the Bible is consistent in its requirement of "two or three witnesses,"[39] the Rabbis allowed one witness to suffice in certain cases where hardship would accrue if the biblical rule was strictly adhered to;[40] and there appears to have been a time when three witnesses was the rule for capital cases instead of the biblical "two or three."[41] This care for witnesses and defendants (with the exception of premeditated false witnesses) shows an enlightened concern for each individual in the judicial process that goes well beyond the biblical record.

Divorce

Deuteronomy describes the circumstances under which a man could give his wife a bill of divorce and send her away.[42] To be sure, there was much controversy in the rabbinic schools as to what constituted proper biblical grounds for the giving of the bill of divorcement. However, one fact is clear. In later times the Rabbis were enacting legislation to prevent abuse of this law. For example, it became the rule that witnesses had to sign the writ.[43]

36. Deut. 19:18–19; M. San. XI, 1.
37. Shebu, 26a.
38. San. 9b.
39. Deut. 17:6, 19:15.
40. M. Ed. I, 12.
41. Damascus Document IX, 17–22; Josephus, *Ant.* VIII, xiii, 8.
42. Deut. 24:1 ff.
43. Giṭ. 36a.

Again, the practice which had developed of merely calling together a local *Beth Din* in order to cancel a bill of divorce was stopped by a ruling of Rabban Gamaliel the Elder in order to prevent the abuses latent in such a practice.[44] These rabbinic rulings reflect an ethical concern for the rights of the parties to a divorce, especially the woman's rights, which is not apparent in the deuteronomic law.

Surrender of Legal Rights

The Hebrew Scriptures placed great stress on the keeping of the law.[45] It was not permitted to add to or take from the law, according to Deuteronomy 4:2.

However, according to rabbinic teaching, it was this very strict adherence to the letter of the law in the legal process that had caused Jerusalem to be destroyed.[46] They held that one could act within the "margin of the judgment" by surrendering one's legal rights on behalf of another. This ethical thrust was based on consideration of others and was often reflected in legal enactments.[47] Thus, in Scripture the emphasis with respect to the various laws of the Torah was, "Hear therefore, O Israel, and be careful to do them . . ." (Deut. 6:3a); the Rabbis, on the other hand, taught that doing the "right thing" included going beyond the letter of the law, or not insisting on the letter of the law if such action would benefit others.[48]

Checks and Balances

The legal enactments of the Pentateuch fall into two classes of law, the apodictic and the casuistic. The apodictic laws are direct com-

44. M. Giṭ. IV, 2.
45. Deut. 5:1, 6:1–9, etc.
46. B.M. 30b.
47. Ket. 97a.
48. B.M. 83a.

mands or prohibitions of Yahweh.[49] The casuistic laws have a conditional clause in them,[50] and deal with specific situations or conditions under which the law is operative. This served as a control in the application of the law in that the conditions had to be taken into account.

The Sages recognized, of course, these two types of law in the Torah, and were cognizant of the type of control inherent in casuistic law. However, they evolved a system of checks and balances which had even wider application. In rabbinic thought, the violation of a negative biblical command was a criminal act. If such a violation occurred, the biblical injunction against that act could be carried out. Thus, the rabbinic requirement for both a biblical negative command and a penalty provision for its violation worked as checks and balances in the penal law.[51]

Prosbul

The deuteronomic law established a Sabbatical year of release,[52] which included an annulment of all monetary obligations, thus legally debarring creditors from collecting debts. This was obviously a humane law with the ethical motive of relieving hardship on the poor. As if in anticipation of the difficulty of maintaining this law, the warning was given that one must not harden one's heart against the poor man and refuse to lend him money simply because the year of release was drawing near.[53]

However, in later times the law became oppressive, since in a more urbanized and commercialized society, nonpayment of loans on a large scale was economically disastrous, and did the poor more harm than good, since it deprived them of all credit. Therefore, to prevent suffering to the poor Hillel enacted the *Prosbul.*

49. Exod. 20:1–17, etc.
50. Exod. 22:1 ff.
51. Mak. 13b.
52. Deut. 15:1–2.
53. Deut. 15:7–11.

This was a legal instrument executed and attested in court by which the lender retained the right to collect a debt at any time he chose. Thus, the lender was not tempted to refuse a loan simply because the year of release was near.[54] This is a classical example of Hillel, who undoubtedly believed in the divine origin of the Torah, effectively circumventing the biblical law with a *takkanah* in the spirit of the law, designed as it was to help the poor secure loans.

Summary Actions

The Torah and the Talmud emphasize law. Judicial procedures are provided for. There was to be an accounting for those who violated the law. However, both in Torah and Talmud allowance was made for summary action, based on ethical and moral considerations, which caused justice to swiftly prevail, e.g., the action of Phinehas in spontaneously slaying an Israelite man and a Midianite woman for gross immorality,[55] and the rabbinic ruling which acknowledged this same principle by allowing the zealots to kill one caught in the act of cohabiting with a heathen.[56] In each case the law provided judicial procedures for such violations; yet, at the same time, allowance was made for summary action separate from legal procedure. Thus, one notes in both Torah and Talmud a recognition that the exigencies of the moment must be considered in the attempt to maintain high moral, ethical, and legal standards.

Taking Life for Protection of Life and Property

Both the Hebrew Scriptures and the rabbinic literature recognized the sanctity of individual human life. However, there was also another principle at work that called for each individual to live his life in harmony with others and with God. When this principle was

---

54. Sheb. X, 3–4.
55. Num. 25:6–13.
56. M. San. IX, 6.

violated in utter disregard for the dignity and property of others, as in the case of breaking in and stealing, the Bible allowed the owner of the property to take the life of the thief without incurring guilt.[57] A rabbinic ruling went further and permitted anyone to kill the burglar in defense of the owner of the property being burglarized, on the grounds that the thief was a potential murderer.[58] The rabbinic extension of this biblical law illustrates the talmudic concern for human rights as basically ethical in nature, showing desire for justice for the victim of a crime.

The Perspective of Kingship

The Bible, generally speaking, presents a pragmatic historical view of kingship in Israel. With the exception of the idealization of Solomon's reign, the Scriptures are rather straightforward with reference to the kings, their rule, qualities, power, etc. There is an attempt by Samuel to "write in" some safeguards to prevent the king's abuse of power,[59] and Deuteronomy is concerned with the duties and conduct of the king.[60] The king's power is, at least in theory, restricted.

By contrast, rabbinic law, written at a time when anarchy was considered the worst possible danger,[61] tends to increase the authority and power of the king.[62] This trend is even more pronounced in Maimonides.[63]

The Stranger and the Proselyte

In one respect there may have been a regression in talmudic law;

---

57. Exod. 22:2 (Heb. 22:1).
58. San. 72b.
59. I Sam. 10:25.
60. Deut. 17:14–20.
61. M. Ab. III, 2.
62. M. San. II, 2–5; San. 20b.
63. Maimonides' *Code,* bk. XIV, treatise V, chaps. iii, iv, v, vi, viii, ix.

viz., with regard to the legal safeguards for the resident alien (גר).
In biblical law, the alien is treated on terms of complete equality.[64]

The Rabbis, as well as the Aramaic, take the biblical *ger* to
mean גִּיּוֹרָא = proselyte.[65] While it may not have been the intention
of the Rabbis, the effect of this misinterpretation was to restrict the
legal safeguards provided in the Torah for the stranger to prose-
lytes, who were, of course, Jews, not Gentile aliens residing in the
land of Israel.

The Yearning for Peace

Peace is a prominent theme in both the Hebrew Scriptures and
rabbinic literature. In both bodies of literature it was viewed as a
gift of God.[66] Thus, it was seen by both biblical and talmudic
writers not merely as the absence of war, but in a theological
dimension.

It is not surprising, then, to find a biblical connection between
peace and justice and truth,[67] and a relationship between God, his
covenant with Israel, and peace.[68]

Neither is it surprising to note that the Sages continued their
quest for peace with many legislative rulings having peace as their
motive.[69] Thus, the subject of peace in the Scriptures was stressed
with equal, if not more, force in rabbinic literature; and the people
of both the biblical and talmudic ages were encouraged by the
prophetic message that a new era of peace would one day be
realized.[70]

64. Exod. 12:49; Lev. 24:16, 22, etc.
65. San. 56a.
66. Hag. 2:9; Giṭ. 59b.
67. II Kings 20:19.
68. Isa. 54:10.
69. Yeb. 14b–15a; M. Giṭ. V, 8.
70. Isa. 2:1–4; Hos. 2:18–20, etc.

CONCLUSION

These selected illustrations have shown the similarities and differences between Torah and Talmud, between the Hebrew Scriptures and rabbinic literature. Also, the judicial and governmental ethics of the two literatures have been compared and contrasted. It has been noted that, generally speaking, the halakhic work of the Sages reflects a more detailed concern with the ethical ramifications of judicial legislation and procedures than do the Hebrew Scriptures.

BIBLIOGRAPHY

Reference Works

"אדם יודע". *Encyclopedia Talmudica,* vol. 1. Jerusalem: Talmudic Encyclopedia Publishers, 1969.

Baron, Salo Wittmayer. *A Social and Religious History of the Jews.* Vol. 1, *To the Beginning of the Christian Era.* Rev. ed. New York: Columbia University Press, 1952. Vol. 2, *Christian Era: The First Five Centuries.* 2d ed. New York: Columbia University Press, 1962.

Bennett, W. H. "Crimes and Punishments (Hebrew)." In *Encyclopaedia of Religion and Ethics,* ed. James Hastings, vol. 4. New York: Charles Scribner's Sons, n.d.

Benzinger, Immanuel. "Law and Justice." In *Encyclopaedia Biblia,* eds. T. K. Cheyne and J. Sutherland Black, vol. 3. New York: Macmillan Co., 1902.

Berman, Saul. "Law and Morality." In *Encyclopaedia Judaica,* vol. 10. Jerusalem: Keter Publishing House, 1971.

"Bet Din and Judges." *Encyclopaedia Judaica,* vol. 4. Jerusalem: Keter Publishing House, 1971.

Brown, Francis, S. R. Driver, and Charles A. Briggs, eds. *Hebrew and English Lexicon of the Old Testament.* London: Oxford University Press, 1951.

Driver, S. R. "Law (in the Old Testament)." In *A Dictionary of the Bible,* ed. James Hastings, vol. 3. Edinburgh: Charles Scribner's Sons, 1900.

Fuchs, Hugo. "Halachah." In *The Universal Jewish Encyclopedia,* ed. Isaac Landman, vol. 5. New York: Universal Jewish Encyclopedia Co., 1941.

Gray, G. B. "Law Literature." In *Encyclopaedia Biblia,* eds. T. K. Cheyne and J. Sutherland Black, vol. 3. New York: Macmillan Co., 1902.

Greenberg, M. "Bloodguilt." In *Interpreter's Dictionary of the Bible,* ed. George Arthur Buttrick, vol. 1. New York: Abingdon Press, 1962.

Greenstone, Julius H. "Gezera." In *The Jewish Encyclopedia,* ed. Isidore Singer, vol. 5. New York: Funk & Wagnalls Co., 1916.

"Halakhah." *Encyclopaedia Judaica,* vol. 7. Jerusalem: Keter Publishing House, 1971.

Jacobs, Louis. "Torah, Reading of." In *Encyclopaedia Judaica,* vol. 15. Jerusalem: Keter Publishing House, 1971.

————. *What Does Judaism Say About . . .?* In Library of Jewish Knowledge, ed. Geoffrey Wigoder. New York: Quadrangle/The New York Times Book Co., 1973.

Kleinknecht, Hermann, and W. Gutbrod. "Law." Trans. Dorothea M. Barton. In *Bible Key Words from Gerhard Kittel's "Theologisches Worterbuch zum Neuen Testament,"* ed. P. R. Ackroyd. London: A. & C. Black, 1962.

Licht, Jacob. "Biblical Ethics." In *Encyclopaedia Judaica,* vol. 6. Jerusalem: Keter Publishing House, 1971.

Mantel, Hugo. "Sanhedrin." In *Encyclopaedia Judaica,* vol. 14. Jerusalem: Keter Publishing House, 1971.

Montefiore, C. G., and H. Loewe. *A Rabbinic Anthology.* London: Macmillan, 1938.

Oded, Bustanay. "Tribes, The Twelve." In *Encyclopaedia Judaica,* vol. 15. Jerusalem: Keter Publishing House, 1971.

Pritchard, James B., ed. *Ancient Near Eastern Tests Relating to the Old Testament.* 2d ed. Princeton, N.J.: Princeton University Press, 1955.

"Takkanot." *Encyclopaedia Judaica,* vol. 15. Jerusalem: Keter Publishing House, 1971.

General

Abel, F. M. *Histoire de la Palestine Depuis la Conquête d'Alexandre Jusqu'a l'Invasion Arabe.* Vol. 2, *De la Guerre Juive a l'Invasion Arabe.* Paris: J. Gabalda et Cie, 1952.

Albright, William Foxwell. *History, Archaeology and Christian Humanism.* New York: McGraw-Hill, 1964.

————. *New Horizons in Biblical Research.* London: Oxford University Press, 1966.

————. *Samuel and the Beginnings of the Prophetic Movement.* Cincinnati: Hebrew Union College Press, 1961.

————. *The Biblical Period.* Pittsburgh: Presbyterian Board of Colportage of Western Pennsylvania, n.d. Reprint from: *The Jews: Their History, Culture and Religion,* ed. Louis Finkelstein. New York: Harper & Brothers, 1949.

————. *The Biblical Period from Abraham to Ezra.* New York: Harper & Row, 1949. Rev. ed., 1960. Torchbook ed., 1963.

————. *Yahweh and the Gods of Canaan.* Garden City, N.Y.: Doubleday, 1968. Anchor Books, 1969.

Apocrypha, The. Ed. Bruce M. Metzger. New York: Oxford University Press, 1965.

Aristotle. "Politics." In *The Basic Works of Aristotle,* ed. Richard McKeon. New York: Random House, 1941.

Berkovits, Eliezer. "The Centrality of Halakhah." In *Rabbinic Judaism from Talmudic to Modern Times,* ed. Jacob Neusner. New York: KTAV Publishing House, 1974. Reprint from: "Authentic Judaism and Halakhah." *Judaism,* 19, no. 1 (Winter 1970).

Bialik, Ḥayyim Naḥman, and Joshua Chana Ravnitzky. *Sefer Ha-Aggadah.* Tel Aviv: Dvir, 1947.

Bible, New American Standard. Carol Stream, Ill.: Creation House, 1960–71.

Bible, Revised Standard. Old Testament, 1952; New Testament, 1946. Philadelphia: A. J. Holman Co., 1962.

Biblia Hebraica. Eds. R. Kittel, P. Kahle, A. Alt, and O. Eissfeldt. Stuttgart: Privileg. Wurtt. Bibelanstalt. 7th ed. New York: American Bible Society, 1951.

Bickerman, Elias. *From Ezra to the Last of the Maccabees: Foundations of Post-Biblical Judaism.* New York: Schocken Books, 1947.

Box, G. H., and W. O. E. Oesterley. "Sirach." In *The Apocrypha and Pseudepigrapha of the Old Testament,* ed. R. H. Charles. Vol. 1, *Apocrypha.* Oxford: Clarendon Press, 1913.

Bright, John. *A History of Israel.* London: SCM Press, 1960.

Broude, Samuel G. "Civil Disobedience and the Jewish Tradition." In *Judaism and Ethics,* ed. Daniel Jeremy Silver. New York: KTAV Publishing House, 1970.

Büchler, A. *Studies in Sin and Atonement in the Rabbinic Literature of the First Century.* The Library of Biblical Studies, ed. Harry M. Orlinsky. New York: KTAV Publishing House, 1967.

Carmichael, Calum M. *The Laws of Deuteronomy.* Ithaca: Cornell University Press, 1974.

Caro, R. Joseph. "Laws of Judges." In *Code of Hebrew Law—Shulḥan 'Aruk, with Glosses of R. Moses Isserles,* trans. and commentary by R. Chaim N. Denburg. Montreal: Jurisprudence Press, 1955.

Cohen, A., ed. *The Soncino Chumash: The Five Books of Moses with Haphtaroth.* Hindhead, Surrey: Soncino Press, 1947.

Cornfeld, Gaalyahu, ed. *Daniel to Paul.* Tel Aviv: Hamikra Ba'olam Publishing House, n.d.

Cross, Frank Moore. "The Early History of the Qumran Community." In *New Directions in Biblical Archaeology,* eds. David Noel Freedman and Jonas C. Greenfield. Garden City, N.Y.: Doubleday, 1969.

Dailey, Robert H. *Introduction to Moral Theology.* New York: Bruce Publishing Co., 1970.

Danby, Herbert, trans. *The Mishnah.* Rev. ed. London: Oxford University Press, 1958.

Daube, David. *Studies in Biblical Law.* New York: KTAV Publishing House, 1969.

———. *The New Testament and Rabbinic Judaism.* London: Athlone Press, 1956.

de Vaux, Roland. *Ancient Israel: Its Life and Institutions,* trans. John McHugh. New York: McGraw-Hill, 1961.

———. *Bible et Orient.* Paris: Éditions du Cerf, 1967.

Driver, G. R. *The Judean Scrolls.* Oxford: Basil Blackwell, 1965.

Epstein, I. *Judaism: A Historical Presentation.* Baltimore: Penguin Books, 1959.

———., ed. *The Babylonian Talmud.* 18 vols. London: Soncino Press, 1961–.

Finkelstein, J. J. "Some New *Misharum* Material and Its Implications." In *Studies in Honor of Benno Landsberger on His Seventy-fifth Birthday, April 21, 1965,* eds. Hans G. Güterbock and Thorkild Jacobsen. Assyriological Studies 16. Chicago: University of Chicago Press, 1965.

Glueck, Nelson. *Rivers in the Desert: A History of the Negev.* New York: Farrar, Straus & Cudahy, 1959.

Goetze, Albrecht, trans. "The Laws of Eshnunna." In *Ancient Near*

Eastern Texts Relating to the Old Testament, ed. James B. Pritchard, 2d ed. Princeton, N.J.: Princeton University Press, 1955.

Goldin, Hyman E. *Hebrew Criminal Law and Procedure.* New York: Twayne Publishers, 1952.

Goldman, Solomon. *The Ten Commandments.* Chicago: University of Chicago Press, 1956.

Guttmann, Alexander. *Rabbinic Judaism in the Making.* Detroit: Wayne State University Press, 1970.

Herford, R. Travers. "Pirkē Aboth." In *The Apocrypha and Pseudepigrapha of the Old Testament,* ed. R. H. Charles. Vol. 2, *Pseudepigrapha.* Oxford: Clarendon Press, 1913.

———. *Talmud and Apocrypha.* 1933. Reprint, New York: KTAV publishing House, 1971.

———. *The Ethics of the Talmud: Sayings of the Fathers.* New York: Schocken Books, 1962.

Herzog, Isaac. *The Main Institutions of Jewish Law.* Vol. 1. London: Soncino Press, 1936.

Higger, Michael. "Intention in Talmudic Law." In *Studies in Jewish Jurisprudence,* ed. Edward M. Gershfield. New York: Hermon Press, 1971.

Hitti, Philip K. *History of the Arabs.* London: Macmillan, 1940.

Hoenig, Sidney B., ed. *The Book of Joshua: A New English Translation of the Text and Rashi with a Commentary Digest,* trans. P. Oratz, A. J. Rosenberg, and Sidney Shulman. New York: Judaica Press, 1969.

———. *The Great Sanhedrin.* Philadelphia: Dropsie College, 1953.

Horowitz, George. *The Spirit of Jewish Law.* New York: Central Book Co., 1953.

Jacobs, Louis. *Jewish Law.* New York: Behrman House, 1968.

Johnson, A. R. "Hebrew Concepts of Kingship." In *Myth, Ritual, and Kingship,* ed. S. H. Hooks. Oxford: Clarendon Press, 1958.

Josephus. *Against Apion.* Loeb Classical Library, vol. 1. Trans. H. St. J. Thackeray. New York: G. P. Putnam's Sons, 1926.

———. *Jewish Antiquities.* Loeb Classical Library. Vols. 7 and 8, trans. Ralph Marcus and Allen Wikgren. Vol. 9, trans. Louis H. Feldman. Cambridge, Mass.: Harvard University Press, 1963–65.

Kadushin, Max. *The Rabbinic Mind.* New York: Jewish Theological Seminary, 1952.

Kaplan, J. *The Redaction of the Babylonian Talmud.* New York: Bloch Publishing Co., 1933.

Kaplan, Mordecai M. "The Legal Foundations of Rabbinic Judaism." In

Understanding Rabbinic Judaism from Talmudic to Modern Times,
ed. Jacob Neusner. New York: KTAV Publishing House, 1974.
Reprint from *The Greater Judaism in the Making.*

Kaufmann, Y. *The Religion of Israel,* trans. Moshe Greenberg. Chicago:
University of Chicago Press, 1956.

Kent, Charles Foster. *Israel's Laws and Legal Precedents.* New York:
Charles Scribner's Sons, 1907.

Kramer, S. N., trans. "Lipit-Ishtar Lawcode." In *Ancient Near Eastern
Texts Relating to the Old Testament,* ed. James B. Pritchard. 2d ed.
Princeton, N.J.: Princeton University Press, 1955.

Lauterbach, Jacob Z. *Rabbinic Essays.* Cincinnati: Hebrew Union College Press, 1951. Reprint, New York: KTAV Publishing House,
1975.

————. *Studies in Jewish Law, Custom and Folklore.* New York: KTAV
Publishing House, 1970.

————. ed. *Mekilta (de Rabbi Ishmael).* Vol. 2. Philadelphia: Jewish Publication Society, 1933.

Lazarus, M. *The Ethics of Judaism.* 2 pts. Philadelphia: Jewish Publication Society, 1900–1901.

Levinthal, Israel Herbert. "The Jewish Law of Agency." In *Studies in
Jewish Jurisprudence,* ed. Edward M. Gershfield. New York: Hermon Press, 1971.

Lewis, Bernard. *The Arabs in History.* Tiptree, Essex: Anchor Press,
1950.

Lewittes, Mendell. "The Nature and History of Jewish Law." In *Rabbinic
Judaism from Talmudic to Modern Times,* ed. Jacob Neusner. New
York: KTAV Publishing House, 1974.

Maimonides. *Code,* book XIV, "The Book of Judges," trans. Abraham
M. Hershman. Yale Judaica Series 3. New Haven: Yale University
Press, 1949.

Mantel, Hugo. *Studies in the History of the Sanhedrin.* Harvard Semitic
Series # 17. Cambridge: Harvard University Press, 1965.

Margolis, Max L., and Alexander Marx. *A History of the Jewish People.*
New York: Jewish Publication Society of America, 1927. First
Atheneum printing, Forge Village, Mass.: Murray Printing Co.,
1969.

Meek, Theophile James. *Hebrew Origins.* New York: Harper & Brothers,
1936.

————, trans. "The Code of Hammurabi." In *The Ancient Near East: An*

Anthology of Texts and Pictures, ed. James B. Pritchard. Princeton N.J.: Princeton University Press, 1958.

Mendelsohn, Isaac. *Slavery in the Ancient Near East.* New York: Oxford University Press, 1949.

Mendelsohn, S. *The Criminal Jurisprudence of the Ancient Hebrews.* Baltimore: M. Curlander, 1891.

Mendenhall, George L. *Law and Covenant in Israel and the Ancient Near East.* Pittsburgh: Presbyterian Board of Colportage of Western Pennsylvania, 1955.

Miller, Patrick D., Jr. *The Divine Warrior in Early Israel.* Cambridge, Mass.: Harvard University Press, 1973.

Moore, George Foot. *Judaism.* 2 vols. Cambridge, Mass.: Harvard University Press, 1927.

Neusner, Jacob. "Archaeology and Babylonian Jewry." In *Near Eastern Archaeology in the Twentieth Century,* ed. James A. Sanders. Garden City, N.Y.: Doubleday, 1970.

————. *Invitation to the Talmud.* New York: Harper & Row, 1973.

————, ed. *Understanding Rabbinic Judaism from Talmudic to Modern Times.* New York: KTAV Publishing House, 1974.

Noth, Martin. *The Laws of the Pentateuch and Other Studies.* German ed., 1957. Enlarged ed., 1960. Philadelphia: Fortress Press, 1967.

Orlinsky, Harry M. *Understanding the Bible through History and Archaeology.* New York: KTAV Publishing House, 1972.

Paul, Shalom M. *Studies in the Book of the Covenant in Light of Cuneiform and Biblical Law.* Leiden: E. J. Brill, 1970.

Rabinowitz, Jacob J. *Studies in Legal History.* Jerusalem: R. H. Cohen Press, 1958.

Redford, D. B. "Studies in Relations Between Palestine and Egypt During the First Millennium B.C." In *Studies on the Ancient Palestinian World,* eds. J. W. Wevers and D. B. Redford. Toronto: University of Toronto Press, 1972.

Robinson, Theodore H. *A History of Israel.* Vol. 1. Oxford: Clarendon Press, 1932.

Rosenblatt, Samuel. *Hear, Oh Israel.* New York: Philipp Feldheim, 1958.

————. *The Interpretation of the Bible in the Mishnah.* Baltimore: Johns Hopkins Press, 1935.

Russell, D. S. *Between the Testaments.* Rev. ed. Philadelphia: Fortress Press, 1965.

Schatz, Elihu A. *Proof of the Accuracy of the Bible Based on Chronologi-*

cal, Organizational, Prophetic and Legal Analyses. Middle Village, N.Y.: Jonathan David, 1973.

Schechter, Solomon. *Studies in Judaism. Third Series.*1924. Reprint, Philadelphia: Jewish Publication Society, 1945.

Speiser, E. A. "Background and Function of the Biblical *Nasi'.*" In *Oriental and Biblical Studies,* eds. J. J. Finkelstein and Moshe Greenberg. Philadelphia: University of Pennsylvania Press, 1967.

Steinberg, Milton. *Basic Judaism.* New York: Harcourt, Brace & World, 1947.

Sulzberger, Mayer. *The Am Ha-Aretz: The Ancient Hebrew Parliament.* Philadelphia: Julius H. Greenstone, 1909.

Wald, M. *Jewish Teachings on Peace.* New York: Bloch Publishing Co., 1944.

Waxman, Meyer. *A Handbook of Judaism.* New York: Bloch Publishing Co., 1947.

———. "Civil and Criminal Procedure of Jewish Courts." In *Studies in Jewish Jurisprudence,* ed. Edward M. Gershfield. New York: Hermon Press, 1971.

Wright, G. Ernest. *The Old Testament Against Its Environment.* Chicago: Henry Regnery Co., 1950.

Yaron, Reuven. "The Goring Ox in Near Eastern Laws." In *Jewish Law in Ancient and Modern Israel,* ed. Haim H. Cohn. New York: KTAV Publishing House, 1971.

Zeitlin, Solomon. *The Rise and Fall of the Judaean State.* Vol. 1. Philadelphia: Jewish Publication Society, 1962.

Commentaries

Boling, Robert G. *Judges.* The Anchor Bible, vol. 6A, eds. William Foxwell Albright and David Noel Freedman. Garden City, N.Y.: Doubleday, 1975.

Bright, John. "The Book of Joshua." In *The Interpreter's Bible,* ed. George Arthur Buttrick, vol. 2. New York—Nashville: Abingdon-Cokesbury Press, 1953.

Burney, C. F. *Notes on the Hebrew Text of the Books of Kings.* Oxford: Clarendon Press, 1903.

Cassuto, U. *A Commentary on the Book of Exodus,* trans. Israel Abrahams. Jerusalem: Magnes Press, 1951.

Driver, Samuel Rolles. *Deuteronomy.* The International Critical Commentary, eds. S. R. Driver, Alfred Plummer, and Charles A. Briggs, 1895. 3d ed. Edinburgh: T & T Clark, 1902.

Freedman, H. "Joshua." In *Joshua and Judges,* ed. A. Cohen. London: Soncino Press, 1950.

Goldman, S. *Samuel.* London: Soncino Press, 1951.

Gray, George Buchanan. *Numbers.* The International Critical Commentary, eds. Charles Augustus Briggs, Samuel Rolles Driver, and Alfred Plummer. New York: Charles Scribner's Sons, 1903.

Gray, John. *I & II Kings: A Commentary.* The Old Testament Library, eds. Peter Ackroyd, James Barr, John Bright, and G. Ernest Wright. 2d rev. ed. London: SCM Press, 1970.

Hirsch, Samson Raphael. "Exodus." In *The Pentateuch,* trans. Isaac Levy, vol. 2. London: Isaac Levy, 1960.

Hyatt, James Philip. "Jeremiah." In *The Interpreter's Bible,* ed. George Arthur Buttrick, vol. 5. New York–Nashville: Abingdon Press, 1956.

Jamison, Robert, A. R. Fausset, and David Brown. "Deuteronomy." In *Commentary Critical and Explanatory.* Grand Rapids, Mich.: Zondervan Publishing House, n.d.

Lange, John Peter. *Commentary on the Holy Scriptures: Kings,* ed. Philip Schaff. Grand Rapids, Mich.: Zondervan Publishing House, n.d.

McKane, William. *I & II Samuel.* London: SCM Press, 1963.

Manley, G. T. *Deuteronomy.* The New Bible Commentary, eds. F. Davidson, A. M. Stibbs, and E. F. Kevan. 2d ed. Grand Rapids, Mich.: William B. Eerdman's Publishing Co., 1954.

Marsh, John. "Numbers." In *The Interpreter's Bible,* ed. George Arthur Buttrick, vol. 2. New York–Nashville: Abingdon-Cokesbury Press, 1953.

Mauchline, John. "Hosea." In *The Interpreter's Bible,* ed. George Arthur Buttrick, vol. 3, New York–Nashville: Abingdon Press, 1956.

———. *I & II Samuel.* New Century Bible, eds. Ronald E. Clements and Matthew Black. London: Oliphants, 1971.

Mays, James L. *Leviticus.* The Layman's Bible Commentaries, ed. Balmer H. Kelly. London: SCM Press, 1964.

Micklem, Nathaniel. "Leviticus." In *The Interpreter's Bible,* ed. George Arthur Buttrick, vol. 2. New York–Nashville: Abingdon-Cokesbury Press, 1953.

Montgomery, James A. *The Book of Kings.* The International Critical Commentary, ed. Henry Snyder Gehman. Edinburgh: T & T Clark, 1951.

Redford, R. A. "Leviticus." In *The Pulpit Commentary,* eds. H. D. M. Spence and Joseph S. Exell, vol. 2. Grand Rapids, Mich.: William B. Eerdman's Publishing Co., 1950.

Rylaarsdam, J. Coert. "Exodus." In *The Interpreter's Bible,* ed. George Arthur Buttrick, vol. 1. New York–Nashville: Abingdon-Cokesbury Press, 1952.

Silbermann, A. M., ed. *Pentateuch with Rashi's Commentary,* trans. and annotated by M. Rosenbaum, A. M. Silbermann, A. Blashki, and L. Joseph. London: Shapiro, Vallentine, 1929 (Genesis), 1930 (Exodus), 1934 (Deuteronomy).

Simpson, Cuthbert A. "Genesis." In *The Interpreter's Bible,* ed. George Arthur Buttrick, vol. 1. New York–Nashville: Abingdon-Cokesbury Press, 1952.

Skinner, John. *Genesis.* The International Critical Commentary, eds. Samuel Rolles Driver, Alfred Plummer, and Charles Augustus Briggs. New York: Charles Scribner's Sons, 1910.

Smith, Henry Preserved. *A Critical and Exegetical Commentary on the Books of Samuel.* The International Critical Commentary, eds. Charles Augustus Briggs, Samuel Rolles Driver, and Alfred Plummer. New York: Charles Scribner's Sons, 1902.

Snaith, Norman H. "I Kings." In *The Interpreter's Bible,* ed. George Arthur Buttrick, vol. 3. New York–Nashville: Abingdon Press, 1954.

Speiser, E. A. *Genesis.* The Anchor Bible, eds. William Foxwell Albright and David Noel Freedman. Garden City, N.Y.: Doubleday, 1964.

von Rad, Gerhard. *Deuteronomy: A Commentary,* trans. Dorothea Barton. The Old Testament Library, eds. G. Ernest Wright, John Bright, James Barr, and Peter Ackroyd. Philadelphia: Westminster Press, 1966.

———. *Genesis: A Commentary,* trans. John H. Marks. Philadelphia: Westminster Press, 1956.

Wright, G. Ernest. "The Book of Deuteronomy." In *The Interpreter's Bible,* ed. George Arthur Buttrick, vol. 2. New York–Nashville: Abingdon-Cokesbury Press, 1953.

Zeitlin, Solomon, ed.-in-chief. *The First Book of Maccabees,* trans. Sidney Tedesche. Dropsie Hebrew Edition, Jewish Apocryphal Literature. New York: Harper & Brothers, 1950.

Journals

Blidstein, Gerald J. "Capital Punishment—The Classic Jewish Discussion." *Judaism* 14 (Spring 1965): 159 and (Winter 1965): 165–166.

Guttmann, M. "The Term 'Foreigner' Historically Considered." *Hebrew Union College Annual* 3 (1926): 1–20.

Hertz, J. H. "Ancient Semitic Codes and the Mosaic Legislation." *Publication of the Society for Jewish Jurisprudence* (reprint from *Journal of Comparative Legislation*), November 1928, 220.

McCarthy, D. J. "The Symbolism of Blood and Sacrifice." *Journal of Biblical Literature* 88, pt. 2 (June 1969): 174, 176.

Mantel, Hugo. "The Nature of the Great Synagogue." *Harvard Theological Review* 60 (January 1967): 87.

Miklisanski, J. K. "The Law of Retaliation and the Pentateuch." *Journal of Biblical Literature* 66 (1947): 296, 300.

Milgrom, J. "The Biblical Diet Laws as an Ethical System." *Interpretation* 17 (January 1963): 291, 294, 300.

Rackman, Emanuel. "Talmudic Insights on Human Rights." *Judaism* 1 (April 1952): 161.

Schiffman, Lawrence H. "Qumran Law of Testimony—Damascus Document IX, 17–22," trans. B. Levine. *Revue de Qumran* 8 (December 1975): 603–605.

Newspaper

Aberbach, Moses. "Jewish Attitude to Capital Punishment." *Jewish Chronicle,* (London), November 28, 1952, p. 15.

INDEX

HEBREW SCRIPTURES

11:38	206
12:ch.	195
12:11	244
12:16–19	244
12:18	198
12:24	249
13:6	249
14:7–16	249
14:30	249
15:27–30	249
16:1–4	250
16:26	43
20:ch.	186
20:13	250
20:22	250
20:28	250
20:31	186
20:34	186
20:35	250
20:42	250
20:43	250
21:8–10	125
21:8–13	138
21:24	250
21:27	250
22:1–28	255

II Kings

1:1–16	251
3:12–14	251
3:19	185
3:24–25	185
5:1–14	252
5:25–27	118
6:8–10	252
6:18–31	252
6:21–23	187
8:1–6	237
8:7–15	252
9:1–13	252
9:7	160
12:12	121
13:6	43
13:14	252

13:20	252
14:5–6	223, 242
14:25	255
16:1–4	255
17:23	22
18:13–37	256
19:ch.	256
20:1–11	256
20:12–19	256
20:19	199, 267
22:ch.	22
22:18–20	252
23:3	21
23:1–25	252
25:1–21	22

I Chronicles

22:9	199

II Chronicles

15:6	208
19:5–8	87
19:11	87
24:20–21	254
36:11–13	253
36:17–21	22

Ezra

6:15–21	135
7:6	23
7:10–11	23
7:11–18	24
9:ch.	135
10:ch.	24
10:1–14	135
10:8	37, 217

Nehemiah

4:ch.	30
8:ch.	135
8:9–18	24
9:ch.	135
10:ch.	30, 135
10:32	126

TALMUD

NEW TESTAMENT SCRIPTURES

ANCIENT WRITINGS

APOCRYPHA

SUBJECTS

Great, 31–32, 37, 87, 91–94, 96,
101, 104, 137, 139–140, 164, 210,
217, 221–222, 224, 258
Savoraim, 34, 216
Scholars, 78–79, 106, 134, 230, 245,
261
Rabbinical, 31, 41, 77, 91, 108,
220, 222, 226
Scribes, 23, 46, 107
Scriptures, 26, 28, 31, 46, 62, 75, 77–
78, 80, 82, 98, 107, 111, 127, 141,
145, 154, 171, 195–196, 217, 223,
227, 236, 257, 259, 263, 266–267
Hebrew, 1, 3, 5, 28, 42, 45, 113,
159, 169, 199, 216, 232, 254–255,
257, 260, 263, 265, 267–268
Shofar, 38
Shunammites, 244
Sin, 131, 160, 179, 184, 188, 224, 248
Consequences of, 95, 160, 179,
242
Removal of, 50, 131, 209, 224
Sinai, 12, 24, 29, 35–36, 44–46, 60, 77,
81, 118, 216–217, 220
Slavery, 14, 55, 120, 130, 227, 244
"Scorpions", 244
Society, 1, 4, 14, 18, 20, 27, 47–49, 55–
56, 58, 65, 96, 110, 116, 119, 158,
203, 215, 217, 223, 228, 233, 260,
264
Statutes, 9, 19–20, 23, 81
"Stubborn and Rebellious Son", 124,
138, 239
Sumerians, 235
Synagogue, Great, 29–30, 77, 117
Syrians, 186–187, 252, 254

Takkanah, 36–37, 39–41, 80, 217, 265
for Changing Times, 38–39
"for Good Order", 38
Talmud, Babylonian, 1, 5, 25, 34–35,
39, 41–43, 45, 56, 59, 68–69, 94,
101, 140, 142, 155–156, 199–201,

203, 210, 216–217, 225, 228–231,
257, 261–262, 265, 268
Tannaim, 74, 97, 211, 217, 229
Temple, 26, 96, 116, 161, 228, 236
Second, 28, 34, 37, 50, 92, 135,
139–140, 201, 217, 224
Theocracy, 11, 114–116, 247
Theology, 10, 16, 24, 42, 109, 114, 170,
176, 180, 184, 215, 225–226, 228,
267
Moral, 3
of the Jews, 3, 109
Torah, 1, 3, 17, 23–28, 32–39, 41–42,
46, 50, 60, 69, 72, 76–80, 106–108,
110, 114, 116–118, 120, 122–124,
126, 132, 134–135, 141–144, 159,
163–165, 167, 169, 176, 198, 201,
210, 215–216, 219–220, 223–225,
227, 229–232, 236, 258–259, 261,
263–265, 267–268
"Making a Fence Around", 33,
36, 41, 71, 217, 258
Tradition, 3, 36, 45, 48, 74, 77, 80, 194,
198, 218, 228, 236
Oral, 28, 31, 231
Rabbinic, 7, 20, 23, 28–31, 42,
216, 231
Trial, 99, 258
Truth, 207, 228, 267

War, 6, 36, 96, 122, 132, 169–170, 178,
181–182, 185, 191, 195–196, 199,
205, 208–209, 228–229, 237, 250–
251, 267
Civil, 190, 227, 240, 248
Leaders (Officers, Commanders), 82, 170–174, 176, 180, 221,
243
Unethical Actions of, 189–
193, 227
of Free Choice, 95–96, 197
Prisoners of 186–187
Rules for, 6, 170, 172, 176, 185,

PERSONS

BIBLICAL

AUTHORS

RABBIS

EDITORS

TRANSLATORS

OTHERS

PLACES

GLOSSARY

Amoraim—Originally, speakers or interpreters who attended upon the public speaker to expound the discourse at greater length. Eventually, the rabbinic authorities responsible for the Gemara.

Amphictyony—A tribal confederation, originally referring to a league of ancient Greek states ruled by a council composed of deputies, or amphictyons, from each state.

Baraitha—A teaching or a tradition of the Tannaim that is not found in the Mishnah but is found in a later literary collection, usually introduced by the phrase "Our Rabbis taught," or, "It has been taught."

Beth Din—Literally, a house of law or judgment. A gathering of three or more men acting as a Jewish court of law.

Gemara—Completion, learning. The traditions, discussions and rulings of the Amoraim based chiefly on the Mishnah and forming the Talmud.

Gerousia—The aristocratic council of the high priest prior to 165 B.C.E. which had jurisdiction over civil matters in Palestine.

Gezerah—Legislative enactment in halakhic Judaism that was preventive in nature, usually thought of as "making a fence around the Torah."

Giṭ—A deed or legal document; usually referring to a writ of divorce.

Haggadah—Interpretation and exposition of Scripture by the Rabbis for the purpose of edification. Also, those portions of rabbinic literature containing stories, legends, folklore, maxims and anecdotes.

Halākhāh—Rule, custom, or decision in rabbinic law; the portion of the Talmud concerned with legal matters.

Haliẓah—The ceremony of "drawing off" the shoe of the man who refused to marry his brother's childless widow.

Ḥanuth—A place on the Temple Mount that served as a temporary residence for the Great Sanhedrin after this court moved from the Hall of Hewn Stones in about 30 C.E.

Hierocracy—A rule or government by a priesthood.

Kabbalah—An esoteric theosophy based on a mystical interpretation of the Scriptures originally handed down by oral tradition.

Kareth—A "cutting off"; or, divine punishment for many sins which had no specified human penalty prescribed by law.

Lèse-majesté—Injury or insult to majesty.

Log—Two litras; or, the space taken up by the contents of six eggs.

Midrash—Interpretation or exposition of Scripture, usually with a verse-by-verse commentary format.

Misharum—An economic reform institution dating as early as the Old Babylonian kingdom that had much the same function as the biblical "jubilee land release" laws found in Lev. 25:28 ff.

Mishnah—Repetition or teaching, especially the legal traditions explaining or supplementing the pentateuchal laws or the principles derived therefrom as compiled by R. Judah the Patriarch near the end of the second century C.E.

Mishpāṭ—Judgment.

Mu'ad—Forewarned. Applied to an animal that had gored or injured on three successive occasions, causing the owner to be liable to pay full damages done by the animal.

Nāsī—Great leaders in ancient Israel (Num. 34:17–18, etc.). Also, according to M. Ḥag. II, 2, the rulers of the Great Sanhedrin began to be called Nāsī beginning with the Zuggot. After the demise of the Great Sanhedrin, the head of Palestinian Jewry was called Nāsī.

Peruṭah—The smallest copper coin.

Prosbul—A rule enacted by Hillel which allowed a creditor to present a declaration before a court of law, properly signed by witnesses, stating that his loan would not be remitted as required by the law stated in Deut. 15:1–2, 9.

Savoraim—Later rabbinic scholars who contributed to the redaction and formation of the Talmud in the late fifth and early sixth centuries C.E.

Shālōm—Peace!

Shebuth—An act forbidden by the Rabbis to be performed on the Sabbath.

Shechinah—The abiding of the Divine Presence; the spirit of God as manifested on earth.

Shofar—Ram's horn blown for military or religious purposes, especially in the course of the Temple or Synagogue service connected with New Year and at the conclusion of the Day of Atonement.

Takkanah—Legislative enactment in the halakhic system of Judaism, especially in the public, criminal, and civil areas of Jewish law.

Talmud—Learning, study of the Law. With reference to documents, it is the comments and discussions concerning the Mishnah found in the Gemara, as expounded by the Babylonian and Palestinian Rabbis from the third to the fifth century C.E.

Tam—Perfect. Applied to an animal which had not injured more than twice; thus, its owner paid only half damages.

Tannaim—Those who repeat or teach. Rabbis quoted in the Mishnah or Baraitha. In the Amoraic period, scholars whose special responsibility was to memorize and recite Baraithas before other teachers.

Tartemar—Fifty zuz, or denarii; or, twenty-five common shekels.

Zuggoth—Pairs of leaders who, according to the tradition, presided over the Great Sanhedrin from about 160 B.C.E. until near the close of the first century B.C.E.